DE LOS

OTROS

D1510283

BETWEEN MEN ~ BETWEEN WOMEN
Lesbian and Gay Studies
Lillian Faderman and Larry Gross, Editors

BETWEEN MEN ~ BETWEEN WOMEN
Lesbian and Gay Studies
Lillian Faderman and Larry Gross, Editors

DE LOS OTROS

Intimacy and Homosexuality

Among Mexican Men

Joseph Carrier

COLUMBIA UNIVERSITY PRESS

New York

COLUMBIA UNIVERSITY PRESS

New York   Chichester, West Sussex

Copyright © 1995 Columbia University Press

All rights reserved.

Library of Congress Cataloging-in-Publication Data

Carrier, Joseph.

De los otros : intimacy and homosexuality among Mexican
men / Joseph Carrier

p.   cm. — (Between men—between women)

Includes bibliographical references and index.

ISBN 0–231–09692–5. — ISBN 0–231–09693–3 (pbk.)

1. Homosexuality, Male—Mexico—Guadalajara.   2. Gay
men—Mexico—Guadalajara—Sexual behavior.   3. Gay liberation
movement—Mexico—Guadalajara.   I. Title.   II. Series.

HQ76.2.M62G813   1995

305.38′9664′0972—dc20   95–6244

CIP

●

Casebound editions of Columbia University Press books are
printed on permanent and durable acid-free paper.

Printed in the United States of America

c 10 9 8 7 6 5 4 3 2 1

p 10 9 8 7 6 5 4 3 2 1

BETWEEN MEN ~ BETWEEN WOMEN
Lesbian and Gay Studies
Lillian Faderman and Larry Gross, Editors
Eugene F. Rice, Columbia University Advisor

Between Men ~ Between Women is a forum for current lesbian and gay scholarship in the humanities and social sciences. The series includes both books that rest within specific traditional disciplines and are substantially about gay men, bisexuals, or lesbians and books that are interdisciplinary in ways that reveal new insights into gay, bisexual, or lesbian experience, transform traditional disciplinary methods in consequence of the perspectives that experience provides, or begin to establish lesbian and gay studies as a freestanding inquiry. Established to contribute to an increased understanding of lesbians, bisexuals, and gay men, the series also aims to provide through that understanding a wider comprehension of culture in general.

Contents

I became an anthropologist and a researcher on human sexual behaviors late in life. It came about as a result of being dismissed at the age of forty from my job with the RAND Corporation in Santa Monica, California, in late July 1967, just one week after I had returned from an extended assignment as a counterinsurgency specialist in South Vietnam. Although I was originally told by my department head that I was being "let go for economic reasons," I learned later that I was dismissed because they believed that I was a "homosexual" and thus a security risk. Some RAND staff members in Saigon had reported to the head of security in Santa Monica that I had been having an ongoing homosexual affair with a Vietnamese Air Force officer. I admitted nothing, but knowing that my days at RAND were over—the mere hint of homosexuality was grounds for dismissal—I made a bargain with the administration that I would leave after I had completed my Vietnamese research project.

Being terminated by RAND turned out to be one of the best things that ever happened to me, since it led to my going back to graduate school to study anthropology, something I had thought about doing for some time but never had the courage to do. Being forced out of my job not because of performance but because of homosexuality also motivated me from the very beginning of my graduate program to study human sexual behaviors.

I was lucky that the Irvine campus of the University of California system was new and looking for graduate students, had an interdisciplinary program in the social sciences, and had a professor of anthropology, Duane Metzger, who was interested and willing to sponsor a student who was determined to study male homosexuality. In order to get a commitment of acceptance to the graduate school, however, it was necessary for me to meet and be approved by the dean of the School of Social Sciences. Enroute to the dean's office, Professor Metzger suggested that it would be okay to mention that I had worked in Vietnam for RAND but not to say anything about my interest in doing research on homosexual behaviors. In the 1960s homosexuality was still considered too risky and odious a topic for a graduate student to pursue.

Another benefit of undertaking a graduate program in social sciences at UC/Irvine was being able to have one off-campus expert serve on my committee. I was thus able to get Dr. Evelyn Hooker, a professor at UCLA and an acknowledged research authority on homosexuality, to serve as an adviser. She was very interested in my proposed study and gave me the guidance and backbone needed to undertake what turned out to be the first Ph.D. field research in anthropology focused on homosexual behaviors.

My original study plan was to make cross-cultural comparisons of the homosexual behaviors of low-income Latino, black, and Anglo men living in Los Angeles. Very little was known about their sexual behaviors at that time, so it was an open area for research. It soon became obvious, however, that because so little was known my investigation needed to be narrowed. In early 1968 Professor Metzger suggested I limit my study to Mexican men and spend the summer in Mexico making some preliminary observations about their homosexual behaviors.

Accompanied by a young gay Anglo friend, who was well experienced in developing sexual relationships with macho Mexican men, I spent the months of July and August 1968 collecting participant observation data on male homosexuality in Mexico. During the first month we traveled south from the U.S.-Mexican border by car through Mexico's northwestern states to Guadalajara via Hermosillo, Guaymas, Culiacán, and Mazatlán. The second month we traveled on south to Mexico City, Oaxaca, San Cristobal de las Casas, and to the Mexican/Guatemalan border. Retracing part of our route, toward the end of the second month we returned to Mexico City and then on north up the center of Mexico to the U.S. border at Ciudad Juárez–El Paso via Aguascalientes, Durango, and Chihuahua.

Information collected during those two months convinced me that a field study of male homosexuality in Mexico could certainly be done for my Ph.D. dissertation. My gay Anglo friend had been a great teacher, helping me acquire a view of Mexican homosexual worlds that would have taken much longer to get on my own. Among the important things he taught me that summer, for example, were the rules that must be followed to safely initiate homosexual encounters in locations—like straight cantinas, bars, and nightclubs—that would seem to most people improbable places for finding male sex partners. So even though little was then known or published about Mexican homosexuality in the English- or Spanish-speaking world, my preliminary fieldwork in Mexico meant that I did not have to start my graduate study from scratch.

Information collected that summer also convinced me that in order to complete the project in a reasonable period of time, I had to delimit the research in terms of who was to be studied and in what location. Given the amount of time I had available to do fieldwork—at most two years—I decided to restrict the study to the sexual behaviors of mainly poor urban Mexican men of mixed Spanish and Indian ancestry (mestizos) living in Guadalajara, the second largest city in Mexico. I chose Guadalajara because its size—close to two million inhabitants at that time—would allow me anonymity. I would thus be able to keep a low profile and conduct my study in an environment where not too many people would be curious about what I was doing. In addition, of all the Mexican cities I had visited that summer I felt most at ease there and had already established a friendship with a young man who knew about my proposed study, seemed comfortable with his homosexuality, and promised to introduce me to his family and his homosexual world.

After successfully defending my research proposal to my committee and obtaining a two-year predoctoral fellowship from the National Institute of Mental Health, I moved to Guadalajara and started my fieldwork in the fall of 1969. As promised, my Mexican friend from the previous summer introduced me to his mother, father, and nine brothers and sisters. Shortly after I got to know the family, they graciously invited me to move from my hotel to their house and stay with them until I found an apartment. This was an auspicious beginning for what proved to be a successful research project and one of the most fulfilling, happiest times of my life.

I finished my fieldwork in Guadalajara in the spring of 1971 and returned to Los Angeles to analyze the data collected. I completed my dissertation and received my Ph.D. in the summer of 1972. Since few university positions in anthropology and almost no jobs for sex researchers were available at that time, I worked the next year and a half in Vietnam and Washington as a staff officer for the National Academy of Sciences' committee studying the effects of herbicides used by American military forces in South Vietnam.

After returning to California at the end of 1973, I began a professional association and lifelong friendship with Laud Humphreys, a professor of sociology at Pitzer College and internationally known researcher on Anglo male homosexuality in the United States. He was interested in my research and encouraged me to continue my fieldwork on male homosexuality in Mexico as long as possible. To make it financially possible, he subcontracted part of his consulting work to me evaluating Los Angeles County–funded juvenile delinquency projects. For the next fourteen years, I continued to support myself financially as a part-time evaluator of experimental law enforcement programs throughout the state of California.

With this ongoing employment and income, I was thus able to resume my study of male homosexualities in Mexico in early 1974, but only part time. I continued my fieldwork in Guadalajara and expanded it over the years to include several cities and towns in the northwestern states of Sonora, Sinaloa, and Nayarit (shown on the map in figure 1), which I passed through while driving back and forth to Guadalajara on coastal Highway 15. My fieldwork outside Guadalajara was initially unplanned and came about as a result of finding myself in interesting homosexual situations.

In the mid 1980s my research was spurred on and given a saliency it would not otherwise have had by the beginning of the AIDS epidemic. It soon became obvious that a popular male-to-male sexual practice in Mexico, anal intercourse, put some Mexican men at high risk for HIV infection and that as a result there would in the future most likely be a serious AIDS epidemic. At that time I also became aware of the need to study the gay liberation movements in Guadalajara and elsewhere in Mexico since they were having an important impact on the lives and homosexual behaviors of many Mexican men. Additionally, gay liberation groups were in the forefront of the fight on AIDS and helping those infected with the virus.

Finally, in the fall of 1987 I received, as a result of my ongoing research on Mexican male homosexual behaviors, my first full-time job as a sex researcher. Raúl Magaña, a fellow graduate student in anthropology at UC/Irvine who knew of my work in Mexico, invited me to do research with him on sexual behaviors and HIV infection of men of Mexican origin living in California. As director of the Orange

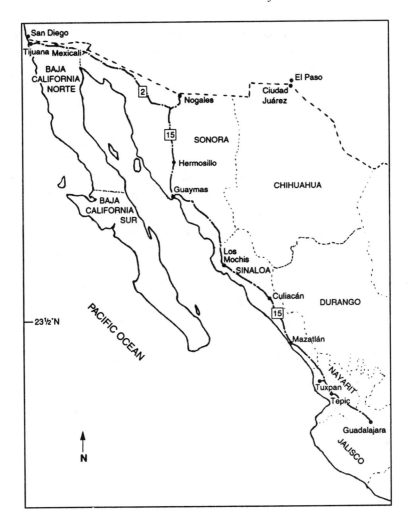

Figure 1.
Fieldwork sites in northwestern Mexico.

County Health Care Agency's AIDS Community Education Project (ACEP), he knew additional information on the sexual behaviors of southern California's large Mexican population was needed to prepare culturally relevant educational materials on HIV infection and AIDS.

I did research on sexual behaviors and HIV infection for ACEP until I terminated my employment with the health care agency at the end of 1992. For four of those years my research had focused mainly on sexual behaviors of men of Mexican origin. In my last year I also directed an ethnographic study of the sexual behaviors of men of Vietnamese origin and HIV infection in Orange County. During those years my fieldwork in Mexico continued intermittently. And in March 1994 I gathered some additional information on male homosexual behaviors in Ho Chi Minh City (Saigon), Vietnam.

Because of the AIDS epidemic, in recent years I have focused on gathering information on high-risk male and female sexual behaviors that may be of use to health care workers who are planning and conducting frontline HIV-prevention programs. More applied sex research needs to be done to help these people carry out their mission. Working with small budgets, they need better support from sex researchers. During a conference on Mexican immigrants and HIV infection and AIDS held at Loyola Marymount College in April 1994, the audience—composed mostly of people working at the community level—made clear their need for better information on the sexual behaviors of minority populations and their impatience with so many sex research projects in the social sciences that yield so little usable results for their HIV-prevention programs.

For the foreseeable future I plan to continue my research on the sexual behaviors of Mexican and Vietnamese men and to help gay activists and community workers utilize the data available on high-risk sexual behaviors to plan and conduct culturally appropriate HIV-prevention programs in California, Mexico, and Vietnam.

Acknowledgments

I am most grateful to the Mexican men who have participated in my study over the past twenty-five years and generously allowed me to learn about and participate in significant parts of their private lives. As my book will show, many of them have become close personal friends, and during the years we have known each other they have shared their families with me as well. I am deeply indebted to them and their families because they have taught me so much about the meaning of love and family in Mexico and showed me such great hospitality. I wish I could identify them all, but because of the subject matter of my book and for reasons of confidentiality I cannot. I can, however, give the first names of a particularly important few: Gonzalo, Felipé, Enrique, José, Francisco, and Arnoldo. And I can openly acknowledge the assistance given me by the leader of gay liberation in Guadalajara, Pedro Preciado, and by my research assistants, José Moreno and Pepé Jimenez.

I am also grateful to colleagues and friends who helped me start my fieldwork and have encouraged me along the way to publish and continue my study of male homosexuality in Mexico. My professors at the University of California, Irvine—Duane Metzger and Kim Romney—and Evelyn Hooker helped launch my study. Clark Taylor and I have been competitive researchers on Mexican male homosexuality but have maintained a close friendship and have always shared our field research findings. Gilbert Herdt has often given me the extra push I needed to write up my findings and continue my research. Ralph Bolton, Michele

Shedlin, Laud Humphreys (deceased), Paul Abramson, John DeCecco, and Holly Magaña have also encouraged me to continue publishing. Raúl Magaña, who was born and raised in Guadalajara, became an especially valued colleague when we worked together and enlarged the scope of my study to include the homosexual behaviors of men of Mexican origin living in southern California.

Among my close personal friends, I would like to thank Ron Emler, Tom Filer, Ynez Johnston and John Berry, Burr Singer and Harry Friedman, Molly and Dennis Fredrickson, Enrique Oliveros, Chris Torres, Edwin Sojo, Lucy Thunder Sanchez, and Armida Ayala for their heartening support. Jeanne Heller, a very special friend, gets a thousand blessings for doing the first edit of this book and helping me improve my writing skills over the years. My sister, Betty Smiley, also deserves praise for putting up with me during difficult times.

Finally, I want to give special thanks to Steve Murray, Carter Wilson, and Ralph Bolton for good counsel and editorial suggestions on several important chapters of this book; to Ann Miller at Columbia University Press for her guidance, editing, and welcome advice; and to Walter Williams for many fine suggestions in a review of the book for Columbia University Press.

Introduction

In my study of homosexuality in Mexico over the past twenty-five years I have focused on the various ways Mexican men involved in homosexual encounters are able to accommodate themselves satisfactorily to their overt homosexual behaviors. Put in very general terms, the principal question of my study has been, How do mestizo Mexican men—men of mixed Spanish and Indian ancestry—who have sex with men cope with their homosexuality in their everyday lives in a society that censures such behavior?

A major premise of mine has been that most Mexican men who have other men as primary or secondary sexual partners are able over time to come to terms with homosexual behaviors which, although legal in Mexico, are still considered reprehensible and deviant in their society. My study has therefore focused on learning about the coping strategies, lifestyles, and sexual behaviors of ordinary men (that is, men not in psychotherapy or institutionalized settings) who are actively involved in homosexual encounters.

To understand how Mexican men deal with their homosexual behavior, we need to know something about the social forces that make coping necessary. So I have also focused on those social forces most important to an individual when coming to grips with his homosexuality in society.

In gathering data for this study, I have mainly used participant observations and structured interviews. Participant observation is the primary method used in field research and may be performed several different ways. I chose the role of "participant-as-observer"—that is, I participated fully with the groups of men under study but made it clear that I was also undertaking research. The structured interviews differed from the observations and brief inquiries I made as a participant observer in that they focused on some unanswered questions raised by the observations and made it possible to gather comparative information about the sex lives of the men being studied. I prepared the questionnaires I used only after almost a year of participant observations. Their refinement over time mostly reflected what I had learned from living among my respondents. Both research methods, however, were important. I obtained valuable information through participant observations that I could never have learned through structured interviews alone; and much was learned from the questionnaire data that was not revealed by participant observations.

Serendipity has also played an important role in my research. Being gay has meant that my private sex life with Mexican men helped to reveal important information about their homosexualities. Moreover, my "private" social outings with gay and/or straight friends in Mexico always had the potential for providing me with additional valuable research leads and a useful understanding of the meaning of behaviors I was observing.

It has thus never been possible to totally separate my fieldwork from my private life. In truth, I am not sure it is really possible for anthropologists making ethnographic observations to maintain complete separation. As the founder of Mesoamericanist anthropology once wrote, "In me, man and anthropologist do not separate themselves sharply; I used to think that I could bring about that separation in scientific work about humanity. Now I have come to confess that I have not effected it, and indeed think it is not possible to do so" (Redfield 1953).

Studying human sexual behaviors, heterosexual or homosexual, adds yet another difficulty because of moral judgments made against studying them by society in general and by professional colleagues in particular. The ethical issues related to this kind of field research must be continually dealt with squarely and morally. I have always obeyed local laws dealing with sex between males and have taken care to protect the privacy of information gathered on the sex lives of respondents. By being a participant as well as an observer, there is the additional problem of biasing the data. This problem, however, can be taken into account when the researcher begins to analyze his or her findings, and is far outweighed, in my opinion, by the potential contribution made by this kind of serendipitous knowledge.

Let me give an example of the useful contribution one's private life can make to collecting data. In the summer of 1982 I began a study of adolescent attitudes and joking about male homosexuality in an old upper-lower / lower-middle-class barrio located close to downtown Guadalajara. My access to the barrio was through a twenty-five-year-old homosexual respondent named Alberto, one of ten with whom I had maintained contact since my study began. He was born and grew up there, and as time passed all his friends in the barrio came to know about and accept his homosexuality. He never denied to any of them that he was homosexual, so he was made the butt of their jokes and teased about his sexual orientation. Nevertheless, he insisted and they accepted, however, that he should be treated with a certain measure of respect.

As the study progressed, Alberto told his young male friends in the barrio about my sexual orientation and that it was alright to tease and joke with me. Letting them know that I was homosexual made it possible for me to experience firsthand what it was like to be on the receiving end of these often daily events. Further, on several occasions sexual overtures were secretly made to me, one-on-one, by some of the young men in the barrio. What I learned from my personal encounters with these young men I could not have learned any other way.

The major objective of this book is to present intimate views of some of the Mexican men I have studied and their homosexualities. Except for fictional accounts in novels and plays, very little has been written in detail about the intimate lives of homosexual people in most societies around the world. Excerpts from my journals and audiotapes are used to illustrate the ordinariness and diversity of men who seek homosexual encounters with other men. The impact of homosexuality on their daily lives is seen through their interactions with family, friends, workmates, and strangers. I also present the social and cultural settings in which these activities take place and show how they affect individual behavior.

No attempt is made in this book, however, to extrapolate from the lives presented here to the larger society of men who have sex with men in Mexico. Rather, the vignettes and four profiles of lives and activities selected are used to illustrate the kinds of accommodations made by these men in response to societal disapproval, and how they may thus behave and be affected differently by their family life and social and cultural imperatives. In the concluding chapter I briefly sum up some of my major findings on Mexican male homosexualities and make some conjectures about the AIDS epidemic and gay liberation in Mexico and how these two events have affected the homosexual behaviors of Mexican men and societal attitudes toward male homosexuality. Readers interested in more detailed discussions can refer to my journal articles listed in the bibliography.

As noted, my research on male homosexuality in Mexico has been conducted mainly with lower-middle-class and upper-lower-class Mexican males of mixed Spanish and American Indian ancestry. Referred to as mestizos, people with this background make up a majority of the Mexican population, which numbers close to ninety million at present. The national culture reflects this ancestry, and most Mexican mestizos proudly accept their mixed Spanish and Indian heritage. Indian subpopulations of varying size continue to live in all regions of Mexico but most are concentrated in the southern Mexican states. I have not studied them and there have only been a few limited studies of their sexual behaviors to date; see, for example, Chiñas (1985), Williams (1986), and Wilson (1995).

I specifically defined my research population as that segment of the mestizo male subpopulation who have homosexual encounters, regardless of their sexual identity. This was a deliberate decision made at the outset of the study in order to put aside the difficult questions of who is homosexual and what is homosexuality. Respondents thus cover the spectrum: some identify themselves as gay; others as homosexual, bisexual, or as being in a state of flux; and still others as heterosexual. This was an important decision because the findings of my research would have been considerably more limited had I focused, for example, only on men who identified themselves as gay—a relatively small minority of the subpopulation of Mexican men who have sexual encounters with other men.

One final note: When I embarked on my study of Mexican male homosexuality in the summer of 1968, I was surprised to find that no graduate student in anthropology had ever done a Ph.D. dissertation on homosexual behavior. I also discovered that few anthropologists up to that time had had the courage (or interest?) to study human sexual behavior in other cultures as a major focus of their research; even fewer had had the courage to study highly stigmatized (by *our* culture) homosexual behavior. Sex research concerning homosexuality in different societies and cultures around the world was not legitimized until the mid-1980s when, as a result of the AIDS pandemic, such information became extremely important in the design of intervention programs to help prevent the spread of HIV, the virus that causes AIDS.

I thus had to start my Mexican study twenty-five years ago essentially from scratch. No previous study of any aspect of homosexuality had been made in Mexico. A literature search revealed only a few impressionistic statements on male homosexuality (Paz 1961; Klapp 1964; and Kiev 1968) and a collection of homosexually oriented word games and jokes from the study of a village located in southern Mexico (Ingham 1968).

Since then, however, a number of excellent field studies and surveys of male homosexuality have been conducted in Mexico and other parts of Latin America. Taylor (1978a) did a pioneering study of male homosexual life in Mexico City in 1974–75. Three Mexican sociologists—Gomezjara, Barrera, and Perez (1978)—gathered some interesting data on male homosexuality in their monumental study of male and female prostitution in Mexico in the late 1970s. Murray (1987) did some systematic data collection on male homosexuality and the family in Mexico City and Guatemala City intermittently between 1973 and 1984. Alonso and Koreck (1989) gathered some data in the mid-1980s on the symbolic meaning of sexual relations between macho men and effeminate homosexual men (labeled *jotos*) in some rural towns in northern Mexico. Lancaster (1988) studied the construction of male homosexuality and stigma in Nicaragua in the 1980s. And Parker (1989) started his study of the social and cultural construction of sexual life in contemporary Brazil in the early 1980s. Additional research has been done by Arboleda (1987) in Peru, Kutsche and Page (1992) in Costa Rica, and Fry (1987) and Whitam (1987) in Brazil.

The AIDS epidemic has also led to some interesting survey and field research on Mexican male homosexuality in Mexico and southern California. For example, GOHL (Grupo Orgullo Homosexual Liberación), the gay liberation organization in Guadalajara, collaborated with Dr. Eduardo Vázquez-Valls, director of the Institute of Infectious Diseases (Instituto de Patología Infecciosa Experimental) at the University of Guadalajara, in a longitudinal study of male homosexual behavior and infection by the AIDS virus from 1984 to 1990. González Block and Liguori (1992) did both field and survey research on homosexual behaviors, HIV infection, and AIDS in working-class populations in Mexico City in the late 1980s. Epidemiological surveys were also conducted in the late 1980s in Mexico City, Merida, Acapulco, Tijuana, and Monterrey by staff members of the Mexican Ministry of Health and reported on by Izazola-Licea et al. (1991), Garcia et al. (1991), and Hernandez et al. (1992). And Raúl Magaña and I (1991) conducted an ethnosexual study of immigrant Mexican male homosexual behaviors and HIV infection in southern California in the late 1980s.

During the 1970s and 1980s, before the AIDS epidemic, more open discussions about sexual behaviors had started to take place in Mexico. The results of Quijada's small survey of male and female sexual behavior in Mexico City was published in 1977. The first openly distributed explicit novel about male homosexuality, Zapata's *El Vampiro de la Colonia Roma*, was published in 1979. Del Rio published a book of his Mexican caricatures about love in the time of AIDS (*El Amor en los Tiempos del SIDA*, 1988). And the literary magazine *Nexos* published a special issue on sex in Mexico (*El Sexo en México*) in 1989.

Findings from all the above-mentioned studies and literary works will be discussed in the concluding chapter of this book, which will present an overview of current knowledge about Mexican male homosexuality. There I will compare these findings with my own field research and life history profiles to show how an understanding of human sexual behaviors is facilitated by the diverse approaches used by social scientists and writers.

DE LOS

OTROS

PART ONE

Sex Between Men in

Guadalajara and

Northwestern Mexico

ONE | *Sex Roles, Family Life,*

and Homosexuality:

The Sociocultural Background

The following description of those sociocultural factors particularly relevant to male homosexual behaviors in Mexico draws upon the ground-breaking studies of the typical middle-class Mexican family by McGinn (1966) and Peñalosa (1968) and includes some items not cited in their papers as well as some of my own analyses of Mexican census data. I should also note that the family roles described represent the normative ideals of the dominant Mexican national culture of the mestizoized majority of the population. For a critical review of these "normative cultural ideals," see the polemical essay by Kinzer (1973).

Sex Roles and the Family

The Importance of Manliness

The Mexican mestizo culture places a high value on "manliness." A salient feature of the society is a sharp delimitation between the roles played by males and females. In general, men are expected to be dominant and independent and females to be submissive and dependent. The distinct boundary between male and female roles in Mexico appears to be due in part to a culturally defined hypermasculine ideal referred to as *machismo*. The ideal female role is generally believed to be the opposite of the ideal male role and may be referred to as *marianismo*.

Machismo is most often characterized by describing the attributes of the macho male. In thinking about manliness, a Mexican male may measure himself, his sons, and his male relatives and friends in terms of such qualities as courage, dominance, power, aggressiveness, and invulnerability. The following statement by a Mexican boxer (quoted in Ross 1966) illustrates how *machismo* may be conceptualized: "*Machismo* means manhood. To the Mexican man *machismo* means to have the manly traits of honor and dignity. To have courage to fight. To keep his word and protect his name. To run his house, to control his woman, and to direct his children. This is *machismo*, to be a man in your own eyes" (p. 386).

As a noun, *macho* is defined in English as "a male animal; in particular, a he-goat," and as an adjective, as "masculine, vigorous, robust, male" (Velázquez 1967). Although not all males in Mexico (probably not even a majority) aspire to actually play the macho role in its extreme form, the available evidence suggests that the folk concept of machismo continues to operate as a principal force dominating the learned part of the Mexican male gender role.

As a consequence of the high status given manliness, Mexican males from birth onward are expected to behave in as manly a way as possible. Peñalosa sums it up as follows: "Any signs of feminization are severely repressed in the boy." McGinn concludes: "The young Mexican boy may be severely scolded for engaging in feminine activities, such as playing with dolls or jacks. Parents verbally and physically punish 'feminine' traits in their male children." He also notes that in a 1964 study of the Mexican family in Guadalajara, Villasenor found that ninety-four of the one hundred middle-class mothers making up her sample believed it important for a boy "to be manly." The importance of manly behavior continues throughout the life span of Mexican males.

The opposite of machismo is the female stereotype of the ideal woman, often referred to as *marianismo*. Stevens (1971) points out that like its macho counterpart it

> is ubiquitous in every social class. There is near universal agreement on what a "real woman" is like and how she should act. Among the characteristics of this ideal are semidivinity, moral superiority, and spiritual strength. This spiritual strength engenders abnegation, that is, an

infinite capacity for humility and sacrifice. No self-denial is too great
. . . no limit can be divined to her vast store of patience with the men
of her world. . . . She is also submissive to the demands of the men:
husbands, sons, fathers, brothers. (pp. 94–95)

But she also points out:

Beneath the submissiveness, however, lies the strength of her conviction—shared by the entire society—that men must be humored, for
after all, everyone knows that they are *como niños* (like little boys) whose
intemperance, foolishness, and obstinacy must be forgiven because
"they can't help the way they are." (p. 95)

No one knows precisely how these stereotypes affect the social behaviors of mestizo males and females living in Mexico today. Everyone
can point out important changes that have taken place in male and
female gender roles in contemporary Mexican society as a result of
more open discussions about women's rights and sexual behavior. Most
of the Mexican people I know, however, say that the effects of these
two stereotypes remain important and will continue into the future.

"Good" Women and "Bad" Women

Another prominent feature of Mexican society is the categorization
of females as being either "good" or "bad." A "good" woman is
represented as being basically the reciprocal of the macho male—that
is, she must be submissive and dependent. Before marrying, according
to the normative cultural ideal, she must also be chaste and faithful.
After marriage she must continue to be faithful and should not demonstrate excessive sexual interest, even in her husband. The categorization "good" thus comes down to a basic belief that a woman cannot
be considered a prime sexual target and still be considered good. Any
woman may therefore be labeled "bad" if she is primarily thought of
by males as being immediately exploitable as a sexual outlet. It is interesting to note that even female prostitutes may be responsive to the
cultural ideal of female passivity. Roebuck and McNamara (1973), for
example, reporting on female prostitution in a Mexican border city,
noted that they played "a more feminine and passive role" in the houses
of prostitution patronized exclusively by Mexican men.

A related aspect of the "good-bad" dichotomization of females is a
double standard of sexual morality that favors Mexican males. The

double standard begins prior to marriage. In the Mexican courtship system the prospective bride is labeled a *novia,* the prospective groom a *novio.* The Mexican couple can be said to have an understanding. McGinn notes that "this arrangement is more serious than the American steady system, yet less formal than an engagement."

The period of courtship may last five years or more. Since she may one day be his wife and the mother of his children, a *novia* must in the eyes of her *novio* fall into the category "good"; she obviously cannot be considered a *primary* sexual target before the marriage. Under existing mores, however, at the same time a Mexican male is courting a *novia* he may have a series of sexual contacts with whatever outlets are available. Girlfriends considered appropriate for sexual seduction are referred to as *amigas;* lovers are referred to as *amantes.* After marriage the double standard is maintained and the husband may continue to seek sexual outlets in addition to his wife.

Several of my Mexican respondents claimed that they did not consider it important for their *novias* to be chaste and faithful. They felt that this aspect of courtship is breaking down in the large urban areas. Nevertheless, they still believed it to be an important factor for most Mexican males. Taylor (1974) suggests that heterosexual anal intercourse—considered to be a common occurrence by his Mexico City respondents—may in Mexico be "a method of maintaining the female's status as a vaginal virgin during courtship and a common form of birth control." Hernandez et al. (1992) report in their study of bisexual men in Mexico City that close to 5 percent of their sample (70 of 1,431) had practiced anal sex half the time or more with their female sex partners. This incidence of anal sex reported between bisexual men and their female partners, however, may just reflect the fact that a large majority of the men responding to the survey always practice anal sex with their male sex partners.

Separate Social Networks

Another feature of Mexican society very relevant to patterns of male homosexual behavior is the separate network of friends retained by males after marriage. Peer group relationships, of particular importance in adolescence, may remain essentially unchanged by marriage. Peñalosa sums it up as follows: "In social life a Mexican man's marital status is of little practical importance, as a man carries on virtually the same sort of social life after marriage as he did before—and one in which the women have little part." Social relationships of Mexican males tend to be all male in character both before and after marriage. Men feel free to spend a lot of their spare time with their male friends rather than with their wives.

Drinking establishments in Mexico—cantinas, bars, and night-clubs—are popular locations where Mexican males spend free time away from their families. With few exceptions, these establishments by convention are restricted to male customers. Females who go generally have working relationships as dance hostesses or prostitutes. They obviously fall into the "bad" category. A "good" woman in Mexico would never be seen in a public drinking establishment, except possibly in cities that have hotel bars or nightclubs for tourists. Even there, however, a Mexican woman would have to consider herself "liberated" in order to frequent such establishments alone on any regular basis.

Proportion of Unmarried Males

Still another important characteristic of Mexican society is the proportion of single males past the age of puberty. Although in any given age group the proportion that is single varies over time and within and between states or regions, marriage patterns in Mexico today lead to a sizable percentage of males in the northwestern states of Jalisco, Nayarit, Sinaloa, Sonora, and Baja California not marrying until in their late twenties. In a 1990 national census the proportion of single males distributed in the total population in Guadalajara by age groups between twelve and thirty-nine were as follows:

Age Group	Percent Single
12–14	99.2
15–19	96.1
20–24	71.4
25–29	38.2
30–34	18.2
35–39	10.5

Although a majority had married or were in some kind of consensual union, it is interesting to note that close to 40 percent of the males in their *late twenties* were still single. Moreover, compared to thirty years ago, the percent of Guadalajaran single males in their early and late twenties has increased: in the age group from twenty to twenty-four, single males increased from 66 percent in 1960 to 71 percent in 1990; and in the age group from twenty-five to twenty-nine, from 33 percent in 1960 to 38 percent in 1990.

The Importance of the Family

Yet another relevant factor of Mexican society is the tremendous hold of the family on its members, single or married, throughout their lives. Although individuals may move away from home because of marriage, quarrels, or for economic reasons, contact with parents, siblings, and other family members is, in the long run, most always closely maintained and cherished. An important tradition in many Mexican families is for "adult children" to gather together at their parental home on weekends, usually Sundays, to eat, enjoy one another's company, and discuss mutual problems. Most men are believed to have a special bonding with their mothers and so take care to visit them as often as possible while their mothers are alive.

It is also important to note that while single, a large majority of Mexican males—a little over 80 percent according to the 1970 census—continue to live in some kind of family grouping. This pattern apparently holds true even when single males are in their late twenties or thirties. The general belief is that the only way a single person is able to move away from his or her family, even if he or she wants to and can afford to, is to move to another area too far away for coresidence to be practical. But even those that move away may at some future point choose to move back home.

Distribution of Income

The final characteristic of Mexican society that is important to consider is distribution of income. Inequalities in income distribution combined with high birthrates result in large segments of the urban as well as rural Mexican population living on incomes that barely provide the basic necessities of life. Although most city dwellers may fare better than rural folk, the available data suggest that a majority of the population, urban and rural, still tend to be in marginal situations economically.

Census data on the distribution of income in Guadalajara are not available. Inequality in income distribution is suggested by such factors as generally low wages for the working class, high rates of unemployment (12 percent) and underemployment (40 percent), and relatively low levels of education received by a large proportion of the population (six years is the mandatory requirement). Riding (1984) reports that, according to estimates made by the Mexican government in 1977, the wealthiest 20 percent of the population controlled 54.4 percent of all income. Some changes have taken place over the past thirty years, notably the expansion of the middle class, which has gained a greater share of income at the expense of both the top elite and the chronically poor: between 1968 and 1977, the income share of the top 5 percent fell from 27.7 to 23.9 percent, and that of the bottom 50 percent from 18.3 to 16.2 percent. But in practice even the middle classes—professionals, well-placed bureaucrats, middle-level company executives, owners of small businesses—still belong to the wealthiest 30 percent that earn 73 percent of the country's total income. Thus, while Mexico's very rich live in a style that would put all but a few American millionaires to shame and the middle class enjoy the standards of suburban Americans, its majority lives in degrees of poverty ranging from mere survival to outright misery.   (p. 319)

A significant outcome of the inequitable distribution of income in Mexico is crowded living conditions. Census data suggest that a little over two-thirds of the Mexican population in January 1970 lived in one- or two-room dwellings. Although the percentage of inhabitants living in such small quarters in urban areas is less than in rural areas, urban crowding is nevertheless extensive. For example, in Guadalajara 43 percent of the population in 1970 lived in one- and two-room dwellings. Leyva (1970) compares population density per room for a number of countries, and Mexico ranks among the highest in the world. The average number of persons per room in Mexico in 1960 was estimated by the Mexican National Institute of Housing to be 2.6 in urban areas and 3.4 in rural areas (comparable figures for the United States are 0.6 in urban areas and 0.7 in rural areas). With high rates of inflation and the deteriorating economic situation in Mexico since that time, the housing situation has probably worsened in Guadalajara and other fast-growing cities in the northwestern states of Mexico.

Furthermore, Mexico's economy turned sharply downward in late 1981 and 1982, and over the next eight years the country suffered its worst economic crisis since the revolutionary period of 1910–1921. One effect of this economic slump in Guadalajara was the migration of large segments of the population to the United States. Escobar Latapí (1993) notes in an article on changing socioeconomic conditions and migration patterns in Mexico that at the nadir of the Mexican crisis of the 1980s, the only good news one heard in popular neighborhoods in Guadalajara had to do with "El Norte," which usually meant California. Whether people talked about opening a small business, making an improvement to their house, or taking a vacation, the United States was usually a part of the story. For the first time, it seemed that success in metropolitan Mexico depended not on "making it" there, but on having California connections or going there oneself. . . . Access to U.S. remittances, together with an intensification of local paid work, was one of the key elements allowing these households to survive the 1980s. International migration became a significant source of income for the popular urban sector and thousands of rural settlements. (p. 75)

A recent economic study of one hundred poor households in Guadalajara, cited by Escobar Latapí, "revealed that over a quarter of them received dollar remittances systematically at one point or another from 1982 through 1987" (p. 75). And studies of workers in Guadalajara found that "twenty-eight percent of household heads interviewed in 1990 had immediate kin living in the U.S., and a further 32.2 percent had other relatives there" (p. 76).

These findings will help the reader understand why so many of my Guadalajaran respondents have lived and traveled back and forth to the United States. It is thus not unusual, for example, that three of the four Mexican men profiled in the second part of this book had during some part of their lives lived north of the border.

Mexico and Homosexuality

Now I will turn to some aspects of the sociocultural setting in Mexico which relate more specifically to Mexican male homosexuality. The homosexual labels, beliefs, and joking relationships to be considered here make up the background setting of homosexuality with which the majority of males in the society must contend throughout their lives. No Kinsey-type survey of male or female sexual behavior has been conducted in Mexico. As a result of the AIDS epidemic, epidemiological surveys of sexual behavior have been conducted in some of Mexico's largest cities in the past ten years, but they have been based on skewed samples that cannot be used to make general estimates of the distributions of sexual behaviors in the society at large. It is therefore possible to make only "guesstimates" about the distribution of different types of sexual behaviors. Nevertheless, as will be seen, there appears to be an awareness and certain kind of openness on the part of Mexican society with regard to homosexuality that suggest that perhaps a larger percentage of Mexican males have at some time been involved in homosexual behaviors than have Anglo-Americans.

Deserved or undeserved, Guadalajara has a special reputation for homosexuality in Mexico. Although males from other parts of Mexico visit the city expressly in search of homosexual encounters, Guadalajara, unlike Mexico City, does not have a large subcultural grouping of homosexual males who have moved in from out of state. However, there appears to be a sizable number of males from rural and small urban settings living within a two- to three-hour bus ride who come into the city regularly on weekends in search of homosexual encounters.

Terms for Homosexuality

Several Spanish terms are used in Mexico to describe male participants in homosexual encounters. Of particular interest to this study is the fact that in popular usage the terms clearly distinguish the passive "effeminate" participants from the active "masculine" participants. Most of the popularly used terms, however, are not usually used in the presence of women or in social situations calling for refined manners.

Maricón and *raro* are the only reasonably polite words used to designate a homosexual male. Both connote male effeminacy as well as homosexuality. According to Velázquez (1967), the first definition of *maricón* is "sissy." Colloquially, it is used to mean "fairy" or "queer," i.e., homosexual. *Raro* translated into English can mean strange, odd, or queer. Used in a certain context with a certain inflection, it can also suggest an effeminate homosexual male. For example, I heard the mother of one of my respondents say to him that she thought one of his friends, who had come to his birthday party, was *raro*. My respondent told me later that she was really suggesting that his friend was homosexual.

Puto, *joto*, and *mayate* are probably the Spanish words most widely used by males in Guadalajara and the northwestern states to describe participants in homosexual encounters. It is the consensus of my respondents that though these terms are widely known they are derogatory, vulgar words, generally not used in polite company. *Puto* and *joto* designate passive effeminate homosexuals. *Mayate*, on the other hand, designates the active masculine participant in a homosexual pairing but does not connote him homosexual. As far as I can determine the evolution of this word, *mayate* was first used to signify a bright green poisonous beetle. Applied next to human beings, at first it designated a male who likes to wear loud, flashy clothes; then, a male prostitute for other males; and finally, any male who takes the insertive sex role in homosexual intercourse. Along the U.S.-Mexican border the word is often used as a label for black people.

Although *mayate* may have many meanings, currently in most conversations among men it is clearly understood to mean a young macho heterosexual male who has casual insertive anal sexual contacts with effeminate anal-receptive men of any age. If a young man is consistently paid to have sex with other men he may be labeled *chichifo*, which is the Mexican equivalent for the North American term "male hustler." *Chichifo* may also connote that a hustler is a thief. *Puto* is probably the word most often used in graffiti. During my travels over the past twenty-five years, I have seen it more often than any other word scribbled on the walls of bathrooms in cantinas and bars, public buildings, and houses in all parts of Mexico. The following is an excellent example of bathroom graffiti I saw in a cantina in Guadalajara: *ojo! mayates, soy puto, me gusta la verga* (attention mayates, I'm a puto, I like cock!).

There are many other words used to signify participants in homosexual encounters. Most of them, however, designate only effeminate male participants, and none of them, according to my respondents, is widely known and used. *Picador, vajador,* and *padrote* refer to masculine participants who are assumed to be anal insertors. The last two terms also connote a male who is a pimp and a prostitute for both sexes. *Padrote* is in addition a slang word used by students to denote someone as snazzy or sharp looking. Jiménez (1971) lists forty additional terms for passive male participants. *Pastilla, del otro lado, de los otros,* and *de manita caída* are the terms best known by my respondents. The first term literally refers to a pill or candy; the next two to the "other side" and to the "others"; and the last one to a limp wrist, a sure sign of effeminacy in a male.

There are a number of words special to the homosexual subculture of Mexico. *Ambiente, loca,* and *puta* are three of the most popular ones. *Ambiente* in colloquial usage signifies a lively gay person (the "life of the party," for example, may be referred to as *de ambiente*). Between homosexual males in the know, however, it is the discreet word used to designate a third person as homosexual. For instance, in a discussion about a male whose sexual practices are unknown, one homosexual male may ask another: "Do you think so-and-so is *ambiente?*" *Loca* and *puta* are used mostly by effeminate homosexual males to describe one of their own kind who in their judgment is acting exceptionally flamboyant. In a conversation they will refer to someone outside their conversational group as being *muy puta* or *muy loca*—that is, that person is overdoing his feminine characterization. A *puta* is a female prostitute; *loca* designates a crazy female person. *Muy puta*, then, suggests that the male in question is acting like a female whore; and *muy loca* suggests he is acting like a crazy female. A homosexual male who plays both sex roles (anal insertive and receptive) is referred to as *internacional*. This term became popular in the early 1970s.

Some word combinations used in the homosexual subculture describe specific types and situations. For example, if two passive effeminate homosexual males sleep together and have sex, they are jokingly referred to as *locas manfloras*. *Manflora* is a popular term for lesbian, so they are thus being referred to as crazy lesbians. *Papacita* and *papasote* are words of endearment often used by young homosexual males to refer to older masculine males they think are sexually attractive and would like to have an affair with. *Papacita* literally means "little daddy."

Negative Attitudes Toward Homosexuality

Judging from the behavior and beliefs of my respondents in Guadalajara and in other urban areas in Mexico, from the views presented in Mexican newspapers, magazines, television programs, and motion pictures, and from the operations of the Mexican law authorities, most people in Mexico generally view homosexuality with considerable disapproval. On the surface, in fact, their view does not appear to differ from that of a majority of North Americans. The following observations lead me to this conclusion.

First, only a small percentage of my respondents believed that their families knew about their homosexual behavior. Moreover, it was not something they wanted them to know. And they did not want them to know mainly because of their belief that it is stigmatizing behavior. Not only do they believe that their families would not approve or condone such behavior, but they also fear possible rejection by family and friends or that if their behavior were known they would be forced to leave or be cast out of their family home. Interestingly, however, even respondents who have had their homosexual behavior revealed to their families, and thus are labeled "homosexual," still maintain themselves—or try to—in such a way that revelations about their homosexual involvements are minimized. Since most of these respondents do in fact continue to live with their families—the fear that they will be cast out only rarely appears to be realized—the family must also maintain a front.

The point here is that *none* of my respondents has looked upon his homosexual encounters as behavior generally acceptable to his family, nonhomosexual friends, or to society at large. This view has been substantiated by my own experiences with respondents and their families. None has ever overtly betrayed himself as a homosexual to his family in a group situation, even in those cases where most of the family members knew about his homosexuality. At birthday parties, for example, respondents always invited and danced with neighborhood girls. Even the most effeminate of my respondents presented the most masculine image possible during family gatherings.

Second, although not a taboo subject, homosexuality is either handled as a joke or is ridiculed and condemned in the mass media. For example, variety shows on Mexican television—like *Siempre en Domingos*—often have skits depicting males who are weak, passive, and effeminate, the implication being that they are homosexual. This same general theme may be followed in the stage shows of popular variety theaters, and in Mexican movies. *Los Superfrios*, a popular Mexican comic book series some years ago, once devoted an issue to the story of a Mexican general and his attempts to interest his effeminate son in girls ("El Generalote," 1970). In Mexican novels homosexuality is usually presented as a tortuous, agonizing experience (e.g., see Maldonado 1969). The first Mexican novel to deal with homosexuality in a positive way—Luis Zapata's *Las Aventuras, Desventuras y Sueños de Adonis Garcia, El Vampiro de la Colonia Roma (The Adventures, Misfortunes, and Dreams of Adonis Garcia, the Vampire of Colonia Roma)*—was not published until 1979 and was also the first novel with a homosexual protagonist that was allowed to be freely sold throughout Mexico.

The most denigrating view of homosexuality in the mass media is presented by a tabloid newspaper published every Wednesday in Mexico City and distributed throughout Mexico. Called *ALARMA!*, it focuses on grisly murders, rapes, scandals, and highway accidents occurring all over Mexico. I saw copies of it in practically every home I visited in Guadalajara. During the year and a half I lived there, I read the publication weekly. It had considerable reporting about homosexual activity in Mexico and the United States, and at least once a month it had a banner headline about homosexuals. Headlines and reportage maintained the same general viewpoint that homosexual males are degenerate, vicious, immoral, and effeminate.

The following headlines are representative of *ALARMA!* from November 1969 to July 1971:

> June 10, 1970—EPIDEMIA DE DESVIADOS SEXUALES (Rash of Sexual Deviates)
>
> December 16, 1970—ASQUEROSA DEPRAVACÍON SEXUAL (Disgusting Sexual Depravity)
>
> March 10, 1971—FUROR DE SEXOS EQUIVOCADOS EN LA INMORALIDAD DEL CARNIVAL (Madness of Female Impersonators in the Immorality of the Mardi Gras)
>
> July 7, 1971—ATREVIMIENTO DE DEGENERADOS! BODA DE DOS HOMOSEXUALES! (Boldness of Degenerates! Marriage of Two Homosexuals!)

Photographs of effeminate males or males dressed in female clothes accompanied each of the headlines, along with text on the cover or inside the periodical that tersely described the kind of activity to be expected from homosexual males—that is, lewd, repulsive, bizarre, and so on. Readers were led to believe that homosexuals were commonly involved in murder, robbery, drugs, and other types of criminal activity.

Although the names of some of these publications have changed since these headlines appeared over two decades ago—*Alarde, Angustia,* and *Peligro* are three new tabloids in print—the themes and headlines have not changed. The major difference is that in recent years some responsible newspapers, journals, and television news programs in Mexico City and Guadalajara, such as *El Nacional, La Jornada,* and *Televisa,* have presented much more positive coverage about homosexuality.

Third, although there are no legal sanctions in Mexico against consenting adult males having sexual congress in private, every effort is made by the authorities to keep any behavior that might be interpreted as homosexual as invisible as possible to the general public. Both uniformed and plainclothes policemen enforce this general policy. As previously mentioned, the police are most active in parks and movie houses where they harass or arrest effeminate males in order to suppress open solicitation. They also close down or force a policy change in bathhouses if their reputation for homosexual activity becomes scandalous and thereby known to the population at large.

Additionally, according to my effeminate respondents, during election years the police increase their harassment of males who flaunt their effeminacy in public. I was in Guadalajara during a presidential election year and personally witnessed an increase in police activity. On three separate occasions in the month prior to the election, for example, I saw the police picking up effeminate males on the main thoroughfare of Guadalajara for questioning. The effeminate males were guilty of nothing more than walking down the sidewalk. I later learned that the police had accused them of being homosexuals and threatened them with a fine and jail. Most paid their *mordida* to the police and were let go without formal booking but not until they agreed to point out other homosexual males as they were being driven around the city.

This kind of police activity was one of the motivating factors that led to the Mexican gay liberation movement, which began in the late 1970s in Mexico City and spread by the early 1980s to Guadalajara, Tijuana, and other large urban areas in Mexico. (The evolution of the gay liberation movement in Guadalajara, from its inception to the present, is discussed later in this book.)

Acceptance of Homosexuality

Although Mexican society generally disapproves of homosexuality, it seems to recognize the inevitability of homosexual contacts between men. There seems to be acceptance in Mexico of the reality that most males have multiple sexual outlets both when single and when married. A man's sexual outlets other than his wife are not socially approved, but are nevertheless put up with so long as they are carried out discreetly.

There is some evidence that homosexual contacts between males are thought no better or worse than other kinds of sexual outlets lacking social approval; however, the provision here seems to be that that understanding is extended essentially only to those playing the role of insertors in anal intercourse. For example, a North American respondent who attended public schools in Guadalajara from the age of fifteen told me that homosexuality was a topic of daily conversation among the boys in his *segundaria* and *preparatoria* (equivalent in the United States to junior and senior high schools); and it was not unusual for *activo* (presumably insertor only) boys to relate their sexual contacts with *pasivo* (presumably insertee only) boys. Those relating their same-sex contacts were not considered homosexual by their classmates, he claimed, because they were *macho* (masculine) and *activo*. They might be considered degenerate but certainly not homosexual. An effeminate fifteen-year-old *pasivo* informant provided another bit of evidence when, in response to my question whether he looked for sexual contacts among his schoolmates, he told me: "No! They come looking for me . . . alone, they come and ask for it."

Paz (1961) supports the notion that only the passive male is considered homosexual with the statement that "masculine homosexuality is regarded with a certain indulgence [in Mexico] insofar as the active agent is concerned" (p. 39). Klapp (1964), in a study of Mexican social types, also indirectly provides support when he notes that "Mexicans are severe toward 'unmanly men', such as the homosexual or pimp. They are also severe toward 'women who are too free' and have lost status, especially by sexual promiscuity" (p. 412). This is no doubt true as an expressed attitude but does not preclude the acceptance of these types as sexual objects. In equating "unmanly men" and homosexuals, Klapp points out that in Mexico, as in the United States, the public stereotype of the homosexual as "effeminate" persists.

From early childhood on, Mexican males are made aware of the labels used to denote homosexual males—*puto, joto, maricón*—with the clear understanding that these homosexual males are guilty of unmanly, effeminate behavior. It is important to note that *homosexual* and *afeminado* are synonymous with the more often used colloquial terms *puto, joto,* and *maricón* (see, for example, Jiménez 1971, 199). Since all these terms apply only to those males who play the anal-receptive sex role in a homosexual encounter, the implication is that the anal-insertive masculine male is not homosexual—and separate terms exist to describe him (*mayate, chichifo,* and *picador*). Thus, from an early age Mexican males are likely to be aware of same-sex contacts and of the *activo-pasivo* dichotomy that exists between males having sexual contact, and that there is a stigma associated with the *pasivo* but not the *activo* sex role.

One use of the *puto, joto,* and *maricón* labels is to discipline young boys so that they will conform to the cultural ideals of Mexican masculinity. For example, a father may correct his small crying son by saying, "*Que no eres hombre? Pareces maricón!*" ("Aren't you a man? You seem like a sissy!"—i.e., a homosexual); or a maid may try to quiet a three-year-old boy by saying, "*Callate, maricón!*" ("Shut up, sissy!"). During my years of travel in Mexico, I have often heard small children tease each other with the labels *joto* and *puto;* and when walking through neighborhoods of all social classes, it was not unusual to see *puto* and *joto* scribbled on walls.

As a result of the negative sanctioning of effeminate behavior from childhood on, Mexican males predictably hold effeminate males in low esteem throughout their life. They are always the butt of jokes, teased, and harassed. At the same time, however, there appears to be a tacit understanding that this type of male will come into being regardless of preventive actions taken. One hears such comments as, "Perhaps he was born that way"; or, because of an indulgent mother or sister, "he is becoming that way." The belief that the "affected" male may change his behavior is not given up easily. It is held apparently until the male is in his late teens or even beyond. And his family may still believe that he might outgrow it, might even do "the right thing" eventually and get married. But, gradually, through the day-to-day interaction between son and parents and among siblings, both sides accommodate to the reality of an apparently unchangeable pattern of behavior. Since family life in Mexico is such that the majority of unmarried children continue to live with their families, an accommodation between the affected male and his family is necessary to prevent (or at least to reduce) family discord. The alternative is to cast the son out, but in my twenty-five years of research in Mexico, I found this to be much more an implied threat than a reality.

There appears to be an accommodation not only between families and their effeminate sons and brothers but also between the society at large and effeminate males. The principal tactic, common both to the family and society, is to keep effeminate behavior out of sight as much as possible. An effeminate male tries as best he can, especially in family gatherings, to behave in a masculine way. If he has sexual contacts with males rather than females, he does it discreetly. The fact that the contacts are taking place is ignored by all parties concerned. On a more general level, as mentioned above, the police attempt to keep effeminate male behavior, or any kind of male behavior that might be interpretable as homosexual, out of public view—unless such behavior is clearly a matter of "horsing around."

Jokes and Word Games

The tension that exists between Mexican society and effeminate homosexual males is somewhat relieved, it would seem, by the homosexually oriented jokes and word games that are part of so many Mexican social interactions. During my years of fieldwork, rarely did a week go by that I did not observe one or two such interchanges during business transactions, or while walking around the downtown areas of cities and in neighborhoods, or in bars and cantinas. While most of these jokes and word games occur between men, they also occur between men and women.

The following examples provide some idea of the variety of situations in which the joking and word games take place. One afternoon, while waiting for my car to be repaired, I observed a thirty-year-old mechanic and his eighteen-year-old helper trading homosexual jokes. These centered around the possibility that the younger man was a desirable sex object for *jotos*. On another occasion, in a small cantina in a *zona roja* (red-light district) one night, I observed a well-dressed middle-aged man play a lengthy homosexually oriented word game with one of the bar girls. She had started the word game with this regular customer by suggesting that since he had not paid much attention to her during recent visits, he must be more interested in men. A male may also play the buffoon while with a group of male friends. An informant reported, for example, that in his school a boy might remark to a pretty girl as she walked by, "If I were *really* a man, I would like to go around with you." His male friends would respond by laughing and whistling, and calling him "*Papacito*." The implication of the label is that he is both handsome and desirable. This is then likely to trigger a set of jokes about *jotos*. Another respondent, who to my knowledge had had no homosexual contacts, reported the following sequence of events between him and his *amiga*. He claimed it to be typical of the ways girls joke with their boyfriends about the possibility of their being a *joto*. He was talking to his *amiga* one evening about nine o'clock just outside the main entrance to her house. Her mother called her to come in but she ignored the call. A second call came. Worrying that the mother might get angry with him, he told his *amiga* that he had better leave so she could obey her mother and go inside. His *amiga* responded by saying, "*Ay tú!*"—the literal translation and implication of the exclamation being that "you [are a *joto*] too." He then responded by saying, "Do you really think so?" The conversation then went back and forth with the *amiga* implying that he wanted to leave because he was afraid of her and preferred boys.

Homosexual jokes and word games are not just an urban phenomenon but are also reported as being well developed in rural Mexico. In a study of culture and personality in a Mexican village in Morelos, a small state south of Mexico City, Ingham (1968) collected a number of excellent examples. Referring to word games (*albures*), he offers the following descriptions:

> *Albures* are normally heard in cantinas, on street corners where men gather in the evening, or when they play cards. *Albureando* commonly commences when someone approaches a group. The entering person then grabs the buttocks (or, occasionally, the penis) of someone in the group to suggest he wants to "make" him. As he does this he may say, "Loan it to me," to which the other retorts, "Loan yourself to so-and-so, so he can use you like an animal."   (p. 231)

> A friend named Martin can be abused by saying to him, "*Hola Martin Cholano*," the *albur* of which lies in the syllables *in-cho* (insert) and *ano* (anus). [Literally, *hincho*, so swollen anus.]   (p. 232)

> Once when Carlos approached Miguel he grabbed the latter's buttocks and said, "What is happening, butt," while Miguel protested, saying, "I'm decent, don't be screwing with me," whereupon Carlos grabbed Miguel's chest as if he were a woman and said, "Ay little mother, what nice teats you have." When Carlos, who is a bachelor, intimated that Miguel was a queer, Miguel replied, "But don't sleep with Manuela" (a girl's name but an allusion to masturbation as well from the word *mano*, hand).   (pp. 232–33)

Ingham concludes that the content of *albures* is often homosexual. In the village of his study, however, he claims that the term *homosexual* has a distinctive meaning—that is, a "homosexual is penetrated by others; those who penetrate are not homosexual" (p. 236).

Ingham notes that jokes are told in the same contexts as word games but are more often heard on street corners rather than in cantinas. The following is an example of a homosexually oriented joke:

> There was a burro and a lion, and the burro hadn't had a *burra* nor the lion a *liona*. So the lion say to the burro, "Listen, burro, let's forget ourselves, you and I." The burro says, "Good," and the lion says, "Me first." So the lion mounts the burro, but the burro says, "Hey man, don't dig your claws into me." Anyway, the lion was not big enough for the burro; so it was the burro's turn. The burro mounted the lion and then said, "Give me a kiss." But the lion couldn't turn around because of the burro's member and so he said, "Don't be a damn fool. Your *chile* is all the way up to my neck."   (p. 238)

In general, Mexican culture outwardly exhibits considerable hostility toward and disapproval of homosexuality. The Mexican concept of masculinity (machismo) requires that the division between male and female be clearly defined culturally as the division between those things active and male and those things passive and female. The ideal male must be tough, invulnerable, and penetrating, whereas the ideal female must exhibit the opposite of these qualities. It follows then that only the receptive, anally passive male is identified culturally as effeminate and homosexual. The active male, the insertor, retains his masculinity and therefore cannot be considered homosexual.

The passive homosexual partner, to put it in the words of Paz (1961), is an "abject, degraded being" (p. 39). Since the effeminate male and the homosexual male are considered synonymous, it is not surprising that societal pressures move in the direction of suppressing outward manifestations. Masculine males are willing to play the insertor sex role in homosexual encounters since no stigma is of necessity attached to the active sex role. The constant homosexual word games and joking carried on in Mexican society are not in contradiction to the societal suppression of effeminate male behavior in that they are generally carried on by masculine males in a rough-and-tumble way and help relieve the tension that builds up between men in their constant need to defend their masculinity.

TWO | *The Guadalajara*

Field Study

This chapter describes some of the important observations I made during the participant-observer phase of my original study. The participant observations were carried out in two different time periods: the first and more intensive study covered the nine-month period from December 1969 to August 1970; the second, less intensive study (which took place during the structured interviews) covered the seven-month period from September 1970 to March 1971.

Since this chapter will be in the first person singular and gives names and locations, it is important to note that although the described events are presented as observed by me or as related to me by respondents, the names of individuals and locations have been changed to protect the identity of the people who made the study possible. From the very beginning I made the topic of my study clearly known to individuals who were more than casually involved. For those families studied, however, I asked the individuals concerned if the topic should be revealed to other family members. In no case was this allowed. It was thus necessary for me to pass myself off as a graduate student in anthropology studying Spanish. Most family members were only casually interested in why an older graduate student in anthropology would be studying Spanish in Guadalajara for over a year; none probed into the specific topic of my study or my reason for learning Spanish.

Guadalajara: A Brief Overview

History and Geography

Since being founded in the mid-sixteenth century, Guadalajara, re-
taining much of its colonial charm, has developed into a modern city
of commerce with a uniquely Mexican flavor. Unlike Monterrey, the
only other Mexican city of approximately the same size (close to three
million), it has not developed on the basis of heavy industry. In recent
times Guadalajara has become internationally known for its mariachi
music, its pottery and glassware, and the revolutionary murals of its
famed painter José Orozco. In 1970 it cohosted with Mexico City the
World Cup *fútbol* (soccer) matches, an event of considerable importance.

Guadalajara has two leading universities, the Universidad de Guadalajara and the Universidad Autonoma de Guadalajara, and a major
theater, Teatro Degollado, which attracts leading performers and or-
chestras from the United States and Europe. It also has a cathedral,
dating back to 1571, with a cardinal in residence. On the northwestern
outskirts of the city, a seventeenth-century basilica honors the historical
virgin of Zapopan. Guadalajara's most important religious festival occurs every October when a procession that includes villagers from all
over the state returns the Virgin of Zapopan from the cathedral, where
she makes an annual visit, to the basilica of Zapopan.

Guadalajara is located on a fertile plain in the west central highlands
of Mexico in the state of Jalisco at an elevation of a little over 5,200
feet above sea level. By road it is 369 miles west northwest of Mexico
City. The closest United States border point by road is McAllen, Texas,
about 700 miles to the northeast. Of more importance to the city is the
fact that it is on the main automobile and air route for American tourists
going from California and Arizona to Mexico City. Guadalajara is
about 1,000 miles southeast of Los Angeles. By air it is about two hours
from Los Angeles, by car, about three and a half days. Also important
to the city is the fact that the coastal port of Manzanillo and the tourist
cities of Puerto Vallarta and Mazatlán are only one day away by surface
transportation.

Demographics

Guadalajara is Mexico's second largest city with a population in its
metropolitan area, according to the 1990 census, of close to three and

a half million. The population has approximately doubled in size since I first lived there in 1970, mostly a result of the high birthrate and an influx of rural people from Jalisco itself and from such neighboring states as Zacatecas, Michoacán, and Nayarit. There was also a large influx of people from Mexico City in the 1980s, partly as a result of the devastating earthquake.

Guadalajara has a young population with some 55 percent of the total under the age of twenty and one-third younger than nine. Males outnumber females in the population until the early teens, when a crossover occurs and females outnumber males. About two-thirds of the city's population live in families of six or more; close to 40 percent in families of nine or more. Only 4 percent do not live in family groupings. Despite the prevalence of large family size, close to two-thirds of the population live in three rooms or less and 18 percent in only one room. A comparison of family size with rooms occupied per family shows that the majority of the population live under circumstances of considerable crowding. As a result of the tremendous population growth, Guadalajara now has both slum areas and smog, but neither is as bad as it is in Mexico City.

Over 60 percent of the population were believed to be literate in 1990. The distribution of the population in Guadalajara by years of study shows that a large proportion of the population has completed a relatively small number of years of schooling. A comparison for two age groups suggests, however, that over time a relatively larger number of children from the middle and poor socioeconomic classes are receiving more education. It thus appears that as time goes by a larger percentage of the city's total population is completing more years of schooling.

City Patterns

Laid out in an essentially rectangular pattern, Guadalajara's residential neighborhoods cover a relatively small geographical area. Most of the population live in crowded living conditions within a radius of about seven to eight miles from the center of the city. Since most of the population are without automobiles, a large and efficient, if somewhat dangerous and polluting, network of private bus lines crisscrosses the city. Bus fares, controlled by the government, are relatively low. To help alleviate the smog problem, the city's small underground bus trolley service is currently being expanded to a larger modern subway system.

The combination of a small geographical area, low-cost public transportation, and crowded living conditions results in a highly mobile population. Guadalajarans spend a lot of time in outdoor cafes, parks, plazas, and markets. They support two bullfight rings, a *fútbol* stadium, and a host of other sporting events such as horse shows and cockfights. Since a large portion of the labor force is still on a six-day work week, Sunday is the only day a family can spend together. Sunday afternoon and evening outings by families to the center of the city make Sunday as crowded then as on any other day in the week. Although Guadalajara has several television stations, and—judging from the large number of television antennas throughout the city—many viewers in all socioeconomic classes, the cost of going to the movies is still quite low, and movie screenings are well attended, day and night.

Most of Guadalajara closes down around midnight when the buses stop running. The *ʒona roja* (the red-light district), the mariachi plaza, and some eating places, however, almost never close. The *ʒona roja*, which exists in most Mexican cities of any size, contains the nightclubs and bars with dance girls who are usually available at low cost. The music offered in the bars ranges from "country" Mexican to the latest American and English popular songs. The nightclubs with stage shows usually offer a mixture of Mexican folk music and striptease, the latter being relatively modest since complete nudity is not allowed in Guadalajara. The zone is located close to the center of the city, covers several blocks, and adjoins the plaza where the mariachi musicians serenade their patrons. Unlike the *ʒona roja*, the mariachi plaza is considered respectable and sometimes whole families may appear there as late as one or two in the morning. Since the buses stop running at midnight, it is costly to keep late hours. Taxis are always available but their fares are prohibitive for most of the population except for special occasions.

Establishing Homosexual Encounters

Selecting an Apartment

My first task of course was to find a suitable apartment, a combination living and working space appropriately situated for the kind of study I planned. It had to be located close enough to the center of the city to provide easy access for respondents; it had to be private enough so that the coming and going of respondents would create no problems with neighbors; and it had to have a minimal number of apartments immediately adjoining it. The second criterion ruled out a crowded family neighborhood; the third, a large apartment house. After searching for two weeks, I found a two-bedroom, third-floor walk-up apartment in a middle-class neighborhood that met all my requirements. Located on a main street, it could easily be reached from the center of the city by any of three bus lines in five or ten minutes. There were three commercial establishments on the ground floor and the only adjoining apartment, separated by a staircase, was rented to four university students.

Developing Contacts

I used two strategies to develop contacts with the people I wished to study. First I utilized a respondent I met in a park (Parque de la Revolución) in Guadalajara while doing my pilot study in the summer of 1968. Although he operated alone, through him I met members of friendship circles A, W, and X. Through a member of circle X, I met members of circles E and Y; and through a member of circle Y, I met a member of circle Z. A member of circle W introduced me to a friend in circle F. (See figure 2.)

The second strategy became necessary because I wanted to study additional friendship circles in the lower socioeconomic level and because I wanted to move into a completely unknown network. I thus set out to find new respondents. One afternoon in late January 1970, I

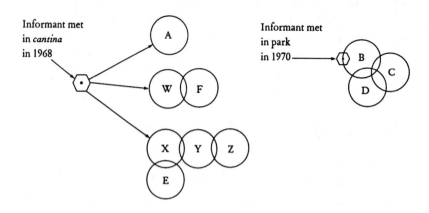

Figure 2.
The friendship circle network.

met a new respondent in a large park near the center of the city. He turned out to be a member of friendship circle B. Through him I gained access to circles C and D. These three circles formed part of a network that at no point touched the three networks I had previously entered. Figure 2 presents the circle of friends and the sequence of contacts.

Setting Up the Respondent Network

During my first participant-observer study, I socialized with ten friendship circles and ten independent respondents—a total of eighty-five people—over varying periods of time. As shown in table 1, the two friendship circles were stratified by age and socioeconomic level, although individual members of some circles were from lower or higher levels than the group in general. I socialized with the ten independent respondents on an individual basis. They tended to search for sex partners alone or at most with one or two friends. Four of the ten belonged to families in the poor class; one in the poor-in-transition class; and five in the middle-solvent class.

Most of the respondents, whether they belonged to friendship circles or operated as loners, lived with their families. Only seven of the seventy-five to eighty-five individuals involved were living in their own rented rooms or apartments. Of the seven, the family of only one lived in Guadalajara. The families of the others lived in other parts of the state of Jalisco or in neighboring states. The individual whose family lives in Guadalajara was cast out at the age of twenty-three for violating his father's weeknight curfew of 10:30 P.M.

I established contacts with six families. Two were families of members of friendship circle B; one was the family of a member of friendship circle W and his brother, an independent respondent; and three were families of individual respondents. Of these six families, I was able to socialize extensively with three—the two families from circle B and the one with the independent respondent and his brother from circle W. I had the most extensive contacts with the latter family and in early 1970 lived with them for two weeks. In terms of their socioeconomic level, two of the six families were in the poor, one in the poor-in-transition, and three in the middle-solvent class.

The amount of time I spent with any one friendship circle or independent individual varied according to the receptiveness of the group or individual concerned. As it turned out, I developed close relation-

Table 1

The Friendship Circles by Socioeconomic Level and Age

Friendship Circle	Socioeconomic Level of Family	Age Range of Members	Close Contacts[a]	Average Number Active Members
A	Poor-in-transition	25–30	2	5 to 7
B	Poor and Poor-in-transition	17–27	7	10 to 12
C	Poor	18–25	3	7 to 10
D	Poor-in-transition	14–16	3	5
E	Poor-in-transition	18–23	1	5
F	Poor	20–23	1	4
W	Middle-solvent	20–25	1	5
X	Middle-solvent and upper-privileged	20–40	3	12 to 15
Y	Middle-insolvent	20–26	3	7
Z	Middle-insolvent and middle-solvent	18–21	2	5
Total			26	65 to 75

[a] The number of individuals in a particular friendship circle with which the author developed a closer association.

ships with five of the ten friendship circles (A, B, D, X and Y), and with three of the ten independent respondents.

Initiating the Encounter

The initiation of homosexual encounters was the first aspect of homosexuality I studied in Guadalajara. Both independent respondents and those belonging to friendship circles introduced me to the methods used for meeting men and the most popular places where the meetings took place. I observed activity with individual respondents, with groups of respondents, and alone. The following general picture emerged.

Homosexual encounters in Guadalajara are initiated on certain streets—while standing, walking, or in automobiles—and in certain plazas, parks, restaurants, cantinas, bars, nightclubs, movie houses, and steambaths. From what my respondents told me, they are also likely to be initiated any place where two or more males come together at home, at work, at school, and so on, but there seems to be a greater likelihood that planned encounters are initiated in particular, known, parts of the city.

Meeting Places

At the time of my original study in Guadalajara (1969–1971), there were no meeting places *exclusively* established for males interested in homosexual encounters. Encounters were initiated in a certain area of the meeting place or at a certain hour, but almost always while the regular business activity of the place was in progress.

The nearest thing to an exclusive meeting place at that time was Bar Pancho, a middle-class bar located in the center of Guadalajara's business district. Bar Pancho closed only for national elections and national holidays, when all bars had to close; otherwise, it was open twenty-four hours a day. During the daylight hours, the bar served a clientele that was about the same as any other located in the city's business district. After dark, however, its clientele changed and it became exclusively a meeting place for men seeking other men as sexual partners; it had an established reputation for this objective throughout the city.

Two other drinking establishments in Guadalajara in the 1970s followed patterns similar to Bar Pancho. One was a lower-middle-class bar (Bar U) located in the business district about eight blocks from Pancho's bar, but its evening clientele was never exclusively composed of men seeking homosexual encounters. The second was a lower-class cantina (Cantina A) located on the edge of the *zona roja* until it was closed by police for the rowdy behavior of its patrons; it later reopened about one mile away on a main road cutting through a poor neighborhood. In the first location its evening clientele was exclusively homosexually oriented, as at Bar Pancho, but mainly from the poor class. In the new location its evening clientele was almost never completely composed of homosexually oriented men. Neither Bar U nor Cantina A was ever supported by large numbers of patrons or ever had the range of patrons from all socioeconomic classes as did Bar Pancho.

Bar Pancho finally faced some competition in the early 1980s when a gay disco, Monica's, opened. Located several miles from the center of the city, it attracted a younger, relatively affluent, gay crowd who could afford to pay the entry fee and taxi fares to get there and back, since buses stopped running at midnight. Although the owner of Monica's supposedly paid off the police, in its early years the disco still operated surreptitiously—screening patrons to make sure they knew they were entering a gay disco. Within a couple of years, several gay establishments opened close to the center of Guadalajara—three discos and a music bar. One of the discos, Boops, was operated by the major gay liberation group in Guadalajara—Grupo Orgullo Homosexual Liberación (GOHL).

There was a winnowing out of gay bars and discos in the late 1980s due to closures by police and lack of customers. More will be said about the openings and closings of these gay drinking establishments in my chapter on gay liberation. Suffice it to say here that the venerable Bar Pancho—the oldest gay institution in Guadalajara, with its diverse clientele, large space, bullfight decor, and popular Mexican music— finally fell victim to its puritanical neighbors and the police (and not to a lack of customers) and was closed permanently in late 1992.

Large numbers of exclusively homosexual meeting places—such as you find in San Francisco, Los Angeles, and New York—have not developed in Guadalajara and other large cities in Mexico primarily because the legal authorities either close down an establishment or force it to change its policy if it caters exclusively to a homosexual clientele. I was told, for example, that in the past several steambaths had evolved to the point where almost all their customers were seeking homosexual encounters rather than steambaths. When their reputations became widely known throughout Guadalajara, they were forced to close.

Since there is no law in Mexico, or in the state of Jalisco, that prohibits adult men from having sexual relations together in private, the legal authorities are reacting to social pressure in not allowing the establishment of exclusively homosexual meeting places. From what my respondents have told me and from what I have observed, the general social pressure is toward the prevention of what is considered objectionable behavior by males in public. Objectionable behavior in this case is defined as effeminate behavior by males or behavior that makes obvious the fact that males are seeking one another for the purpose of sexual contact. Effeminate males in public parks or on the streets late at night, for example, may be harassed by the police if caught loitering. This likelihood may be increased if they are in large groups and acting blatantly effeminate. Several of my effeminate respondents reported being harassed by police at various times. The police monitoring of sexual behavior between males in the upper balconies of movie houses provides another example of an attempt to establish public limits. When the activity in the balcony of a particular movie house becomes too brazen, the police begin to clamp down. The possibility also exists that openly homosexual males may be harassed by students. One of my respondents related that late one evening a group of students threw him into the pond of a fountain in a park located near the center of town and the University of Guadalajara (Parque de la Revolución), which for a long time has been an active place for homosexual cruising.

The lack of meeting places exclusively for homosexual men may also be attributed to the fact that so many all-male environments already exist—in schools, bars, cantinas, and nightclubs. As previously mentioned, females in Mexican society tend to be dichotomized into good and bad, with the result that their behavior is much more closely monitored than that of males. One consequence of this is that men spend much more time together than do women. The possibility thus exists that suitable sexual partners may be found in any of these all-male locations. A good example is that encounters may be initiated in almost any drinking establishment in Guadalajara, according to my respondents. As will be seen in future chapters, this also appears to be the case in many other cities and towns I have studied in northwestern Mexico.

Methods of Initiating Encounters

Although the methods of initiating homosexual encounters vary individually and according to the circumstances of the time and location, the activity appears to follow a general pattern, paralleling in many respects the courting behavior of heterosexual men. For example, a homosexual male interested in a deep emotional and sexual relationship with another male may pursue him with as much intensity as any heterosexual male may pursue a female. And for another example, homosexual flirting by males appears to exhibit a number of similarities to heterosexual flirting. The differences that do exist between homosexual and heterosexual male courting behavior are in part attributable to at least two unique aspects of the Mexican male. First, unlike the Mexican female, he is relatively free to act sexually as he wishes. This means the search by one male for another is not limited by having to deal with a closely watched, cloistered sexual object. Second, by societal definition the Mexican male is considered to be more promiscuous by nature than the female. The relatively free promiscuous male is thus more likely to develop and find multiple sexual outlets. Moreover, the search by promiscuous males for many sexual contacts with other males over time has led to the use of a large variety of locations and situations in which to pursue homosexual encounters. This search in turn has made necessary the private set of cues that allow males to know when mutual sexual interests exist.

One of the most basic cues used in the initiation of homosexual encounters is an intense look, at the core of which is eye contact held between the interested males for a longer duration than is usual between males. The eyes of the two interested males may briefly wander and then lock together a second time. Depending on the situation, this intense gaze may continue at the time of the first meeting or be postponed to some future, hopefully more opportune time. If the males are interested, they will at that time, or at some future time, provide additional cues to make clear their interest. The additional cues may be subtle or bold. Individual style, the situation, location, and timing all dictate the kind of cue provided next. A subtle cue would be to discreetly follow the interested male—a bold one would be to approach the interested male directly and attempt some kind of conversation.

As a means of gathering original data on the "eye-contact" cue and its effectiveness, at various times I used it while walking along some of the main streets and through some of the main parks of downtown Guadalajara. I found that most males indeed do not respond to this cue. I also found that I could increase the response rate by operating in a location considered a meeting place by my respondents. Of those males who did respond, I found that depending on my boldness and on the situation I could more often than not trigger a secondary response. For example, if it was possible to discreetly follow or approach an individual after experiencing eye contact, I would do so. With only a few exceptions (which might be interpreted as a rejection of interest in me as much as anything else), the result of my following or approaching was for the individual to position himself for a second "eye contact" or to approach me directly for conversation. In this way I was able to connect with several respondents for my study. Another interesting finding from these "eye-contact" experiments is that an occasional male will respond while walking with a group of friends, female or male. Before making a secondary response, however, he will use some pretense to move away from the group.

Timing of Encounters

Homosexual encounters are sought by men throughout the week, both night and day. In Guadalajara, however, at least three factors appear to establish general time boundaries. First, a large majority of the single male population continue to live with their families until married. Second, most of the families require their sons, even if in their twenties, to return home at a "reasonable" hour. During weekdays, a reasonable hour is defined as around ten to eleven at night; on weekends this might be relaxed to before the sun comes up, but the son is definitely expected to return home. Third, a large majority of the male population has no access to an automobile and so must depend on public transportation. Since the buses stop running at midnight, males not able to walk home after that hour must pay twenty times as much or more for a taxi; or, if they choose to stay out all night, they must pay the family penalty for doing so. From what my respondents have told me and from what I have observed, the combined effect of these three factors is to establish a midnight curfew for most homosexual and other activity. The major exceptions appear to be Saturday nights and the eves of special holidays.

The rhythm of homosexual activity in the various meeting places is related to the combined effect of such things as individual time away from work, family, and friends; individual motivation to pursue the activity; individual preferences as to meeting places; and the hours the meeting places are open. Some of the peaks of homosexual activity are obviously related to peaks of activity experienced by the general population. For example, in Guadalajara the siesta and the principal meal are still taken each day from one to three o'clock. Those employed then return to work, finishing their day between seven and eight o'clock. Thus it is that after work the favored streets, parks, plazas, and cafes tend to be most active with males seeking homosexual encounters. And then, since the most popular time at the movies is the evening show starting between eight and 8:30 P.M., homosexual activity peaks again when the evening movie finishes between ten and eleven. Homosexual activity in some meeting places, however, peaks when general public attendance is lowest. For example, the best hours for initiating a homosexual encounter in a steambath or a movie house are not when the largest number of regular patrons are there—no doubt because homosexual encounters are not only initiated but also often brought to completion in these meeting places. By operating off-hours, males interested in other males minimize possible interference by uninterested or hostile patrons.

Observations of Men Meeting Men

The following seven observations from my field notes illustrate the variety of circumstances under which homosexual encounters are initiated. An observation is included for each of the important encounter locations. Except for minor editing and a few deletions of irrelevant material, each observation is presented as originally set down in my journal. Since it was rarely possible to take notes on the spot, either by writing or tape recording, my usual practice was to put down my journal observations as soon as possible after the event observed.

The initial cue used by the respondents in each of the locations was eye contact. The steps that follow varied according to location—for example, request for an object or information, light physical contact, or a greeting—but eventually there must be conversation, to solve the problem of whether there is mutual sexual interest and where to go.

LOCATION: Sidewalks, downtown
TIME: Early evening, weekday
RESPONDENT: Pepé, twenty-two, regular masculine
RESPONDENT'S PREFERRED SEX ROLE: *Pasivo* (anal receptive)

We left the mariachi plaza and walked toward the central market. As we passed in front of the plaza Pepé stopped a young man about eighteen for a cigarette and then talked to him for a few minutes. Although close by, I couldn't hear what they were saying. Pepé was propositioning the youth . . . who seemed uncertain about whether he should accept. Pepé turned toward me and we started walking again. The young man went in the opposite direction. I turned around to watch him leave. He turned around at the same time and smiled. Pepé told me the youth had really wanted to come with us, but he had had several experiences with men in the past and had promised his priest in the confessional that he wouldn't have sex with men anymore.

After leaving the young man we headed for a pedestrian bridge that crosses the main thoroughfare of the city, connecting the plaza with the central market. Pepé explained that this is a good place for cruising (*fichando*). We stopped on the sidewalk at the entrance to the bridge. A young man walked by and gave us the long look. We were standing still so Pepé followed him with his eyes. Pepé called out to him for a match. The youth stopped and came over next to us. After a few casual remarks about the weather and the number of people walking around, Pepé asked him if he would like to go to his room for a drink and some entertainment. Pepé, patting his own rear end and saying it was good, indicated the kind of entertainment he was suggesting. The young man smiled but decided he didn't want to go and so walked away. Pepé turned to me and said the young man was stupid for not coming. Another youth was walking by at this point but was not looking our way. Pepé called out to him for a match. He stopped and came over with a light. Pepé followed the same routine as before but made his proposition in a much quicker, blunter, way. The young man just laughed and walked on. He didn't appear upset by being propositioned.

Pepé suggested we walk on across the bridge. While crossing he approached two separate men standing with their backs to the bridge's railing. He used the same approach with each one and was turned down by both. Pepé did not appear upset by the refusals. Each time he referred to their stupidity for not accepting. As we were walking down the steps leading into the market, Pepé spotted a former conquest. He called out to him, and we went over to where he was standing. His former conquest appeared to be about eighteen or nineteen, was poorly dressed, and looked like he was in need of a bath. Pepé introduced me to him and told me his father had a small stall in the market. Pepé told the young man that he was showing me around—that I was a rich gringo from California. Pepé then suggested that we all go to a nearby steambath. I walked over with them and bought a ticket for a private room (*baños privado*). I gave Pepé the ticket and told him to meet me afterward in the mariachi plaza.

LOCATION: Plaza near cathedral, downtown
TIME: Early evening, weekday
RESPONDENT: Unknown youth

This evening around 7:30 P.M. I made observations alone in a plaza near the cathedral. I sat on a park bench not too far from a bus stop. Seated next to me on the bench was a middle-aged couple. The husband was getting his shoes shined. A young man about twenty years old, medium build, masculine in appearance and gesture, walked by. Our eyes met. He looked at me in an interested way but walked on and stood close to a bench nearer the bus stop. He stood there for a short while and then walked close-by again. He gave me another look and this time stopped and stood only a short distance away. He pretended to be just waiting for a bus, opened a book and started to read. The middle-aged couple seemed unaware of us . . . but their presence prevented his making an approach. He returned to his previous place by the other bench. I decided to test my reading of his intentions by moving to a third, empty, bench. After sitting down, I looked over in his direction and caught his eye. He came over and sat down next to me. I started a conversation by asking about the book he had been reading. He said it was a text book and that he had just come from an evening class in his school (a *preparatoria*) and was waiting for a bus home. He asked if I was a tourist staying at one of the nearby hotels. I replied that I was a graduate student from California working on my thesis—that I had my own apartment since I was living in Guadalajara. I then, rather bluntly, asked him if he liked men. He said he did at times. He asked me where my apartment was located. Before I could make a reply, he said if not too far away he had time to go with me. I suggested we go to a nearby cafe for coffee. In hopes that I could enlist him as an informant, I told him about the general nature of my study. He seemed interested so I invited him to talk again after his next evening class. He agreed to meet the following night at the same time, but was obviously disappointed that we weren't going to have sex that night. I walked him back to the bus stop and we parted. He didn't keep the appointment and I never saw him again.

LOCATION: Two different movie houses, downtown
TIME: Two different Friday afternoons
RESPONDENT: Luis, twenty-two, regular masculine
RESPONDENT'S PREFERRED SEX ROLE: *Internacional* (anal receptive and insertive)

First Friday Afternoon

For some time Luis has been telling me about the action in the movie houses. This afternoon I went with him not to watch the movie but to see how the cruising was done. We went first to the place set aside for smokers in back of the seats on the main floor. Men wanting to smoke and watch the movie must stand in a rather narrow area behind a chest-high railing. Although only 3:30 in the afternoon, the main floor was almost full. Spread all along the area in back of the railing, men were two and sometimes three deep in spots. Luis explained that some of the men were there just so they could smoke and watch the movie. He claimed most, however, were only there because they wanted a sexual partner. His claims were supported by the head movements and motions of many of the men. As I stood with my back against the wall and pretended to watch the movie, I noticed a number of men staring at each other and several of them kept walking back and forth. As is the case in most locations where homosexual encounters are initiated, the first cue is the long intense look. But instead of being followed by conversation the next move here was body contact, the two interested men standing next to each other slightly touching. I asked Luis about this. He said that whether standing or sitting—it didn't make any difference—the usual tactic is a slight pressure with the leg. If this gets a positive response, it may be followed by groping the genitals with a hand or by pressing one's genitals on the interested man from the back; or it may be followed just by small talk. In any event, the final outcome was usually an arrangement to go somewhere else for sex, even if only the upper part of the balcony.

Luis then took me upstairs. The lower part of the balcony was almost full, the upper part only half full. Luis and I took seats in the last row where our backs were against the wall. Enroute to the seats, I noticed that several men turned and watched us as we went up. The main feature was in progress at the time. Luis told me that he had had sex several times in this part of the balcony. He said it was too dangerous now though because the *Servicio Secreto* (the city's plainclothes police) were watching this theater. As we were talking, I noticed a man move from his seat on the aisle over next to a man seated alone. Luis left his seat, telling me to wait while he scouted around. While he was gone, I saw only one other interaction between two men. Unless sensitized to the operation I don't think I would have been aware of anything out of the ordinary going on. I told Luis about this when he returned. He replied that maybe this is the usual case in most movie houses most of the time, but at times he had seen it get pretty wild and obvious—and as a result of these wilder episodes the *Servicio Secreto* started checking homosexual activity in this theater. Luis said there was no one in the balcony that interested him. He had also checked the bathroom downstairs. There was one man loitering there but Luis wasn't interested in him.

During the intermission between the two main features, we went to the main lobby of the theater. We stood to one side. Several men were in constant motion, circling the lobby and making eyes at other men. Luis recognized one of them and complained about his obvious effeminate manners. We watched the second movie. On leaving the movie house, Luis, disgruntled, apologized for there not being much activity. He blamed it on the plainclothes policemen.

Second Friday Afternoon

Luis was unhappy that I hadn't seen any real action last week, so he took me to a lower-class movie theater this afternoon where he was sure I'd see some live sex because the police weren't working this theater yet. The action spots here were the same: the smoking area in back of the main floor seats, the downstairs bathroom, and the upper balcony.

Luis scolded me for my performance last week, telling me that I needed to get in on the action to really know about it. He left me on the main floor and went off to scout the balcony and downstairs bathroom. I watched from in back as before. I saw one masculine-looking young man—about eighteen or nineteen—smoking and watching the movie, who was also cruising part of the time. I went over and stood behind him, touching him ever so slightly. Not long after, he turned around and invited me to take his place. He then stood behind me and pretended to watch the movie, gradually pressing against me and getting a hard-on. When I didn't move away, he pressed against me harder as he kept watching the movie. Before the movie ended, he tapped me on the shoulder and motioned me to follow him. As I turned around, I noticed that he had tucked his erection under his belt to conceal his sexual excitement. I followed him to the downstairs bathroom. There were no empty stalls to go in and have sex so he shrugged his shoulders and suggested we go to the upper balcony. The bright neon lights in the bathroom made us both feel a little embarrassed by what we were planning to do and what was obviously going on there.

There were only a few people scattered in the upper balcony so we took two fairly isolated seats together. As soon as we sat down, he pulled my hand over and put it on his crotch. He whispered that he wanted to fuck me. I asked, where? He made it clear he meant right there, in the ass. I had heard how it was done: with both men facing forward, the receptive partner just lowers his pants and shorts, and moves over and sits on the insertive partner's erect penis. The insertive partner is thus able to remain seated and yet still have sexual intercourse. I told him I couldn't, that I was afraid of undercover police, and suggested we go to a *baños privado* instead. He didn't like the idea, so I told him my friend Luis would probably be interested. I found Luis looking for me on the main floor and told him about the hot guy waiting upstairs. We went up and, for the first time, I saw a live demonstration of anal sex between men seated in the balcony of a movie theater.

LOCATION: Small cafe, downtown
TIME: Early evening, midweek
RESPONDENT: Paco, thirty, slightly effeminate
RESPONDENT'S PREFERRED SEX ROLE: *Internacional*

After the movie, Paco and I went to a small nearby cafe that specializes in *carne asada* (roast meat). Their charcoal fires weren't hot enough for cooking when we arrived so we drank beer for about an hour before being served. Seated at the table next to us was a young man about seventeen or eighteen and two older men in their late thirties or early forties. We made contact with the table through the young man. He was very friendly. One of the men was also friendly, the other one seemed disinterested. The young man from time to time would lean back in his chair and talk to us. He and Paco started a long conversation about popular Mexican songs and singers. Based on my previous outings with Paco, depending on the circumstances his behavior might be effeminate or masculine. This time he played it very masculine. After eating our beef we had to leave because between us we had just enough money to pay the bill.

We were just about to leave when one of the older men invited us to stay and have one more beer on them. I gave Paco my last two pesos and and told him to let the young man pick the songs he wanted. Paco and the young man went over to the jukebox. They spent some time together selecting the songs, then went to the bathroom together. While they were gone, I told the two older men about the movie Paco and I had just seen. The two older men seemed undisturbed by the length of time Paco and the young man were in the bathroom. It seemed an unusually long time to me. Paco and the young man returned to the table as though nothing had happened—and were still talking about music. When we finished our beer we thanked them for their hospitality and left. About a block from the cafe, Paco told me that he and the young man had had a little sex play in the bathroom. Paco had tried to get him to meet us later on, but the young man had to return home with his father and uncle. They lived in a rural area in the outskirts of Guadalajara. Paco did succeed in making a date with him the next Friday night. Paco told me later on that the young man had kept the appointment. They went to a cheap hotel to have sex.

LOCATION: Bathhouse, suburb

TIME: Saturday afternoon

RESPONDENT: Juan, twenty-one, effeminate

RESPONDENT'S PREFERRED SEX ROLE: *Pasivo*

Juan went with me to visit this bathhouse, my first time here. Most of my respondents claim it's getting a reputation for homosexual activity. The bathhouse is located in a middle-to-lower-class neighborhood in Sector Juárez. The blank walls of the old Spanish-style houses front on the sidewalk around it. We arrived during the siesta hours so no one was outside as we walked to it down a side street. Once inside you have to make a choice between the *baños general* and the *baños privado,* and no crossing back and forth is allowed without paying extra. Homosexual cruising takes place only in the general part of the bathhouse. Sexual intercourse between men, however, may take place in both general and private rooms.

In the *baños general* there is one large outer room, an open shower room, and three hot rooms. The outer room is circled by two floors of small change rooms. The change rooms are small, barely large enough for two people. There is a small sun deck and swimming pool on the roof. It is reached by a circular staircase from the second tier of change rooms. At the end of the outer room there are two doors into a large room with ten shower heads along the sides of two walls. A masseur operates in a small room off to one side. The three hot rooms are side by side but not connected, each having an exit only into the shower room. Two of the hot rooms have dry heat, the third has live steam.

Each bather is given a small towel in the outer room. It's almost too small to wrap around. Almost no one uses it anyway so most of the clients wander around completely nude. Juan and I left our clothes in a second tier room so he took me first to the sun deck.

There were ten men lying on their towels and two in the small pool. It's possible to order soft drinks, beer, and shrimp cocktails so a lot of homosexual men, Juan claims, spend their afternoons on the roof eating, drinking, and cruising. Juan believes most men who come to the sun deck may be available if approached the right way. He told me that once in awhile there are sexual orgies on the sun deck—with fucking and cock sucking in and out of the pool. A guard is posted on the stairs to alert the participants if unknown persons or employees are about to come up.

We went downstairs to the shower room. As Juan and I showered, he pointed out the "for sure" homosexual men. He said the customers downstairs were always a mix of those looking for a sexual adventure and those in for nothing more than a steambath and shower. One way of telling them apart is to watch how long they stay in a hot room. The ones cruising keep moving in and out of the hot rooms. The live steamroom is preferred over the other two because it is possible to not only find a partner there but to also have sex with him on the spot by building up enough steam to obscure vision. Juan told me he had had sex many times in the steamroom but he really preferred going somewhere else because it had to be such a hurried act in that you never knew who might be coming in.

I asked Juan if he saw any prospect. He said yes and for me to follow him when he went into the steamroom but not to talk to him once inside. I did as he suggested. He followed a middle-aged, husky, very masculine man. I followed them into the room and stood as far away as possible so as not to inhibit either one. Juan sat down next to the man. The room was crowded so he was able to sit very close. Juan pressed his leg against the man. Neither said anything. One by one people left, until there were just four of us. Juan got up and opened the valve to let in more steam. I remained standing but could not see Juan clearly when he sat down again because of the steam. The heat and steam were too much for me so I left to cool off in a shower. The man came out soon after and then Juan. I asked Juan what happened. Juan said the man became partly erected so he put his hand over and played with it. But the man was apprehensive so pushed his hand away and left. I asked Juan what he thought his prospects were now. He said he thought they were good because the man had let him play awhile before pushing his hand away. I had to leave, so I told Juan I'd see him later. Juan followed the man up to the sun deck.

I stayed under the shower a bit longer. While there I noticed several young men, two of them very effeminate, going from one room to another. I also watched a youth about thirteen—whose father had gone to one of the dry heat rooms—gradually get a hard-on as he stood in a nearby shower looking at the young men. He was embarrassed by their stares so he turned his back to them and faced the wall.

Juan told me afterward that in the late afternoon, when the bathhouse was less crowded, he and the man had gone back downstairs and had had sex in the steamroom. I asked him what kind of sex they did. "I sat on it," he said. "That way if someone comes in we're not sure about I stand up, he stays seated—no one knows for sure we were having sex."

LOCATION: Lower-class cantina, downtown (near *ʒona roja*)
TIME: Midweek, 9 P.M.
RESPONDENT: Carlos, twenty-six, regular masculine
RESPONDENT'S PREFERRED SEX ROLE: *Pasivo*

At my suggestion, Carlos and I went to Cantina F after seeing a movie. Cantina F is a medium-sized drinking establishment that features north Mexican country music (*norteña*) and dance girls are available for fifty centavos (about five cents) a dance. A long stand-up bar takes up one end of the room and in a back corner there is an L-shaped open urinal. Tables are spread around the small dance floor in the center of the room. Carlos led me through the tables to the far left side of the cantina. He followed his usual tactic of picking a table near someone that interests him.

Tonight, we sat next to a table with two men who appeared to be fresh in from a small town. One appeared to be around nineteen or twenty; the other older, about forty or forty-one. They had two of the dance girls at their table—one was sitting on the lap of the older man. Loud *norteña* country music was blaring from the jukebox. To me they seemed completely involved with the two dance girls. Carlos positioned himself at the table so that he faced the young man. From time to time he would look over at the young man, smile, and give him a long look. I thought Carlos was really wasting his time. I was wrong.

Carlos started getting friendly responses from both men at the table. When the young man got up and went to the open urinal, Carlos followed him. They had a conversation while urinating. When he returned, Carlos told me that the young man wanted us to go with him and his uncle to a hotel. I asked Carlos where they were from. He said from a small town about fifty miles away. I then asked him whether they planned to bring the two dance girls along. He said no, just us—and they wanted a bottle of tequila.

We walked together with the young man and his uncle to a nearby cheap hotel. En route I bought the tequila. After we got to the hotel and I paid for the room—no questions asked—I chickened out. Carlos tried to lure me up to the room by saying he would take the uncle and I could have his nephew. I told him I just wasn't up to it. He was annoyed with me for not staying but didn't push it. They went upstairs and I left. A few days later Carlos told me that they had spent the night at the hotel. Their room had two beds and, after they finished the tequila, he had slept with both of them. The uncle fucked him first. Then, when the uncle fell asleep, he slipped over into the nephew's bed and got fucked by him. I asked Carlos how they acted in the morning. He said they pretended as though nothing happened. They were hung over and so didn't talk much before leaving.

LOCATION: Bar Pancho, downtown

TIME: Saturday midnight

RESPONDENTS: Memo and Francisco, both twenty years old, regular masculine

RESPONDENTS' PREFERRED SEX ROLE: *Activo* (anal insertive)

[Saturday night was always the "hottest" night at Bar Pancho. It was usually packed with young queens and macho hustlers drinking and often cruising for the same men—many of whom were regular customers—who came from all segments of Guadalajara's society, from the lowest to the highest, and with sexual orientations ranging from homosexual to heterosexual. Most of the men being sought after, however, were usually middle class, regular masculine in appearance, and believed to be bisexual or heterosexual. No one in the bar could be deceived into thinking that the majority of its customers were anything other than men interested sexually in other men. Groups at tables tend to segregate themselves by degree of effeminacy but there was lots of cross-talk and table hopping. The men being sought after were often only interested in cruising each other.]

I was standing at the end of the long mahogany bar when Memo and Francisco came in about midnight. They sat at a table next to a post, alone. Several people stood talking next to me so they didn't see me when they came in. I have seen Memo in Bar Pancho only once before with his older brother; I've never seen Francisco here before. They sat at their table drinking beer, talking to each other. Several young queens made comments as they passed their table, but they were ignored. Seated at one of the tables next to Memo and Francisco were two men in their late thirties and a young man in his early twenties. The young man I know (hustler R who usually works around the mariachi plaza), but the two older men I don't remember seeing before. Seated at another table nearby was a group of very effeminate youths eighteen to twenty years old. Memo and Francisco arranged themselves at their table in such a way that they faced the older men and had their backs to the effeminate youths.

After they had been in the bar about twenty minutes they started interacting with the two older men by raising their glasses of beer and saluting. They did this while hustler R was in the bathroom. When hustler R returned, the interacting stopped. As is usual around this time, Bar Pancho becomes crowded and noisy with conversations, shouted jokes and insults, and music blaring the latest popular Mexican songs from a jukebox. There is constant movement of people back and forth to the bathroom, from one table to another, from one little conference to another. Plans are in progress for the night's sexual activity. After finishing his drink hustler R moved up to the bar and started talking to one of his regular "norteamericano" customers.

As soon as hustler R left the table, the two older men invited Memo and Francisco to join them. It was now about 1:30 in the morning. In his new location, Memo caught sight of me. He pointed me out to Francisco, got up, and came over. I was surprised to find that Memo wasn't embarrassed by my finding him in the bar. I know his family well through his older brother and have been a guest in his home for dinners, fiestas, and so on. He asked me if I knew the two older men. I told him I didn't. He said that he and Francisco were invited to go to the older man's apartment for drinks, but it was so late he hadn't made up his mind whether he should go. He changed the subject and commented about "las reinas" (the queens). He was amused by their feminine talk and gestures. Francisco then came over to say hello. He told Memo that the older men had gone for their car and would take them home if that's where they wanted to go.

Memo came to my apartment a couple of nights later to talk about his adventures in the bar and to make sure I did not say anything to his family about my seeing him there. He knew his older brother had homosexual affairs, but his older brother didn't know for sure about him. He said he and Francisco talked about having sex with me and wanted to know if I was interested. I told him I had to think about it since I was already having sex with his brother. I then asked him about the two men they went home with. Memo said that they were both architects, and that he fucked the one that owned the apartment while Francisco was fucking the other in another bedroom. They were driven home afterward. He said they hope to meet them again.

Completion of Encounters

Two major factors that influence where homosexual encounters are brought to completion are family and income. Because most of the male population either live with their families or are married, the completion of encounters—that is, the carrying out of some kind of sexual activity—is not usually possible in the family residence. The alternatives are to have sex at the place of meeting or to move on to some more suitable private location like an apartment or hotel room. However, only a relatively small percentage of the interested male population has access to private apartments, and even the cheapest hotel room ($5–$10 U.S. equivalent) is expensive given current levels of income. This means then that sex is carried out wherever a private place can be found at the moment and can be afforded. From what I have observed and from what my respondents have told me, Mexican males use a wide variety of places—the outskirts of the city, vacant lots or buildings in the city, church bell towers, isolated parts of city parks, the upper balconies and rest rooms of movie theaters, private and public parts of steambaths, and automobiles. Their order of preference would be something like the following: private apartment, hotel room, private room in steambath, and the outskirts of the city. Men with limited incomes have access to the first two places generally only through contact with men from middle- or upper-income families. As will be seen, there is considerable homosexual contact between social classes in Guadalajara.

Participants

Judging from what I learned both through field observations and through interviews, it is clear that participants in homosexual encounters in Guadalajara come from all socioeconomic levels in the society; have a variety of occupations, from the most humble to the most high and from the most artistic to the most technical; and have physiques and manners that vary from the most effeminate to the most masculine. It is also clear that males from all age groups, both single and married, are involved. The data suggest, however, that at any given time the majority of males involved are single and somewhere between puberty and their late twenties. Since theoretically the sexual activity of males is at a maximum at this point in their lives (Kinsey et al. 1948), it is not surprising that proportionately more males from this age group should be involved in homosexual encounters. But as will be discussed later, there are additional reasons why this should be so in Mexico (for example, the dichotomization of females into those who are sexual targets and those who are not, and the general acceptance by males that there is no stigma necessarily connected with the *activo*—anal-insertive—sex role in homosexual encounters).

I had decided early in my research to select respondents for the interview phase of the study on the basis of socioeconomic level and sex role preference. My preliminary investigation in 1968 had suggested that these two variables were most important in explaining variations in homosexual behavior. My nine months of field observations in Guadalajara, before beginning the structured interviews in the fall of 1970, confirmed the importance of these two variables. My observations further suggested, however, that sex role preference was more important than socioeconomic level as an explanatory variable, and therefore I chose sex role preference as the principal criterion for selecting interviewees for my judgmental nonprobability sample (i.e., a nonrandom sample of men based on my field research knowledge).

How Participants Categorized Men

To get my participants' view of their lives in Guadalajara, I used Metzger and Black's (1965) method of eliciting cognitive categories with several respondents. I asked them initially how they categorized men in general. The first eliciting frame was of the type: What kinds of men are there? What sort of men do you know? The responses given were then incorporated into the second frame; the responses given to the second frame were then incorporated into the third frame, and so on.

The informants' general categorization of the male population was always in terms of sexual orientation: homosexual versus nonhomosexual. They thus see the male world as having similar or different sexual desires and feelings. The following provides a good example of an elicitation:

Q: *Qué clase de hombres están?*
   (What kind of men are there?)
R: *De todas clases.*
   (All kinds.)
Q: *De todas clases de hombres, qué clases tú conoces?*
   (Of all kinds of men, what kinds do you know?)
R: *Conozco de ambiente y serios.*
   (I know gay and serious.)
Q: *Qué clase de ambiente conoces?*
   (What kind of gay men do you know?)
R: *De la clase de ambiente en el sexo hombre y hombre.*
   (The kind of gay men who have sex with other men.)
Q: *De la clase de ambiente en el sexo hombre y hombre, qué clase conoces?*
   (Of the kind of gay men who have sex with men, what kind do you know?)
R: *Toda.*
   (All kinds.)
Q: *Qué clase de serios conoces?*
   (What kind of serious men do you know?)
R: *Serios que no les gusta hombre y hombre.*
   (Serious men in that they don't like man with man.)
Q: *Qué clase de hombres serios estan?*
   (What sort of serious men are there?)
R: *Son serios porque no son de ambiente en la cama.*
   (They are serious because they are not homosexual in bed.)

This general categorization of men by sexual orientation by the respondents, however, must take at least two factors into account. First, all the respondents involved in this elicitation knew about my study. It is therefore likely that in their minds this aspect of their life was always preeminent in my presence. On the other hand, I was constantly impressed during my field observations by the amount of conversation between my respondents directed toward this sexual division of the world. And it was not done just for my benefit. On many occasions when I withdrew from a group of respondents in my apartment on the pretext of working or resting (so that I could listen to their conversation without being present), the sexual orientation of their conversation remained the same. Second, the respondents queried by this method were young (fifteen to twenty years old), unsophisticated, and exclusively homosexual. Respondents differing in any of these three characteristics might utilize other categorizations first. For example, an older, not exclusively homosexual respondent might think of men first in terms of their being single or married rather than the fact of their being homosexual or nonhomosexual.

The respondents' categorizations of that segment of the male population involved in homosexual encounters were in terms of a number of different personal characteristics of the participants. For example, they were categorized into those who were good friends versus those who were not, those who wanted a lover versus those who did not, and those who were both sexually available and compatible versus those who were not.

In a further elicitation of subcategories that make up the sexually compatible versus noncompatible category, I was especially interested to find that many respondents who played both the *activo* and *pasivo* sex roles (*internacionales*) revealed a ranking system that integrates relative degree of masculinity of prospective sex partners with their willingness to play more than one sex role with any one partner. When some *internacionales* judge a potential sex partner to be significantly more masculine than themselves, they expect and will agree to play the anal-receptive role; but if they judge him to be more feminine, they will only play the anal-insertive role. Judgments about a prospective sex partner's relative masculinity or femininity compared to self may thus determine which sex role they will play. Mexican men who play *both* sex roles may therefore be sorted on the basis of sexual behavior into at least two groups: those who usually play both sex roles with all their sex partners, and those who play both sex roles but not usually with the same partner. A possible third group would be comprised of those men whose sexual behaviors do not clearly place them in either of the above groups because of changes in sexual preference over time.

Social Life of Men Who Have Sex with Men

The social life of participants in homosexual encounters appears to depend, aside from personality characteristics, primarily on three factors: family, degree of involvement in homosexual encounters, and available income. I will briefly discuss these three factors and then present some observations from my field journal to illustrate variations of social interaction between encounter participants in Guadalajara.

Because most participants must continue to live with their families until they marry or until they move to another city, interactions with family determine to a large extent the basic structure of the social life of participants from all socioeconomic levels. For example, each night they must return to the family home for sleeping. And for most (and this even includes some in their late twenties and early thirties), they must return home at specified hours or face the anger or scolding of their parents. They must also involve themselves in a lot of family functions such as birthday parties, ceremonial dinners, and entertaining relatives.

The family hold on participants in homosexual encounters almost precludes the sharing of apartments by male friends and the setting up of households by homosexual lovers. During the year and a half I lived in Guadalajara I knew of only one group of single men sharing an apartment. Of the ten homosexual couples I knew, or heard about, that were living together in Guadalajara, only two had families living in the city. The individuals making up both pairs were older—three were in their early thirties and the fourth was forty—and came from well-to-do families and had good jobs. But it is interesting to note that a partner in one of the pairs—in his early thirties—still had to return each evening to his family home to sleep. It was the consensus of my respondents that moving from the city or marrying were usually the only ways to leave the family and establish a separate household. As will be seen from the interview data, however, many men in Guadalajara liked living with their families. They viewed it as a hedge against loneliness as they grew older.

Depending on their degree of involvement in homosexual encounters, the social life of participants is more or less shaped by their homosexuality. Those men who continue socializing with girlfriends on the *amiga* or *novia* level are also more likely to continue socializing with nonhomosexually involved male friends. They are thus less likely to spend much time socializing with their partners in homosexual encounters. The sexual histories of most men in this group would probably place them from 1 to 4 on the Kinsey scale (a seven-point scale with 0 indicating exclusive heterosexual preference, up to 6 indicating exclusive homosexual preference).

As participants start becoming more and more involved in homosexual encounters, they usually must structure their social lives differently. If they want to sustain a large number of different sexual contacts, for example, they must spend more time socializing with or searching for men who are likely to be prospective partners. Moreover, even if they prefer having a sexual relationship with only one male partner, they will still have to diminish their other social contacts as they spend more and more time socializing with that partner. Exclusively homosexual men tend to spend most of their free time—that is, time away from family, work, and school—socializing with homosexual friends.

What participants in homosexual encounters do with their free time depends in part on available income. Most participants regardless of income spend a lot of their free time going to movies, stage shows, outdoor cafes, drinking establishments, and private parties. The more affluent participants are likely to spend additional time going to plays, concerts, and art exhibits, and vacationing in Acapulco and Puerto Vallarta. They are also more likely to have a close friend with an apartment, or they may share the rent on an apartment with friends. In either case the apartment provides a place for parties and for sex. The less affluent participants are likely to spend additional time in free or low-cost public places such as parks and picnic grounds. Given their limited incomes, a surprisingly large number manage vacations in Mexico City and in beach resorts. Almost none of the less affluent participants can afford to rent an apartment, however; and they can only afford to rent a hotel room occasionally. If they should have access to an apartment, they are more likely to have it as a result of being a casual sex partner rather than as a friend of the individual (or individuals) renting it.

Observations of Social Interactions

The following entries from my journal illustrate some social interactions involving encounter participants in Guadalajara. The first two observations focus on parties. They show variations in behaviors between parties organized exclusively for homosexual and in-the-know friends, and parties organized for family members and a mixed group of friends. The final three observations focus on the social interactions of respondents in drinking establishments. The first two describe respondent interactions in Bar Pancho and in an almost exclusively homosexual cantina. The last one describes behavior in a nightclub in the *zona roja*.

SOCIAL FUNCTION: Birthday party (family and friends)
LOCATION: Respondent's married sister's house

TIME: Saturday night
RESPONDENTS: Friendship circle B
INCOME LEVEL: Poor-in-transition

This birthday party was for Ramón's next-to-the-oldest unmarried sister. It was held in the small house of a married older sister. Family members present at the party when I arrived were Ramón, his mother, three sisters (two older, one younger) and two younger brothers. Ramón's father was home with the rest of the younger children; his brother-in-law was out of town. Ramón's closest friends, Arturo and Gilberto (all members of Friendship circle B), were also present.

Shortly after I arrived, four girls from the neighborhood came in. A record player was then turned on loud and the dancing started. Several more neighborhood girls came in. When the girls ran out of male partners they started dancing together. No one danced close! A boyfriend of Ramón's arrived wearing a shiny fancy suit with white ruffled shirt and tie. He went straight over to Ramón's mother and asker her to dance. He was very flamboyant and I thought a little effeminate. Arturo told me he was one of Ramón's ex-lovers and only *activo*.

Arturo's eldest sister came in next with one of her daughters. She looked at me with great curiosity. I noticed her and Ramón in a private conference in one corner of the room. Ramón came over and whispered that she wanted to know if I was Arturo's latest "husband"! Both Ramón and Arturo's families know about their homosexual behavior. No open recognition of the fact is made at the party. Ramón, Gilberto, and Arturo spend all their time dancing with the girls. There are more girls at the party than boys.

The unmarried sister's boyfriend arrived late with a male cousin. The cousin, about nineteen or twenty, was a little drunk on arrival. He sat on the couch and drank tequila and coke. I don't think he danced more than once all evening. He seemed to me to be watching Ramón a lot. Ramón whispered to me in the kitchen that he is a *mayate*. He told me he could have him sexually but was afraid of him because he belonged to a neighborhood gang of toughs.

The neighborhood girls left about ten o'clock. I stayed on, but when the party showed no signs of letting up about midnight I left. Ramón told me later that he and his two sisters and two friends continued to party all night long.

SOCIAL FUNCTION: Surprise birthday party
LOCATION: Colonia Polanco
TIME: Late Monday evening
RESPONDENT: Julio, twenty-seven
INCOME LEVEL: Poor

Though feeling tired and sleepy, I set off with Julio to go to a surprise birthday party for his friend Hector. The party was given at Hector's small apartment: one room, with a large double bed, and a little kitchen at one side and a bathroom on the other—concealed only by a curtain. A couch and two chairs made up the rest of the furniture. The apartment occupied the bottom half of a house, with the connecting stairway closed in.

The usual slow start was under way when we arrived: six guests seated stiffly in chairs drinking warm coke and brandy, one guy lying on the bed. All but one were in their late twenties or early thirties, somewhat effeminate, and chunky. Paco, the youngest one—in his late teens, trim, masculine, and handsome—acted as the host until Hector, who was to be surprised, arrived from work. After several false alarms, just a half hour before midnight Hector finally arrived and was truly surprised. Three more older guests came in—two in their late forties, one in his mid-sixties. The party finally got going, the room now crowded and thick with smoke. A tape recorder loudly played the theme song of the evening, "Despacito, Muy Despacito" (slowly, very slowly), the implication being that fucking and dancing should be done that way. Another guest arrived—Hector's young, macho, *mayate*, neighborhood boyfriend.

From time to time Paco tried—with little success—to get the dancing started. Finally, as the theme song started again for the umpteenth time, he pulled up the oldest guest and slow-danced with him in a tender way. Julio then asked me to slow-dance with him. Suddenly everyone was dancing. Hector's room became like a crowded dance floor in a small nightclub. I wondered what the family sleeping in the upstairs apartment thought about the noise.

Around 2:30 in the morning, at the sound of a car stopping in front of the house, Hector asked everyone to stop dancing and to be very serious (*muy serio*). All dancing ceased and the usual chair and couch sitting resumed with stilted conversations. Five macho men came in and were introduced. All campy behavior ended. Hector comported himself in as masculine a way as possible. Basically a very feminine man, he reduced his effeminate behavior to a minimum. The reason for the change was that one of the macho men turned out to be Hector's brother-in-law and it was his first visit to the apartment. The dancing had stopped but Paco, a bit drunk, continued to do kind of a dance by himself. Several guests left. After about a half hour, dancing resumed in a limited way—"rock and roll" and Latin music, but no close dancing.

Hector need not have worried about his brother-in-law because before the party ended about seven in the morning everyone was drunk, close dancing had resumed, and it was quite clear that the brother-in-law and his friends came prepared to have fun at a gay party. Toward the end, a friend of the brother-in-law and Hector put on a campy show in makeshift costumes.

The lights were turned out in the main room while they prepared for the show in the bathroom. While the lights were out a lot of hugging and kissing went on. Paco and I were dancing close when the lights went out. He pushed me onto the bed and was lying on top of me and kissing me on the mouth when the lights came on. Julio and Hector's *mayate* boyfriend were necking on the other side of the bed. Hector made several caustic remarks about our behavior during his show, but it was all good-natured. Dancing resumed after the show and continued on until the sun came up. As we left, Julio and I wondered how well the family had slept upstairs.

SOCIAL FUNCTION: Drinking
LOCATION: Bar Pancho
TIME: Saturday evening

There are two entrances into Bar Pancho almost side by side. As you enter there is a long sit-down bar to the right. At each end of the sit-down bar there is sufficient room for three tables with chairs. In the rest of the essentially square room about twenty tables with chairs are scattered about. Off to the left, in a kind of alcove, are some rarely used booths and a small kitchen. The bathrooms are off in the right-hand corner. As you enter Bar Pancho you can look right down the sit-down bar into the open men's room, which has a long trough urinal and a toilet enclosed by a swinging door. The men's room is used as a place to meet and negotiate sexual encounters elsewhere as well as a place to urinate. Since February 1970, the bar has employed two uniformed policemen daily to maintain order.

Maintaining order is essentially a problem of controlling the male prostitutes who operate out of the bar from time to time. When they become aggressive and start harassing customers into buying them drinks and cigarettes and giving them money, quarrels and fights are bound to follow. This causes a rapid decline in the number of customers. The owner of the bar thus had no alternative than to hire his own security guards.

I went alone to Bar Pancho about 11:30 P.M. There was the usual large Saturday night crowd. Every table was filled to capacity and the jukebox was playing a favorite popular Mexican romantic song. All the stools at the bar were occupied, so I stood up at the end nearest the bathroom and ordered a *cerveza* (beer). Three of the regular American customers were there, two at tables with young men and one sitting up at the bar but falling-down drunk. I recognized three full-time hustlers sitting at a table with an unknown middle-aged Mexican. Members of Friendship circle A were at a table across the room near the jukebox. I decided to steer clear of both groups. The Saturday night "queens" were out as usual, mincing from table to table and camping. Daniel and Arturo were trading jokes with the "queen of Guadalajara" who had been crowned at Fernando's last party.

Rodolfo, a hustler, came over and asked me to buy him a *cerveza*. I did and he filled me in on his activities for the past week. He specializes in older, well-off American and Mexican men. He made his usual protestation that he was trying to find a job. His pattern seems to be that he holds a job for several weeks then quits or gets laid off. He admitted he doesn't like keeping regular hours. He brought up his wife and child. This is usually preliminary to asking me for money. I had none to spare so I changed the subject and asked him about the three hustlers and the middle-aged man. The man comes from Mexico City to Guadalajara occasionally on business. He always ends up at Bar Pancho looking for a new conquest. Rodolfo observed that he was rich but stingy. *Norteamericanos*, he said, were always more generous.

There was a fight beginning between a young, nicely dressed guy and some slightly older rougher-looking guys at a nearby table. The two regular policemen appeared and quieted them down. As soon as the policemen arrived the younger guy moved quickly away from the table and then walked out the front door.

Salvador (a member of Friendship circle Y) came in with a group of very young effeminate types. He saw me and came over with his friends. Rodolfo left to start looking for a customer. Salvador told me he had just come from the mariachi plaza. He had met the young men there. Since nothing was going on, they decided to move to Bar Pancho. The young men were dressed in expensive-looking clothes. I had not seen any of them at Bar Pancho before. I asked them if it was their first time. One answered saying they had been to the bar before but not often. He said it was "quemado" (i.e., it would "burn" his reputation to go there). Salvador wanted to take them to my apartment—only for dancing and drinking, he said. I begged off saying I was just too tired to start a party. They moved off to another table.

Jesus came into the bar alone. He had just come from work so it was about 1 A.M. He saw me and came over. Rodolfo joined us. Jesus and Rodolfo started joking with each other. Jesus asked Rodolfo how he could get an erection when he had sex with older men. Rodolfo told him he closed his eyes and thought of a girl or his wife. A friend of Jesus, José-Luis, joined us. I've been watching José-Luis for about six months in Bar Pancho. When I first met him he was almost painfully shy. He had changed a lot. He and Jesus joked about the kind of sex they liked. José-Luis groped Jesus's genitals playfully at least twice.

SOCIAL FUNCTION: Drinking
LOCATION: Cantina Y
TIME: Sunday morning
RESPONDENTS: Paco, Jesus, Javier, Miguel, and Luis
INCOME LEVEL: Middle-insolvent and poor-in-transition

From Cantina F we walked three blocks up the street to Cantina Y, a small low-class cantina with a reputation for attracting a poor, rough, homosexual clientele. En route to the cantina Paco and Javier camped down the sidewalk. Paco said loudly, "I'm the prettiest girl in the world!" Two straight couples looked back in amazement as we passed by. We arrived at 3:30 A.M.

Cantina Y had a stand-up bar at one end near the entrance. Five tables with chairs were crowded in the remaining space. An open urinal was located in the back right-hand corner. The bar was crowded. Our entrance created a stir amongst the patrons. Paco minced to a table with no chairs. A man, identified as the owner, brought chairs over and took our order in a friendly way. There was some muttering and a few hostile looks among those standing at the bar. Everyone seemed to be looking through watery alcoholic eyes. Those that seemed hostile turned quickly back to their drinks and intimate conversations. Most of the patrons looked a little seedy. They were physically on the heavy to fat side. None could be considered blessed with good looks.

The six of us gathered around the table, with Miguel muttering that the bar was very dangerous. A man with battery-charged metal handles came through offering a macho test. He was also selling a white rebozo. Paco bought it, wrapped it around his head, and got up and danced between the tables. At a nearby table, a fat queen surrounded by fat middle-aged men yelled at Paco with an effeminate toss of the head, "Andale mi hija!" (Go to it, daughter!). Paco responded with a toss of his head.

A plump mustachioed man (early thirties?) came over and started talking to Miguel. They had not met before. Paco pushed his left hip out and pointed his rear end toward the man and the rest of the bar. Jesus patted it and declared it a good piece. The plump man was interested and walked over for a closer look. Paco responded to his interest by saying, "It's too much ass for you." The man moved closer. Paco said, "Besides, you probably can't get it up." The man fumbled at his fly and pulled it out. Everyone seated at the table nervously hollered at him to put it back in. He did. He sat next to Miguel and started to kiss his neck and cheek with his arm thrown around him. Miguel seemed embarrassed but just sat there.

I looked around the bar at the clusters of men. Some bargaining appeared to be going on. There was only one "queeny" type and even he, Jesus told me later, could play the macho role if he wanted. There were at least five other fairly obvious homosexual men, judging from their comments and actions. Javier used the urinal and as he left it he still had his penis out and shook it at the bar. The plump man was once again over by Paco. This time he unbuttoned his fly and pulled out a semierect penis. Everyone laughed. He put it back in and went away. We decided to leave and visit a few more bars.

SOCIAL FUNCTION: Drinking
LOCATION: Nightclub (*zona roja*)
TIME: Friday morning

RESPONDENTS: Sergio and a doctor
INCOME LEVEL: Middle-solvent and upper

Sergio and I were about to leave Bar Pancho when a doctor I had met at Casa de Julio (a male brothel now closed because of the death of the owner) came by the table. He asked if I remembered him. I said yes. (At the time we met he seemed embarrassed by his presence in a male brothel.) He asked when we were leaving. I said soon, as it was 2:30 in the morning. He sat down and had a drink. He invited us to go with him to a nightclub. We accepted.

We arrived at the club in the *zona roja* about 3 A.M. There were about five tables of customers. At one of the tables two men were talking to one of the young mariachi musicians who worked in the club. One of the two men had his arm around the young man in a very affectionate way, and as we walked over to our table I saw him pat the young man on the rear end. The doctor was known by the mariachis, the club manager, and the bar girls. We sat at a table and he had one of the girls come sit with him. He ordered a bottle of rum and some Cokes. We started drinking—the girl included. She seemed rather shy. Sergio said she was a *puta*. The doctor made a great show of affection toward her with much hugging and soulful looks.

A half-hour stage show started at 4 A.M. Mariachis played and the young man sang. They were followed by a female singer in her late twenties or early thirties. There was a great display of macho from all tables in response to her songs—Sergio and the doctor included. Sergio told me, "Mexicans love to call out to singers." She was followed by a ranchero-type female singer who was greeted even more enthusiastically. All kinds of shouts were hurled at her as she sang. When she completed her set of songs and went behind the curtain, she was brought back by shouts for an encore. All the time she was onstage, the young man who had sung was playing a guitar and flirting with some of the male customers. I asked Sergio if I was reading him correctly. He pretended to be annoyed that I even bothered to ask. He said the young man was *ambiente* (homosexual).

Although there were girls at three or four of the ten tables, now filled, there seemed to be a lot of sexual feelings going back and forth between the men. Two men seated at the next table were in our line of sight to the stage. They started making gestures for Sergio to come to their table (the thumb and forefinger held close together, meaning come over for just a minute). Sergio went over and talked to them. They appeared to be in their late thirties or early forties. Sergio said they were from the northern state of Chihuahua when he returned to our table. The two men started signaling Sergio to return to their table. The doctor, meanwhile, was preoccupied with his girlfriend. Sergio suggested we both go and sit with them for awhile. Both of the men spoke to me in English. They asked me the usual questions as to how I liked Mexico, where I was from, and so on. One of them asked me directly in Spanish, but in a joking way, which I preferred: boys or girls. I was about to give a reply when Sergio said, "Es iqual" ("It's all the same"). Their question annoyed him. He then pushed himself away from the table and said it was time for us to go. The two men seemed startled by our sudden departure. We thanked the doctor, who was still talking to his girlfriend, and left. It was 5 A.M.

Family Relationships

The relationship homosexually active Mexican males have with their parents and siblings depends on such variables as age, degree of masculinity, extent of involvement in homosexual encounters, and the family's knowledge about homosexual behaviors. To understand fully the impact any of these have on the concerned individuals and their families would require a separate study. The following observations thus provide only some general notions.

As mestizo Mexican males grow older, they are under increasing pressure to explain to all concerned why they have not married. To be single until their early thirties is not particularly unusual for them, but even by their late twenties their older brothers are usually married and often their younger brothers may also be starting to marry. Single males thus find it more and more difficult to explain their single state. In fact, simply on the grounds of their being single their families may have suspicions about their sexual orientation. Several respondents in their late twenties replied to the question of whether their family knew about their homosexuality by saying that their family had to at least suspect them because they were still single and had given no positive signs about getting married.

Degree of masculinity may provide families with another clue as to whether a family member is homosexually inclined. Since in Mexico effeminacy and homosexuality are thought to go together, it follows that a son or brother's effeminacy may be interpreted as meaning that he is also a homosexual. From most of my effeminate respondents there is evidence that their effeminacy dates back to a very early age. Moreover, because of their early effeminacy they were sexual targets for some of their older relatives, family friends, or neighbors. There is also evidence that fathers and effeminate sons become alienated at a very early age, and that the effeminate boy establishes a protective alliance with an older sister (who more often than not appears to be the eldest). Some interview data on both these factors will be presented later.

The extent of involvement in homosexual encounters affects family relationships because, depending on the number of encounters and the kind of involvement, the individual concerned is likely to be in a more or less troubled state with regard to himself and to members of his family about his homosexuality. The greater the individual's involvement, the more he jeopardizes having his sexual practices discovered, and the more he must adjust to the shame connected with these. Given the far greater societal disapproval of "effeminate" males, those individuals playing the *pasivo* role theoretically should experience the most shame; those playing the *activo* role the least. My data suggest, however, that it is not the exclusively *pasivo* individuals who experience the greatest shame over their sexual practices. Rather it is those who play *both* the anal-insertive and anal-receptive sex roles. Those who play both sex roles appear on the average to be *more masculine* than exclusively receptive males and do not necessarily think of themselves as effeminate. But they may thus experience more dissonance because although they play the anal-insertive and thus the masculine sex role, they also play the anal-receptive role and must come to terms with the shame associated with playing what is considered to be the female role.

Homosexually behaving Mexican men are usually concerned about how much their parents and siblings know about their sexual behavior. Do they know for sure or only suspect? Do they know anything at all? Which parent knows or suspects? Which sibling knows or suspects? How much do they know or suspect? All these questions surface from time to time as the result of comments or incidents that occur as a part of daily interactions with family members.

The effeminate male obviously has a different set of circumstances to contend with than the more masculine male. The effeminate male's sexual behavior is more likely to be known or at least suspected by family members. While young he may just be suspected of such behavior, and his family may harass him and try to get him to change. Several fifteen- and sixteen-year-old informants reported, for example, that their parents complained all the time about the feminine behaviors of some of their close friends—the implication of the complaints being that they could better improve themselves by associating more with masculine boys. However, when the effeminate behavior persists as they grow older, there appears to be a mutual accommodation between the effeminate male and his family. I observed the family of a very effeminate twenty-two-year-old informant off and on over a period of several months. His parents and older siblings knew about his homosexual behavior. He was allowed by his father, and encouraged by his mother and older sisters, to socialize with his effeminate male friends at home, and who were often invited to such family functions as birthday parties. On several Sunday afternoons I played a bingo like game (*lotería*) with the informant, his friends, and his mother and one or two sisters. The father was always friendly to his son's friends, but very few words were ever spoken between father and son. When the game started, the father always left the house and spent the afternoon with male friends.

The masculine male faces the problem of effeminacy only in that he may worry whether his public image is masculine enough. His principal family problem is more likely to stem from the implications of being single and the amount of interest he is able to display toward women and marriage. The more involved he is in homosexual encounters, the more intense is this problem. If he also vacillates between sex roles, he adds the burden of self-contempt for his passivity. All his problems deepen as he grows older and still finds it necessary or desirable to live with his family.

The kind of family situation a masculine male faces is illustrated by the following conversation (recorded in my field notes), which occurred during the birthday lunch of a very masculine informant:

After finishing our meal the dishes were cleared and the women left. The conversation drifted to sports, automobiles, and jokes about driving. The father then started talking about *jotos* by first telling a joke about the governor of the state. He slowly explained to me that the governor is *soltero* (single) and *dicen* (they say) he is a *joto*. The father talked next about the carnival in Veracruz and the men who went out on the streets dressed as women. He talked about all these things in a very jovial manner. Memo and his younger friend listened and laughed but said nothing. A friend of the father's made a few comments about *afeminados* in Tokyo and then the subject was changed.

For those males who feel that their families at most only suspect or who believe their families know nothing at all, there is the uncertainty of what will happen to them if they are found out. One of the greatest fears of many is that they will have to leave their family home, whether voluntarily because of the shame associated with their homosexual behavior, or following an edict from their father. In either event, the outcome would be the same: leaving home and the ensuing alienation from family. There is insufficient data to reach even a preliminary conclusion about how often this fear of being cast out is realized. It does happen. Over the many years of my research I have known several Mexican men—and heard about others—who were forced out or felt they had to leave home when their homosexuality became known. After some time passed, however, most of them reestablished cordial close relations with their families, and many returned home to live. Additionally, several of my longtime informants, who are known to be homosexual by both parents, have lived most of their lives at home and yet have never been asked to leave. They have worked away from home from time to time but it was always by their choice, and they returned home because they missed being with their families.

THREE	*Smaller Studies: Hermosillo,*
	Los Mochis, Tuxpan,
	Mazatlán and Culiacán,
	and a Guadalajara Barrio

Descriptions and findings of several small unplanned studies I conducted in urban areas in northwestern Mexico in the 1980s are presented in this chapter. They are of especial interest in that they clearly illustrate the ways in which normative social and cultural rules about sex in Mexican society can produce similar male homosexual behaviors in various settings and geographical locations. The opportunities to conduct the studies began by chance while I was making various trips by automobile between Los Angeles and Guadalajara—a 1,650-mile journey that normally takes three and a half days if traveling straight through (see figure 1).

One study in the *zona roja* of Hermosillo, a city with a population of almost one half million and the state capital of Sonora, took place during the summer and fall of 1980. I discovered the unusual goings-on in the bars, nightclubs, and cantinas in the *zona* while stopping off one summer night through a chance meeting with a Mexican professor and his lover in the only gay bar in Hermosillo. The homosexual behaviors turned out to be so interesting and unique that I returned the following fall for a weekend study of the two most active bars in the *district* to gather additional information.

Another study, of a late afternoon and early evening drinking establishment called La Luna, took place during the summer of 1982 in Los Mochis, a large agricultural town about three-hundred miles south of Hermosillo in the state of Sinaloa. I learned about La Luna late one afternoon while looking for a motel to spend the night. My traveling companion had shouted at me to stop the car, jumped out, and walked fast to catch up with what appeared to be an ordinary-looking heterosexual couple ambling down the side of the road holding hands. He saw something I had not noticed—the "lady" was a man in drag. On arrival in a Mexican town for an evening layover, my eagle-eyed Latino friend from Colombia was always on the lookout for "drag queens" since they were usually willing to give him a good rundown on the local homosexual scene. This time he struck gold. The "lady" was a waiter at La Luna. Located on the outskirts of Los Mochis, the bar encouraged local homosexual and bisexual men to congregate and cruise. We ended up spending the rest of the afternoon and evening there. En route back to Los Angeles from Guadalajara three weeks later, we made a weekend stopover in Los Mochis to spend more time at La Luna and interview some of the transvestite waiters.

Still another study took place in the spring of 1987 in Tuxpan, a medium-sized farm town located near the Pacific Coast some four hundred miles southeast of Los Mochis in the state of Nayarit. I spent two weeks there while waiting for a major overhaul of my car's engine, which had broken down nearby on Highway 15. I was headed back to Los Angeles with José, a friend and respondent from Guadalajara. After having the car towed into town and finding the best engine mechanic, we went to an open-air restaurant facing a river for a late Saturday afternoon lunch. As soon as we walked in to La Vitamina and saw it filled with men drinking beer and eating grilled fish tidbits, we knew we had made a good choice. We had no idea, however, of the good luck we were about to have in being befriended by our waiter, Vicente, who within the space of an hour gave us a complete rundown of homosexual behaviors in Tuxpan. José and I were pleased to hear that so much was going on. I knew then that the time spent waiting for engine repairs could be put to good use. José proved to be a valuable research assistant and helped me map out the surprisingly extensive homosexual scene in Tuxpan.

In a later section of this chapter, I will briefly discuss some additional findings made over the past twenty-five years during stopovers in two cities—Mazatlán and Culiacán—on ten round-trips by car from Los Angeles to Guadalajara on coastal Highway 15. Although I had no specific plan to study the homosexual scene in either of these cities in northwestern Mexico, through repeated visits I gathered some additional information about the similarities between Mexican male homosexual behaviors in urban areas distant from each other but connected by Highway 15, which goes in a southeasterly direction down a coastal plain from Nogales at the U.S.-Mexican border in Sonora, to Tuxpan in Nayarit, and then upland to Tepic and Guadalajara.

Finally, at the end of the chapter I will briefly describe and present some findings of an unplanned study of sexual behavior and joking relationships in a lower-middle-class barrio in Guadalajara. The study began in the summer of 1982 when I accidentally ran into an original informant that I had not seen in many years. It has allowed me to view firsthand the various ways that joking relationships of barrio youth may be used by them to initiate sexual activities as well as to defuse allegations about their sexual orientation and availability. At this writing, the study was still in progress.

Cross-Gender Behavior in Hermosilla

The following excerpts from my field notes provide a glimpse of unusual male cross-gender behavior in a *zona roja* located on the outskirts of Hermosillo. The appearance of male transvestites is not uncommon in segregated entertainment areas and red-light districts in most Mexican cities. The transvestite behavior described below is unusual, however, in that the role of "dance hostess" in two of the seven bars that ostensibly cater to heterosexual low-income men from Hermosillo and nearby rural towns is played by men in drag. From what I have observed and read, dance hostesses in *zona rojas* are usually females from the lower-income strata of Mexican society, and they often play the additional role of prostitute.

Hermosillo's *zona roja* is three blocks long and two blocks wide. A high wall separates it from the city's police headquarters. There are fifteen drinking establishments (three nightclubs, seven bars with dance hostesses, and five cantinas), three small eating places, and assorted housing for the hostesses. The district's patrons are all male and mainly from the lower-income strata. Men from all levels of society, however, seek entertainment there. The major difference between the nightclubs and dance hostess bars is quality. The clubs are generally higher class and often feature live music and a floor show. The hostess bar is smaller, has no floor show, and mainly uses a jukebox to dance by. The cantinas have jukeboxes but no dancing. Although the female dance hostesses appear to move with ease between the bars and night-clubs, a majority have a home base at a specific bar or club. They take customers for sex to generally tiny rooms adjacent to their home base. A bouncer often screens the customers going into the prostitutes' rooms. *Zona rojas* are traditionally high-conflict areas, so police patrols are a regular feature of these segregated entertainment areas in Mexico. An informant in Hermosillo told me the city plan called for the *zona* and police headquarters to be located next to each other.

The field notes that follow were made on three separate visits to the *zona roja* in July and September 1980:

FIRST VISIT: July 5 and 6, 1980

There is only one gay bar in this city of 200,000 persons, located in the center of town and serving hard liquor and beer. . . . Enrique and I returned Sunday at 11 P.M. Our visit was limited to one hour since the bar closed at midnight. Luckily, before it closed we met a university professor and his boyfriend (from Guadalajara). The professor suggested we all go to the *zona roja* where the action was just beginning. He said the *zona* had become very liberal about ho-mosexual behavior. The trip by taxi took about twenty minutes. The hard paved road ended just before we reached the *zona*. A new police station, brightly lighted, is located at the end of the paved road.

The professor took us first to a dance hostess bar (Candillas) where *all* the hostesses were drag queens. Although it was hot (about eighty-five degrees), the queens were gussied up like Tijuana whores . . . wigs, sequins by the pound, long sleeves and skirts or hot pants and boots to the knees. The bar was small . . . there appeared to be as many queens as patrons. Three of the queens were dancing close with ranchero-type men. We left the bar abruptly when the professor was recognized by one of the queens. He appeared embarrassed by "her" attention. He suggested we leave, however, because of the possibility of a police raid. He also said he didn't like the place much.

The professor took us next to another dance hostess bar (Car-men's) where the hostesses were female. He said straight men could be picked up here and men oftentimes danced together. A small but loud live rock group assaulted our ears on arrival, but there were only a handful of customers and three *putas*. Shortly after our arrival the rock band mercifully took a break and the jukebox was turned on. Two of the *putas* were arguing and then fighting. One bashed the other with a small chair. The downed one grabbed a nearby chair and retaliated with a blow of her own. Several *putas* came in from the street and a general hairpulling brawl ensued. Within five minutes, however, a patrol car arrived with two uniformed officers. The fight stopped as abruptly as it started. The good professor suggested we move on to a nightclub (Lucilles) catercorner across the main drag, a dirt road.

Lucilles had a cover charge (twenty-five pesos) . . . this obviously limits the clientele. The manager of the club turned out to be a drag queen. She has a very handsome macho-looking boyfriend. Many of the waiters appear effeminate. The professor invited one of the *putas* from across the street to come sit with us. We all took turns dancing with her to the tunes of a rather nice live band. Several straight-appearing but gay men (according to the professor) sat at a nearby table. Two of them were obviously lovers. They danced *close* together out on the dance floor among the male-female couples. This is the first time I've ever seen this allowed or done in a public place in Mexico! The professor was not surprised by what we saw. He did not, however, dance with his boyfriend. Enrique and the boyfriend danced together out on the floor but not close. The club did not have a capacity crowd, but over half the tables were filled and many customers stood drinking next to a long bar on one side of the large room. The professor said the bar was a good place to cruise . . . also the bathroom located at the end of the long bar.

SECOND VISIT: July 23 and 24, 1980

Chris and I returned to Candillas on Thursday night about 10 P.M. . . . too early to find much action. There were again more queens than patrons in the bar (ten queens, three ranchero-type men). The behavior of the drag queen hostesses differs from their female counterparts in that it is far more aggressive. After paying for an expensive round of drinks and cigarettes, we decided to see what else the *zona* had to offer. We looked into Carmen's bar . . . few patrons, loud live rock music. Chris, with his eagle eye, noticed that

there were drag queens in the bar across the road. A relatively good
live band (not too loud) was playing and, as in Candillas, the hostesses were guys in drag. There were four queens and ten patrons in
the bar (El Rio). As is the case in most *ʒonas*, a goodly number of
people were clustered at the windows looking in while drinking beer
from a bottle being passed between friends. They appeared to be
amused by the getups of the queen hostesses, but probably couldn't
afford to buy drinks inside (fifty pesos for a tequila, thirty for a beer).

We settled in at El Rio for about two hours. An older tough-
looking lady managed the bar and kept the drag queens in line. She
chastised one for stealing money from a very drunk young man
(about sixteen or seventeen) who had been dancing with all the
queens and spending a lot of money on drinks. Chris and I invited a
very talkative queen to come sit with us. I offered to buy her a fifty-
peso drink and she ordered a double, which cost me one hundred
pesos. Afterward, I loudly announced we would henceforth drink
only thirty-peso beer. She gracefully accepted but admonished me
that, after all, she had to make a living . . . turns out she got a cut
from the house on drinks bought by patrons she cultivates.

The queen (La Cleopatra) responded to my questions about the
drag hostesses operating in the *ʒona* in a friendly relaxed way. She
said the drag queens were from all over Mexico, not just Hermosillo
. . . and had been working in the *ʒona* clubs for about two years.
From time to time the police (their new station clearly in view of the
ʒona) arrested the drag hostesses, but they were released after paying
a five hundred-peso fine (about U.S. $23). . . . La Cleopatra hinted
that the bar owners were usually good about paying the fine. She
said the police obviously knew about the drag bars and were paid off
by the owners on a regular basis. The police only laid down one restric-
tion: the queens could operate in only two bars, Candillas and El Rio.

I asked La Cleopatra if some of the drag hostesses also worked as
prostitutes. She replied with a dainty giggle that *all* of them did . . .
that's how they earned most of their income and that sex was an extra dividend. I also asked her if she had ever considered having a
sex-change operation. She said absolutely not! She loved having a
cock . . . and some of her macho customers like to take it up the ass.
On the question of price: customers probably have to pay about the
same for a drag queen as they would for a female hostess. The cost
of drinking and dancing is the same. And La Cleopatra claims that
their ass is just as good, if not better and tighter, than the *putas* so

they can get the same money (the range being 100 to 300 pesos per sexual encounter). Given the element of pleasure that lures many of the drag queens to the *ȥona*, one can only suspect that on the average they may be willing to accept lower fees than the professional *putas* who generally have a regular clientele. La Cleopatra is in her late twenties, from Guadalajara, and just getting over a love affair with an eighteen-year-old boy she had lived with in Guadalajara.

THIRD VISIT: September 25 and 26, 1980

Although it was the end of September, Hermosillo was as hot and dry as it was last July. It was ninety degrees when I arrived at the *ȥona* around 10 P.M. There were a lot of customers milling around, but it was not crowded.

I went straight to Candillas. Compared to other bars in the *ȥona*, it is small and sits in the middle of a block down a side street. Two differences from my previous visit: a bouncer screened customers at the door, and there were new tables and an air cooler. As before, when Chris and I visited the bar also on a Thursday night last July, the queens outnumbered the customers and I was hustled to buy drinks by a friendly waiter—thirty-five pesos for a Modelo beer.

The waiter, from Nogales, urged me to pick out a "girl." He made no attempt to clue me in that they really weren't girls. There were ten or eleven hostesses inside and two to four "girls" hanging around outside. In addition to the waiter, there were only three to five customers during the hour I stayed at the bar. A fat woman in her forties was in charge. The customers were a scruffy-looking lot and overweight—probably in their late twenties or thirties. They appeared to be known by some of the hostesses. I wonder how they can afford the high prices! Three military MPs came in shortly after I arrived. I asked the waiter if they caused any problem. He said no (but then I found out he's only worked there four days). I think the bar is off limits to the military, but the MPs were in no hurry to leave.

I bought one of the hostesses a beer. She had pretty blonde hair done up in ringlets and was wearing very short Levi shorts. She said she was from Ciudad Obregón. I asked the waiter where the "girls" came from. "All over," he said, pointing to one who was a Chicana from Arizona. I then asked how much they cost for sex. "Three to four hundred pesos for most, some up to five hundred."

It was not possible to sit in the bar and just casually drink and observe. The hostesses harass you for drinks, dancing, and "more" if you want, as soon as you arrive and sit down at a table. After an hour I decided to leave. I told the waiter I would come back the following night as I was running out of money.

I walked around the *zona*. A slow Thursday night, but it was still early, only 11 P.M. Carmen's bar was empty—no customers, hostesses, or band. The El Rio bar across the road had a number of very drunk customers dancing to a live loud rock band. I returned to downtown Hermosillo to check out Intimo, the only gay bar in the city. By the time I got there around 11:30 P.M., it was already closed.

The *zona* was crowded when I arrived around 11:30 P.M. Friday. I was apprehensive about coming this evening, so decided to start with a couple of beers at Carmen's bar where there is less hustle and the beer is cheaper. The rock band wasn't as bad and loud as on previous visits and there was a bar stool available (half the seats were broken or not there). As soon as I had a bottle of Corona in hand, an old hag with dyed black hair and a long red dress sidled up and asked me to buy her a beer. She took my polite refusal gracefully and danced away. A handsome young man, twenty-two or twenty-three, sat one stool away drinking a large bottle of Corona. He was quietly drunk, introspective, looking only down or ahead. Two young men (lower-lower class from appearance) crowded together on the empty stool and tried to get the old bartender to cash a check. He didn't refuse outright but kept waiting on other customers. Two young boys sat at a table near the bar. They looked to be about fifteen or sixteen but may have been older—eighteen is the legal age for drinking, but is not always enforced. A very young, pretty girl (sixteen–seventeen?) sat alone on a stool at the end of the bar. One of the young men motioned her to come over and talk to his friend, who seemed quite nervous. He got them beer and talking, then moved to a table near the door to start a conversation with the *putas*. All the *putas* in this bar are female.

One of the *putas* I thought to be middle-aged, who turned out to be twenty-eight and from Navojoa, rejected a thirtish bearded man. I moved to a stool at the end of the bar so I could see the action at El Rio across the dirt road. She came to the end of the bar and asked for a cigarette. I gave her a cigarette and bought her a beer. I asked her about El Rio bar with all the "women." When I pretended surprise over the fact that they were really "*jotos*" (her label), she seemed amused. I asked her what she thought about that. She expressed complete indifference to their being at El Rio. It didn't bother her, she claimed. She asked me if I thought the old hag (*bruja*) in the red dress in Carmen's was a man or a woman. I really wasn't sure but replied I thought she was a real woman. She laughed and said no . . . it was an old man.

I started paying more attention to El Rio. Drag queens were inside and outside the bar. Customers with drinks in hand were allowed in. Most of them were young . . . some looked poor, others were affluent-looking. Most seemed to go in and out from curiosity. They didn't stay long. But then there was no band and no one was dancing to the jukebox. Meanwhile, two male-male couples were now dancing in Carmen's, along with a male-female couple. The male-female couple were dancing close; the male couples apart. At the beginning of the next number one male couple cut out . . . each asked female hostesses to dance but were turned down. They returned to the floor and danced together. I left Carmen's and looked in the window of El Rio. Still not too much activity even though it was now close to 1 A.M. One of the drag queens was having her picture taken on the hood of a car parked in front.

En route to Candillas I decided to use the "look in window" strategy as a means of seeing what was going on in different bars in the *zona* and thus cut the cost and consumption of beer. Most bars had customers and dance hostesses who varied in age from quite young to middle-aged, and in looks from quite pretty to rather homely. Most had dumpy bodies and so, even with nice faces covered with makeup, they were not much to behold. Their outfits run the gamut from hot-pants outfits with knee-length leather boots and short shorts to feminine frilly dresses. The drag queens in comparison tended to be trimmer but still shapely, and their dresses though similar in excesses were still a little more tastefully done. Many drag queens exhibited their small breasts (from self-administered female hormones?) by wearing see-through blouses. They hold a common belief that many of their customers choose them because of their better looks and shape.

Candillas bar was jumping when I arrived a little after one in the morning. Two street food-hawkers had parked their carts in front and were doing a booming business with patrons and drag queens. The bar presented a totally different picture compared with previous visits: it was packed! There were at least two customers for every drag queen inside the bar . . . a capacity crowd of about thirty-five people. My first impression on entering was that it had turned into a "semigay" bar; some of the masculine men were using gestures that I would identify as *ambiente*—use of eyes, way of laughing, and other body movements that differentiate them from the majority of men I have seen in this *zona roja*. I reckoned that the ratio of straight to gay male patrons was about half and half (not counting the queens). Some of the *ambiente* men were probably there to see the queens operating as female hostesses and to dance with them; others use it as a meeting place since the only gay bar in Hermosillo closes at midnight.

Cervecería "La Luna" in Los Mochis

Cervecería "La Luna" was in 1980 a popular outdoor beer hall located on the outskirts of the booming farm town of Los Mochis and on the road to the nearby railhead and port of Topolobampo. The population of Los Mochis almost doubled between 1970 and 1980, going from about 68,000 to 130,000 inhabitants. A federal irrigation program brought both people and prosperity to this semiarid agricultural region noted for its production of cotton, wheat, rice, corn, tomatoes, and marigolds. Like Hermosillo, per capita income is higher here than in most parts of Mexico, and it is considered to be a stronghold of wealthy conservative farmers.

La Luna can be best described as an after-work watering hole that attracts macho working-class men, some with good incomes judging from the trucks they arrived in. It featured a live rock band, popular vocalists, and a comedian who sang songs and told jokes that often had homosexual themes. A drag queen, called La Munchie, ran the place. One story had it that she was the lover of the owner—a well-to-do behind-the-scenes agricultural entrepreneur. Two of the three waiters were also drag queens. They did not work in drag, but close to it. Their feminine hairdos, plucked eyebrows, painted nails, rouge, and tight pants made them quite obvious. One of them, La Chepis, who had told my Colombian friend about the bar, was intrigued by our interest and visits to La Luna and took great delight in telling detailed stories about the macho male customers and the homosexual men who pursued them. La Chepis also told us about the active homosexual scene in Los Mochis: where to go street cruising after La Luna closed late in the afternoon, and the names of a "hot" straight bar and the only gay bar in town.

As is usual for beer halls in Mexico, La Luna's customers were mainly men who came to drink with their coworkers and close male friends after a hard day's labor—many stopping off before going home. Most came to enjoy the camaraderie of being together, drinking, joking, telling each other ribald stories, and listening to popular songs about sex, lost love, and treachery. Some came, however, with the additional hope that, before they went home, they might also have sex—their partner preference oftentimes blurring after many beers. Few had problems recognizing people who were presumably there because they wanted to sell or give away sex: all the women (just by being in a beer hall) and all the effeminate men. The unknown sex objects were the regular masculine men who could not be readily spotted as homosexual. According to La Chepis, gossip between regular patrons often revealed the identities and real homosexual intentions of some of these men, especially if they were also regular customers.

The following brief excerpts from my field notes provide some details of my observations in Los Mochis:

First Visit: July 8, 1980

We arrived at La Luna on a Tuesday afternoon. We were surprised to find a full house, and that so many had come to the beer hall in trucks. A live band was playing northern Mexican country music when we entered. Chepis, the drag queen we had met on the road, saw us and came bustling over and took us to one of her tables. She seemed pleased to see us and immediately started gossiping about the customers, pointing out the good guys and the bad guys. The good ones were a mixed lot to look at: all were macho but varying in age, weight, and looks. They were "good" in Chepis's estimation because they gave good sex and afterward treated you right—and most of the time even paid for the drinks. The ones she put in the bad category might be gorgeous and offer good sex, but they were troublemakers. Some would get hostile afterward from guilt, but she thought most of the bad ones just enjoyed making trouble—especially when they were drunk.

Enrique gave a nod and raised his beer bottle to a young man seated at the table next to us. The young man, in his late twenties, was 100 percent Enrique's type: swarthy and very masculine-looking with a dark black mustache and wearing cowboy boots and sombrero. He returned Enrique's *salud* and then, after some time had passed, left the table for the bathroom. As soon as he disappeared in the bathroom, Enrique got up and followed him in. The young man returned to his table. Shortly afterward, Enrique came back to our table. They had connected, but the young man didn't want to be seen leaving with us. We were to meet between 9 and 10 P.M. in the bar of the Hotel Azteca. I reminded Enrique of our nine o'clock date with the two guys we had met earlier on the road. He pointed out that since we were in Mexico we could do both. He would just be a little late meeting his new friend at the Azteca.

Shortly before the bar closed, we told Chepis we would be returning to Los Mochis July 21 en route back to California from Guadalajara and wanted to take her to lunch then. She was very pleased and told us to meet her in the Hotel Azteca bar. I asked her if there was something special about the Azteca. She said although it wasn't a gay bar, cruising did take place and *mayates* hung out there. She said there was a gay bar in Los Mochis, but it didn't open until around 8 P.M.

Second Visit: July 21 and 22, 1980

La Chepis didn't keep our Monday luncheon date at the Azteca bar and didn't show up at work either. We didn't ask the manager, La Munchie, where she was when we got to La Luna in the afternoon since the beer hall was packed and she was obviously angry over being short a waiter. As on our previous visit, there were several tables full of *ambiente* men. And Enrique and Chris—a friend from Los Angeles who was with us on the trip back—had made dates with a couple of macho guys they met while strolling around the beer hall. One was in his late twenties, the other in his early thirties. They both worked at the foreman level in agriculture. Neither were shy about being seen with us so they moved over to our table. I would have liked to ask them a lot of questions about the homosexual goings-on at La Luna but couldn't because they were playing it straight. They laughed along with everyone else in the beer hall when the entertainers hit on homosexual themes, but neither one was interested in talking about his own homosexual experiences in the first person. When La Luna closed, we went to a downtown restaurant for supper and then they went drinking with Enrique and Chris at the Hotel Azteca bar, eventually going back with them for sex at our hotel. I went to the only gay bar in town to see what it was like on a Monday night—only a few people there, so I didn't stay.

La Chepis was at La Luna when we went back for our last visit Tuesday afternoon. Once again, the beer hall had a full house; there were at least a couple of tables of *ambiente* men, and the entertainers did their regular routines. Chepis, looking somewhat disheveled, told us she had done too much fucking and drinking Sunday evening with her boyfriend so she just couldn't pull herself together to work even Monday afternoon. She told me later that it was too bad we couldn't have made it back for the weekend. The hottest men come on Saturday and Sunday afternoons, she said, and when La Luna closes many customers oftentimes just move to the gay bar in downtown Los Mochis or to the Hotel Azteca bar.

Enrique and Chris had evening dates with their boyfriends from yesterday so I went to the gay bar for another look. There were only a few people there but I decided to stay. There was no long bar with stools so I sat down at a table and ordered a beer. The bar had a sterile look with bright neon lights and almost nothing hanging on the whitewashed walls. The jukebox was silent, so I went over to play a few songs to liven the place up. I called to a young guy walking by to help me make a few selections—a lucky move because he turned out to be friendly and spent several hours with me. His name was Manuel. He was a twenty-year-old student, knew a lot about cruising in Los Mochis, and appeared to be comfortable with his homosexuality. Manuel didn't know about La Luna beer hall. He said he never went to those kind of drinking places and wouldn't know how to pick up straight men there. He knew about the Azteca bar but didn't go there because, he said, he didn't like the people—too many *mayates*. He found most of his sexual partners at the gay bar or cruising some of the downtown streets. Manuel liked the location of the gay bar because it was on a side street and he could get in and out without being seen. He lived with his family and left me in time to get home by his parents' curfew, 10 P.M.

Farm Town Homosexuality in Coastal Nayarit

While conducting research in Los Angeles over a period of several years in the late 1970s, I met many bisexually behaving immigrant Mexican men from coastal Pacific farm towns in the state of Nayarit. They turned up as partners of gay men in homosexual encounters more often than could be expected by chance alone in my studies of several straight Mexican bars in central Los Angeles that were cruising grounds for both Anglo and Latino homosexual men.

I wanted to learn more about the bisexual behaviors of men living in these coastal farm towns, so en route to Guadalajara by car in the summer of 1979, I stopped off in Tuxpan for two days to visit a twenty-three-year-old respondent, Luis, who had moved back home to live with his family. Although Luis was open with me about his past and current homosexual behavior, during the short time I was with him in Tuxpan he showed me only the heterosexual side of his life and town. He had come back home to find a wife.

Several years later, en route to Guadalajara by car in the summer of 1986, I visited another nearby coastal town, Santiago Ixcuintla, for a couple of days with two young cousins in their mid-twenties who had been traveling with me since I picked them up hitchhiking in the desert south of Mexicali. Like Luis, they were open with me about their own bisexuality but reluctant to tell me much about homosexuality in their hometown. They preferred talking about their many girlfriends. Once again, I had gotten nowhere trying to get heterosexually identified young men to help me map out the sexual exploits of other bisexually behaving men.

It was not until the following spring of 1987, when my car broke down on Highway 15 and I spent close to two weeks in nearby Tuxpan, that I was finally able to learn something of substance about male homosexuality and bisexuality in coastal Nayarit. The following brief descriptions of events and respondents, and excerpts from my field notes, show that I learned much in a short period of time partly as a result of a chance meeting the first Saturday afternoon in town with Vicente, a queenly waiter, and partly the result of our meeting additional important players in the local homosexual scene—Beto, Eric, and Gilberto—and knowing what questions to ask and what leads to follow.

Vicente not only mapped out for José and me what was going on in his riverfront restaurant sexually—both he and female prostitutes found sexual partners among the men who came in to eat and drink a lot of beer in the late afternoons and early evenings—but he also told us about another restaurant in town, Restaurante Campestre, that had both good food and subtle homosexual cruising. The married owner, Beto, was bisexual. His wife and children were often in the rustic thatched-roof restaurant, but so were some of the young men in the neighborhood with whom he had ongoing sexual relationships. José and Beto, both slightly effeminate, immediately hit it off, so we became good friends and regular customers. Beto eventually confided a lot about his private sex life and the availability of young men in his neighborhood for homosexual encounters. Quite often at breakfast he would give us a complete rundown on his sexual adventures the previous night.

Vicente gave us directions to a drinking establishment in Tuxpan's small *zona roja* that was a standard bar for female prostitutes in the first room you entered, but had a secluded gay bar in a separate room tucked away behind a fairly large open patio. At his urging—he said the bar was always crowded on Saturday nights—we went there to celebrate our first night in town. We were again blessed with good luck and that evening met Eric, the manager of the bar, Noa Noa, and self-described leader of gay liberation in Tuxpan. Looking back, I am still astonished that on my first day in town I met three such interesting and important players in the local homosexual scene.

Just a few days before leaving Tuxpan, I had another bit of good luck. I was crossing a street near the center of town when a voice to my rear shouted, "Hey, what are you doing in my hometown?" I turned around expecting it to be Luis, whom I had looked for since arriving. Instead, it was Gilberto—one of my original research respondents in Guadalajara—who had returned to his hometown to take care of his aging mother. He was involved in local politics, so was able to give me some important historical information about official attitudes toward male homosexuality in Tuxpan.

La Vitamina

La Vitamina is a popular open-air fish restaurant and beer hall located near the center of Tuxpan, yet close to the river with a clear view of the small ferryboat carrying passengers back and forth to the little town of San Luis on the other side of the river. Although officially not a beer hall, nearly all its late afternoon and early evening customers are men who come to drink beer with their buddies after work as well as to flirt and make dates with female prostitutes who discreetly hang around the restaurant. Like La Luna in Los Mochis, La Vitamina attracts homosexual men as well who discreetly cruise straight customers and treat them with food and beer.

The couple that owns and manages the restaurant—and always seems to be there with a few of their children—appear to be indifferent to their customers' beer-drinking and other activities, and to the way Vicente camps and carries on as he waits on some of their customers. There is nothing discreet about Vicente, who is openly effeminate while he works. He takes great pleasure in teasing some of the straight regular patrons he has had sex with. He also acts as a pimp for homosexual customers. On one of our weekday late afternoon visits to La Vitamina:

> The restaurant was full when José and I arrived. Vicente and a waitress were scurrying about trying to keep up with customers' orders. Some of Vicente's regular customers made rude remarks to him about the slowness of his service. He responded by campily saying such things as, "Well, if we hadn't drunk so much and had so much sex together last night, I could move faster" and "We sure did drink a lot together last night, I wouldn't be so tired if you had gone home instead of sleeping with me."
> Vicente finally took a break and came over and sat down at our table. He gave us a coy look, knowing that we overheard his remarks: "It's true, I've made a lot of sex with them."

On another late afternoon visit:

> José and I had just seated ourselves when Vicente came bustling over and moved us to another table right next to two macho-looking guys in their early twenties. He chided us for not being more selective: "Don't be stupid, look before you sit! They're handsome and available for just a few beers. Invite them over." I somewhat timidly suggested that they were probably more interested in the female prostitute they seemed to know and were talking to. Vicente pursed his lips, threw back his head in a very feminine way, and said, "That's true, but what'll they do for money?" When the prostitute left it took only a *salud* with our bottles of beer and a nod of our heads and over came Leonardo and Oscar. They were farm workers and showed us their rough hands to prove it. Vicente was right. After several rounds of beer they quite happily came back with us to our motel. No subterfuge was necessary; we left the restaurant and walked back to the motel together.

Restaurante Campestre

Restaurant Campestre is located in the middle of a Tuxpan neighborhood, about a ten-minute walk from the center of the geographically small town. It is a family-style restaurant run by Beto and his wife—both in their late twenties—who do the cooking and waiting on seven tables. They serve good food at reasonable prices so José and I regularly ate breakfast and supper there.

By our second visit, whenever he was not busy, Beto would come sit at our table and gossip with us. He was slightly effeminate but always conducted himself in a serious regular masculine way inside the restaurant even when he was giving us intimate details of his wild homosexual encounters with neighborhood youth. In telling us about his sex life he did not seem at all inhibited by the presence of his wife and two small children who were usually there during the supper hour. He spoke low, however, and given the large space between tables and the kitchen, nobody in the restaurant could possibly overhear our conversations.

Given José's appearance—his tight pants and flamboyant ways—I often wondered what Beto's wife thought when he was with us, but she never reacted hostilely and always greeted us when we arrived, and she seemed pleased that her husband enjoyed our company. Shortly before leaving, I asked Beto how much his wife knew about his homosexual life. He said he was certain she knew he was fooling around with some of the neighborhood youth, because they came into the restaurant and got free meals, but she did not know for sure what they were doing sexually and never questioned him about it. Beto believed she was content staying with him because he was a kind husband and a good provider and father.

Unfortunately, while in Tuxpan I learned very little about Beto's early sex life or his family. In the short time I was there, I never had the opportunity to talk with him outside the restaurant. He told me he had been born and raised in Tuxpan, had had sexual relations with men only a few years older from a very early age, and had married because he wanted children and the stabilizing influence of a wife. He had slipped across the border and worked several years in Los Angeles as a waiter and cook to get experience and money so that he could return to Tuxpan to open his own restaurant. After he got Restaurante Campestre up and running, he decided to get married. Before marrying, practically all his sexual experiences were with men; his heterosexual encounters were limited to prostitutes in Tuxpan.

From my conversations with Beto, it was clear that he accepted the fact that he enjoyed men sexually more than women. As he got older, he knew as well that it was getting more and more difficult and riskier to find the kind of sexual partners he enjoyed most—young masculine men who would penetrate him anally. How long could he continue to find partners, he asked himself, and how long before he got himself into trouble. As the following journal entries illustrate, he was already experiencing the good and the bad:

TUESDAY EVENING: March 24, 1987

José and I had supper at Beto's restaurant. He told us about a trip he had made to the beach alone last Sunday. There were all kinds of young men there. He picked up a good-looking one about eighteen or nineteen and spent a pleasant afternoon with him, buying all the beer and food he wanted. Beto doesn't like beer so he drank vodka instead with disastrous physical results. He got sick and thus lost the chance to have sex with the young man. Beto said that next time he would stick to *mota* (marijuana).

WEDNESDAY EVENING: March 25, 1987

Before going to Noa Noa bar, José and I had supper at Restaurante Campestre. Beto was waiting for a twenty-three-year-old boyfriend to show up. He told us he had been fucked twice by him the previous night. The young man was coming back for a free meal and, Beto hoped, more sex. He arrived shortly before we finished our dinner and was rather good-looking. Beto was pleased that we had a chance to see him. When Beto came over with our check, he pointed out another handsome young man—about nineteen—who was eating his supper alone and told us, "He's believed to go both ways."

THURSDAY EVENING: March 26, 1987

Once again dinner at Campestre. José and I looked forward to hearing Beto's story about last night's sexual encounter with the young man. But Beto was slightly depressed because after really good sex the youth had said he needed some money. Beto ended up giving him 5,000 pesos [about U.S. $4.50].

FRIDAY EVENING: March 27, 1987

José left by bus late last night for Guadalajara so I had to eat alone this evening at Campestre. Seeing that I was sad about José's leaving, Beto came over and had supper with me. Between courses, he took me to the door of his restaurant and pointed out a cluster of young men about half a block away. As we started our second course, he gave me a detailed account of how he got out of his depression last night. He had had sex with the three neighborhood youths he pointed out to me—two brothers and their cousin. The older brother was twenty-two and married, the younger brother and his cousin were about nineteen and single. After closing the restaurant, Beto took them in his car—with some beer and *mota* (pot)—to a secluded woodsy spot on the outskirts of Tuxpan. Beto had anal sex with them in the bushes one at a time. Beto explained, "Only the one fucking me left the car, the other two smoked *mota* or drank beer in the car and listened to music." Beto concluded his story by making sure I understood that none of them had asked for money. Beto had had sex with the older brother before and now felt sure he would have all three again soon.

Noa Noa—The Gay Bar

José and I made our first visit to the Noa Noa late one Saturday night (March 14, 1987). We were both surprised to find a "gay bar" in a relatively isolated moderate-sized farm town like Tuxpan. Even the state's capital city, Tepic, with a population close to 200,000, did not have a gay bar then. We were further surprised to find a gay liberation group in Tuxpan and that its leader, Eric, managed the Noa Noa. He had named the bar after a popular 1980s song about gay life in a bar in northern central Mexico written by Juan Gabriel, a nationally known singer reputed to be homosexual.

The small *zona roja* in Tuxpan, located on the southern edge of town, contains only four bars and is relatively quiet for this type of entertainment area. From outside, the bars appear quite ordinary. Unless you were told, you would not know that the back room of one of the bars is for gay clientele. Female prostitutes work the straight front barroom, which has about eight or nine tables and a short sit-down bar with wooden stools. More tables are available in back in a large open patio with a fountain on one side. Noa Noa is located in a small room down a short walk from the other side of the patio. You must walk through the front bar and patio to reach the gay bar so customers "not in the know" generally would not stumble onto it accidentally.

We got a royal welcome at Noa Noa. Eric came over and introduced himself and, because tourists never come to Tuxpan, asked us a lot of questions: Why were we there? Where were we staying? How long would we be there? He was also curious how we found his bar on our very first night in town. We told him that Vicente had recommended we have supper in Campestre and then go to Noa Noa. Eric knew Vicente but did not know Beto or his restaurant.

José and I became habitués of Noa Noa and the front barroom. After just a few visits, we could see there was a lot of moving back and forth by gay patrons. The female prostitutes almost never left the front barroom. The "straight" men rarely went into Noa Noa, but when the front barroom was full they would sit and drink at tables in the patio. The patio, especially on busy weekends, thus often became a low-key cruising area—like La Luna in Los Mochis—for men interested in discreetly initiating sexual encounters with other men.

The prostitutes were in the know, but they did not show any open resentment toward the gay men who flirted with their potential customers. They often called out to José and me as though we were potential customers when we passed through their area en route to Noa Noa. Although they usually wanted us to buy them drinks, on a few occasions they bought us drinks and insisted we sit and gossip with them about Tuxpan men.

During weekday nights, when business was slow, there was more mixing of customers in the front barroom. The following journal entry illustrates one such occasion:

As José and I were passing through the front bar Wednesday night, Eric, who was waiting tables, invited us to sit with him for a few drinks and enjoy the view: four young macho men drinking at a nearby table. When one of the young men called out for more beer, José jumped up and volunteered to act as their waiter. Eric signaled the bartender to give José the beer so off he went. José was wearing his tight white pants. Eric turned and joked loudly with a young rancher customer seated at the bar about "José's nice ass." The four guys at the table propositioned José, saying that he should come with them when they left, that all he had to do was bring some beer and they would show him a good time. José told me afterward that he was sure he could have negotiated a sexual encounter with them, but it would have meant that he had to take them all on—too risky a venture.

José and I stayed late that night. After the young macho men left, Eric told us about his role as leader of gay liberation in Tuxpan. One of the things that concerned him most was AIDS. A lot of sexually active young gay men in Tuxpan had asked him for information, but he said he knew very little and so could not tell them much about how best to protect themselves from getting infected with the AIDS virus. Eric then went on to tell us what he knew about the sexual transmission of HIV between men. He was dangerously misinformed. He mistakenly thought that oral sex was the most dangerous ("all those germs going in your mouth while sucking"), and receptive anal sex the safest, since "after having sex all the semen comes out when you take a shit." José and I gave him a brief rundown on HIV infection and AIDS, and before I left Tuxpan I gave him a complete set of instructional pamphlets in Spanish put out by GOHL, the gay liberation group in Guadalajara. En route back to our motel, José, chuckling about Eric's naïveté about the safeness of anal sex, said it was probably a product of "wishful thinking."

Renewed Friendship with Gilberto

I was glad to run into Gilberto before leaving Tuxpan, but sad that it happened so late in my stay that we were able to spend only a few days and nights together catching up. When I first met him in Guadalajara in the summer of 1970 he was twenty-six years old, worked as a labor organizer for a union, and studied law part time. I had last seen him in Los Angeles in 1976, where he had just moved and was living with an Anglo lover. He lived in Los Angeles ten more years before returning to Tuxpan, after the death of his father in the summer of 1986, to take care of his eighty-one-year-old mother. The youngest of five children, he was estranged from his two sisters and remaining living brother because of his homosexuality. He further alienated them when he moved back to Tuxpan by kicking his nephews and other hangers-on out of his mother's house, which he now owned.

Gilberto had been an excellent respondent in my original study in Guadalajara. Sexually active, he took great delight in showing me the homosexual side of his life in Guadalajara. In the fall of 1970 we took an interesting trip together to La Barca, a farm town about two hours' drive away, to see if its reputation for having a lot of sexually available young men was true. (It was, and probably still is.) Given the similarities between La Barca and Tuxpan, I now understand how Gilberto could read the sexual scene so fast and was such an expert in negotiating homosexual encounters with farm town men.

Gilberto took it upon himself to make sure I clearly understood what was going on sexually and politically in his hometown. He was a farmer, growing sorghum as a cash crop on land he owned near Tuxpan. He was also involved in local politics, sponsoring a female candidate for "Presidente de Tuxpan." He made strong speeches on her behalf to farmers in nearby villages. He carefully noted that he was always very macho when making these speeches in the countryside.

Gilberto then changed the subject and talked about the annual "Queen of Tuxpan" contest—when he was the opposite of macho. Eric had already told me about the *travesti* show held in the large patio of Noa Noa every December, but had not given me details as to how it could be legally carried out in a farm town like Tuxpan. I asked Gilberto for more information. He said it was the result of goodwill of some town officials who took it as a spoof and gave the gay group a special permit every year to put it on. Gilberto briefly described the contest held in 1987: "I was mistress of ceremony at the crowning of the 'queen of Tuxpan' last December. My hair was beautifully done— a big bouffant wig actually—and I wore a stunning green gown. The patio was packed with straight and gay people. My *travesti* cousin— Miss Tepic of 1986—was there in drag. Even the police chief was in the audience."

José had to return to Guadalajara the day we met Gilberto, so after supper at Campestre we walked him to the bus station. Afterward, Gilberto went with me to Noa Noa. He liked cruising in the front barroom, so we took a table there. Shortly after our arrival, Gilberto's *travesti* cousin in male garb—thin, plucked eyebrows, and very feminine—came over to our table with two plump queens. One of the queens, a dressmaker, was moving to Hermosillo where she could make more money selling her much sought-after *travesti* gowns. I invited them to join us for a drink, but they declined, saying they would meet us later in the back barroom.

After they left, Gilberto talked a long time about male homosexuality in farm towns like Tuxpan. The following journal entry summarizes the important points of his monologue:

Gilberto talked at length about his belief that in smalltown Mexico it is very important to play *only* one sexual role in anal intercourse. The consequences of fucking a *mayate* when he is drunk may be severe. As an example he related the details of a murder late in 1986 of a relatively young queen (about twenty-eight or twenty-nine) across the river from Tuxpan in San Vicente. "She" was found shot in the head. Gilberto thinks the murder might be the result of a vendetta by

a *mayate* the queen had fucked. Gilberto said that although he personally was *internacional* while living in California (that is, he played
both sex roles), he is *puro pasivo* (only anal receptive) with men in
Tuxpan. He related how easy it was for queens to find sexual partners in the farm towns he knew along the coast in Nayarit, many (or
most?) of whom are free. He told about having sex with young
groups of guys down at isolated parts of the river that runs through
Tuxpan.

When Gilberto finished, we moved to the back barroom to see what
was happening—only two drunken queens arguing about some missing
jewelry. We left, and Gilberto walked me back to my motel. En route
we stopped off at a small cantina in the center of Tuxpan for last call.
A thin man I recognized from the gay bar was there with a friend.
When we arrived at the motel, Gilberto and I agreed to spend the next
evening together at Noa Noa. He was going to be out of town during
the day making political speeches for his candidate, so I would have
to spend Friday, my last day in Tuxpan, alone.

Last Day in Tuxpan

While walking to breakfast early Friday morning I was followed by
a twenty-year-old youth on his bicycle. After several blocks I stopped,
turned around, and motioned him to come over and talk. He explained
that he had lived with his brother in Los Angeles for a month and
wanted to practice his English with me. I asked him to join me for
breakfast at Campestre. It was not yet open so he guided me to a small
restaurant close to the central market. During breakfast he talked about
wanting to move to Los Angeles. He was already married with two
children, the youngest being only fifteen days old. He knew the routine:
work and live alone in Los Angeles, send for the family later when he
had money. When my car was ready, he wanted to travel with me
north to the border. He was sure I could get him into the United States.
I told him I could not get him across legally and that only "coyotes"
knew how to get people across the border illegally.

When we finished breakfast I shook his hand, wished him well, and
told him good-bye. I tried to make it clear that I had work to do. He
stuck with me and kept talking all the way back to the motel. When
we arrived, I said good-bye again and went into my room. About five
minutes later, there was a knock on my door and there he was again.
He had parked his bicycle near the motel's reception desk for security

and come back. This time he made it clear he wanted to come in for sex, not talking. His original motive for interacting with me, I think, was for a free ride and help in getting across the U.S. border. When it became obvious that he was not going to get that, he decided he might as well at least have some sexual pleasure. On seeing the book *The Many Faces of Homosexuality* in my room, he said wryly, "Homosexuality is very common in Tuxpan."

I spent my last evening in Tuxpan drinking with Gilberto and Eric at Noa Noa. As I passed through the front barroom, a table of female prostitutes hollered at me to come sit with them. They had heard I was leaving the following morning so wanted to buy me a drink. It was early evening and few men were at the bar, so the women were gossiping and waiting for their regular Friday customers. I sat down and ordered a gin on the rocks. They wanted to know what kind of men I liked and offered, for a fee, to fix me up. There was some boisterous arguing among them as to whether Jaime or Jorge would do and which one was best suited for me. About this time, Gilberto came into the bar. He jokingly accused me of being a *manflora* (lesbian) and pulled me away from the table, telling the ladies that we had some important business to discuss.

After I finished my drink, we walked on to the back barroom. Eric was there talking to a couple of middle-aged, rather masculine men I had not seen before. Gilberto whispered in my ear that they were relatively prosperous married ranchers who came in on weekends every once in a while to drink and have sex with one of the drag queens. Gilberto was sexually attracted to both of them, but they were not interested in him.

Eric came over to ask if I could send him more AIDS pamphlets in Spanish when I returned to Los Angeles. I assured him I would. He and Gilberto were friends, but I got the feeling from the way they greeted each other that there was some rivalry between them. Gilberto reminisced about the good times we had had together cruising for men in La Barca and Guadalajara; Eric said he would fix me up with a handsome youth for my last night in Tuxpan.

By midnight there was a full house in both the front and back barrooms. The two ranchers were now drinking and joking with two effeminate young men. Gilberto had gone to talk with several queens he had met during the last *travesti* contest. They were just short of being in drag. Eric, meanwhile, sent several young men in their late teens to my table. Gilberto looked at me, obviously annoyed that they were now seated at my table and that I seemed to be enjoying their company. They were not the kind of men he was attracted to; he preferred older rancher types. He came over and suggested we move back to the front barroom and see what kind of "real men" might be available there. I told him to go ahead and do some cruising, that I would join him later.

I stayed and talked with two of the young men for about half an hour. They asked lots of questions about gay life in San Francisco and Los Angeles. I told them the good and the bad about gay life in the United States, that the AIDS epidemic had changed many things and that they should learn about safe sex from Eric. They in turn told me some stories about themselves—that they were just school friends, not lovers. Like the bicycle youth, they thought homosexual behavior was widespread in Tuxpan.

About a quarter to one I told the two young men I had to spend some time with my old friend Gilberto and then go back to my room at the motel. They offered to walk me back when I was ready, and something more (*algo más*) if I wanted. I thanked them, but said I had to leave early in the morning so had better just visit with my friend en route back to the motel and then go to bed alone.

When I returned to the front barroom, Gilberto was in heavy conversation with a rancher I had not seen before. Neither had Gilberto, and he said to me in an aside that he wanted him and was almost certain he was available. I wanted to give Gilberto an excuse for not having to leave his new friend and walk me to the motel, so I told him the guys in Noa Noa wanted to take care of me. It was a perfect solution. We said our good-byes and both of us ended up going our separate ways and doing what we really wanted to do. The two young men readily agreed to escort me back to my room. I did not, however, get to bed early or alone.

The Homosexual Scene in Mazatlán and Culiacán

Random observations I have made since 1968 of the homosexual scene in the two largest cities in the state of Sinaloa—forty-five cumulative days and nights in Mazatlán and fifteen in Culiacan—provide additional circumstantial evidence about the similar ways Mexican men in different locations in northwestern Mexico search for and carry out sexual encounters with other men. Mazatlán, a prime beach tourist city, is located on the Pacific Coast; Culiacán, the state capital and a major center for drug trafficking, is located inland, about 140 miles northwest of Mazatlán.

The easily observable homosexual scene in both cities is about the same—meager. There is usually only one gay bar open and major cruising areas are limited to a few places in nearby parks and streets. As is the case in so many cities and towns I know in Mexico's northwestern states, however, a closer look reveals a lot of homosexual encounters going on, not only in the "gay scene" but also in bars, cantinas, and nightclubs in the *zona roja* and elsewhere in Mazatlán and Culiacán. And every spring, during Mardi Gras, there is a peak of homosexual activities in Mazatlán when gay men come from all over Mexico to cruise and participate in its well known pre-Lenten festivities.

Except for Mardi Gras, the pattern of homosexual behaviors in Mazatlán and Culiacán appears to be about the same as I have observed in Hermosillo, Los Mochis, and Tuxpan. Cruising in straight drinking establishments is usually carried out between homosexually or gay identified men and "straight" men—who for a variety of reasons may be interested in having a sexual encounter with another man—in locations where the activity is tolerated or encouraged by managers or owners who look upon it as a way of increasing business. Customers' attitudes toward homosexual cruising determine how openly it may be carried on and for how long. If the cruising or effeminate behavior becomes blatant enough to cause a decline in business, it may be stopped overnight. Whenever I returned to certain "hot" bars or cantinas in Culiacán and Mazatlán after a long time, I often had to search for the new "in" drinking establishments.

There has been more stability in the location of gay bars in Mazatlán and Culiacán, but one may also have to look for them under new names and in new places after a prolonged absence. The reasons for closing are almost always the same: pressure from police and civil authorities on the owner of the building not to renew the lease. Bribes are usually paid to relevant city officials by the operators of gay bars in Mexico. But if the behavior in and around a gay bar becomes too scandalous— too much fighting, camping, and cross-dressing—even a bribe will not be enough to overcome community pressure to close it down.

An interesting fact about the young men I have met in gay bars in Mazatlán and Culiacán over the past twenty-five years is that a sizable minority come from rural areas and small farm towns into the cities— sometimes a long bus ride away—expressly to find sexual partners. Some come looking for a good time and new faces; others because, although they can find men to have sex with in their home territory, they want to cruise in an anonymous place where they do not have to worry about having their reputations spoiled or being found out by family members and friends.

"Straight" male rural migrants coming into the city looking for work are another interesting set of participants in homosexual encounters in Culiacán and Mazatlán. During my stopovers in these cities, most of the sexual partners I found while cruising in bars and cantinas fall into this category. One of my respondents from Guadalajara, Federico, who works half the year in Mazatlán, told me when I passed through in 1987 that he had almost daily homosexual encounters with migrant young men he met in his neighborhood near the central bus station. Although Federico always gives these men five or six thousand pesos (five or six dollars at the time), he made clear to me that they were *mayates*, not *chichifo*—the distinction in his mind being that they were horny macho men, not male prostitutes.

A Mini Barrio Study in Guadalajara

While having a beer one night in Bar Pancho in Guadalajara early in 1982, I had the good fortune to meet Alberto, one of my original informants. We had not seen each other for a long time (about eight years, we thought), and we were both happy to be back in touch again. I had lunch with Alberto the next day and afterward went home with him to give my regards to his parents and his many brothers and sisters. I had visited them only a few times in 1970 during the early months of my friendship with Alberto, who was only seventeen at the time. I was surprised and pleased to receive such warm and friendly greetings.

Later in the afternoon Alberto gave me a tour of his barrio, pointing out that—like many old neighborhoods close to downtown Guadalajara—it dated back to the early eighteenth century when the small Catholic church located at its center was built. He told me that even though his neighbors were poor they still thought of themselves as being middle class and maintained most of the old Mexican traditions. He said a lot of social activities in the barrio, for the young as well as the old, are intertwined with church activities. As is the case in many old barrios, for example, the church's student choir (referred to as the *estudiantina*) not only performs music for Sunday masses and special occasions but also provides barrio youth a means for getting together for all kinds of social activities.

The modest houses in the barrio are separated from the streets only by sidewalks. The interior courtyard and rooms are small and the average family size large (about seven members), so most families live in crowded circumstances. A lot of socializing by the young people takes place on sidewalks in front of the houses and in two small parks—one located in front of the church, the other down a side street a block away. Barrio youth often use the side street park for volleyball and softball games in the afternoon, and for conversation, singing, and guitar playing in the evenings.

We spent the rest of the afternoon walking around the barrio. By sunset Alberto had introduced me to many of his barrio friends—male and female, young and old. He received some gentle ribbing from a few of his young male friends, who wanted to know if I was one of his rich North American boyfriends. From the content of the joking back and forth between them, I gathered that Alberto's homosexuality was not a barrio secret. I asked him about this later on. He said that over the years he had had sexual affairs with many boys in the barrio and still continued to do so, but he did not run around broadcasting his sexual orientation, nor did he try to hide the fact that within his clique of barrio friends, male and female, he preferred having sex with men.

Sensing my interest in knowing more about male homosexuality in his barrio, Alberto suggested I spend some time studying it and volunteered to help as much as possible. I told him I wanted to do the study, but it would just be a small one since I would be able to do it only sporadically during my annual visits to Guadalajara. And I wanted to focus it narrowly on how it felt to be known as a *joto* by men in the barrio and to be the butt of their homosexual jokes. Alberto replied that we could do it together and I could get information firsthand, since he could spread the word that I was also a *joto*.

I started the mini barrio study when I returned to Guadalajara for a month in the summer of 1982. At Alberto's suggestion, I drove down so I could have a car available to take his friends around the city on their many social outings. It turned out to be a clever strategy for both participant observation and acceptance by Alberto's friends. One of the most sought-after uses of my car was to take young men and their friends to serenade their girlfriends late at night. Since the serenades often ended after the buses stopped running, and because the girlfriends sometimes lived several miles away, the young men were quite happy to be taxied back to the barrio. As a result of being able to use my car for *serenatas* and many other different kinds of social outings, I was

quickly accepted as an adjunct member of their group. By the end of my monthlong visit they felt comfortable enough having me around to start making me the butt of their homosexual joking. I had established my reputation in the barrio as a *joto*.

As a fifty-four-year-old *norteamericano*, I was initially uneasy hanging around with Alberto and his young group of barrio friends. He was twenty-five, and they ranged in age from fifteen to twenty-seven. I wondered what their parents and older siblings thought about my constant presence in the barrio. What did they think I was doing? By the time I left, however, it became clear that no one seemed hostile over my presence and I was usually invited along with Alberto to attend family-sponsored fiestas and ceremonies. It was Alberto's barrio, so I decided at the end of the first month of study to let him decide whether I should continue. I made it clear to him that I wanted to go on with the study and felt comfortable being around his family, friends, and neighbors, but that if it was causing him any problems at all, I wanted to stop the study straightaway. When I posed the question to Alberto, he responded immediately: "Please, don't stop now. My friends and I will be very disappointed if you don't come back next year."

I continued the study for six more years, driving down to Guadalajara and spending about a month on each visit. I was unable to return in 1983, so I resumed the study in the summer of 1984 and returned to the barrio every year until 1989. I sampled all the seasons: a winter, spring, and fall—and three summers. During 1983 three barrio youths moved to southern California to work, and we kept in touch through visits and by telephone. All but one became homesick and returned to Guadalajara before the year ended. I have kept in touch with Alberto and his barrio friends up to the present through letters and through the young man who still lives and works in Los Angeles.

All in all, for this study I totaled close to six months hanging around the barrio with Alberto and his friends. Each year I returned for a visit I was greeted warmly, as though I was one of their older relatives working in Los Angeles for the money although preferring to live in Guadalajara. Because the families lived in such crowded circumstances, I was never able to find a place to stay in the barrio. The truth is that some of my young friends in the barrio really liked my staying in a hotel so they could hang out with Alberto and me there and take warm showers, watch television, and drink beer. Luckily, I was always able to get the same back room in a small hotel, and the desk clerks never complained about my constant stream of male visitors.

Although Alberto and his group of friends remained relatively close and the same over the six years the study took place, each year I was able to see differences in attitudes and behaviors related to age (Alberto was twenty-five when I met him again in 1982 and thirty-two by the end of the study in 1989); there were also some changes in group cohesiveness related to work, marriage, and different interests. Yet the core barrio group remained essentially the same at the end of the study as it was at the beginning in 1982. Even at the beginning of 1994, eleven years later, my Los Angeles informant from the barrio group told me that he is still in touch with many of his old friends and is thinking about moving back to Guadalajara. Alberto also keeps in touch with his old friends but is no longer as close as he once was with them because he and his family had to move, for financial reasons, to another barrio in the nearby town of Zapopan.

Having set the stage, I will now present in narrative form brief representative selections of some of the more interesting participant observations made in the barrio. Although at times I was alone with some of the young men, when I hung around with them as a group Alberto always accompanied me. He thus appears in most of the events described. As a result, I must assume that what I experienced with the group may in part be colored by Alberto's being there. I was never quite sure, for example, how much of the kidding directed at me was to impress Alberto and how much was just being lifted off him and put on me.

Serenatas

One could never predict the preparation time required to put together a *serenata*. These events became a regular feature of my interaction with Alberto's friends in the barrio when I returned in the summer of 1984, but I never knew until the guys would suddenly pile into my car that it was time to go. The targeted girlfriend usually knew in advance that she was going to be serenaded on a particular night. And during the serenade her parents and siblings often hovered in the background; some mothers occasionally prepared a snack for the boyfriend and his fellow singers. The most time-consuming task before the serenade was the selection of musicians. Who should be asked to sing along? Would the best *estudiantina* singers really show up if asked? There was frequently a great flurry of activity as the time for departure grew near. Unless the *serenata* was called off for peevish reasons, it usually took place—but there was often a "make do" quality about it.

Alberto was a pretty good singer so the guys generally asked him to come along. His motive for going was commonly twofold: he liked pleasing the girlfriends and liked doing favors for the guys. And then, as I witnessed myself, there was also the wonderful camaraderie of being with the young men in an all-male singing event.

Sometimes, during the alcoholic drinking bouts that often followed the *serenatas*, opportunities for sex arose for Alberto and me (be it very late in the evening or early in the morning). Homosexual joking invariably surfaced with the second round of *cervezas* or tequila. It was never mean-spirited, but at times, with drunkenness, individual sexual requests made to me in jest could be quite crude. Once inebriated, several of the guys—who as far as Alberto and I knew had never had sex with another male—would ask me how much I would pay "to suck their cocks." I would reply something like "I'm really *surprised*, here I thought you were *mayates*, now you disappoint me by showing me what you really are: *chichifos*." My quick response amused them, and then they wanted to know what kind of sex I liked best and had I ever been with a woman sexually.

The guys who were really interested in having sex with me and Alberto would also enter into the joking and be quite crude, but when they wanted to negotiate a sexual encounter it would be done discreetly, out of earshot from the others. They never wanted any of their friends to know *for sure* that sex had taken place, so some nonsexual pretext was always made for going off alone with either of us. One favorite strategy was for me to arrange my dropoff route so that at the end of the outing I would be taking the interested sex partner (or partners) home last—and it would of course be via my hotel or wherever it was we were to have our sexual encounter. I believe everyone in the group knew what was going on, but everyone pretended nothing was actually happening.

A New Year's Eve Party

A New Year's Eve party I attended at the beginning of 1986 illustrates how a barrio heterosexual event may end up having a touch of homosexuality once the girls leave and it becomes an all-male party. Two young brothers in their late teens, whose family had gone to their native village for the Christmas holidays, organized the party at their house. From the start, the boys outnumbered the girls, and most of the girls had to return home before midnight. The few that did stay on to see the new year in were able to do so only because Alberto promised their parents he would promptly escort them home just after midnight.

Like most barrio parties, this one got off to a slow start about eight-thirty with guests sitting on borrowed metal folding chairs arranged in a circle, and chatting and drinking soda pop over loud disco music. The dancing finally started after about an hour and continued until the first group of girls left just before midnight. Tequila, rum, and beer were brought out in time for New Year's Eve toasting, but heavy drinking did not start in earnest until the last girls left and the new year began. There was a letdown in the party after the girls left. The dancing stopped and there seemed to be some confusion among the guys as to what to do next. A few left, but most stayed (about fifteen) and continued drinking. A new guest arrived with a bottle of brandy and some more sodas. He was loudly cheered.

There was a second peak of activity when Alberto returned from his chaperon task. Pablo, one of the most macho guys at the party, came up with the idea of a "strip show" and said Alberto and I should be the strippers. The age range of the partygoers was about sixteen to twenty-five, with most being in their late teens, so I tried to wriggle out on the grounds that I was too old. I was hooted down. Alberto came over and whispered in my ear, "We both have to do it, José, things might get out of hand if we don't. They might get angry."

Alberto moved away from me and loudly announced to the group that we would do the strip show, but insisted the macho instigator had to be the first stripper. To my surprise Pablo made no objections at all. He jumped up, moved to the front of the living room, and with music blaring did a first-class striptease with hips gyrating and clothes tossed to the audience. When he got to his shorts I hoped he would stop. But the guys kept egging him on until he stripped nude. Alberto stripped next and was greatly applauded as he tried to outdo Pablo with even more exaggerated wiggles and gestures. He also had to strip naked. I hoped to be let off after their great performances, but the hooting started and there was no escape. I was pushed to the front of the room to perform. I downed another tequila, threw my glass to the audience, and did my strip to the buff—much to the delight of the guys who expected me to chicken out.

Afterward there was more disco dancing, with Alberto and me being sought out as dance partners. Everyone, to put it mildly, was plastered. It was now close to two in the morning and I was ready to return to my hotel room for a good sleep. The party was not yet over, however, and I was put through one final incident that went much further than

I wanted it to go. One of my dance partners suddenly pulled me onto a bed in one of the small rooms adjacent to the living room saying he wanted to have sex. I protested that there were too many people around, we would be seen. He said nobody cared what we were doing and pulled down his jeans so I could go down on him. I got up from the bed and turned to leave. As I did so, I looked up to see two guys at the doorway watching us. Instead of helping me get away, however, they pushed me back on the bed laughing and saying I should make my partner happy and they would be next. Luckily, Alberto pushed into the room at that moment and turned the whole thing into a joking situation. En route back to my hotel, Alberto and I talked about the incident. He said the guy was not trying to embarrass me, he was "just drunk and hot" and probably thought I was as interested as he was in having sex.

A Mooning in the Choir Loft

From time to time on Sundays some of the guys who were in the *estudiantina* would invite me to come up to the choir loft to listen to their performances at the morning masses. The choir loft, which overlooked the main length of the sanctuary and altar, was on a second-story level of the barrio's early eighteenth-century Catholic church and could be reached only by two narrow circular stone staircases, one on each side as you enter the building. The staircase on one side continues on up to the roof of the church and a bell tower.

There was an equal number of males and females in the *estudiantina*, ranging in age from about fourteen to twenty-five. Since they were out of view of the congregation below, they dressed informally and some of the guys only wore shorts, T-shirts, and sandals. In between the songs they sang for the mass, they would relax and gossip; a few would engage in horseplay. Whatever they did it was not supposed to disturb the worshipers below.

Since I felt I would be out of place as a nonperformer, early on I turned down invitations from some of the guys to come listen to their music and view the mass from the choir loft. Alberto insisted, however, that I had to go there to witness firsthand the homosexual joking that was part of the horseplay between the guys. Alberto sang with the choir so he knew about and participated in the joking.

The "jokers" always used the circular stairway to the right; the girls and the more serious guys the stairway to the left. I was always ushered upstairs on the stairway to the right because that is where much of the joking took place. The stairway was so narrow that people had to go up or down single file. To pass anyone meant that there had to be some body contact. One of the fun things the guys liked to do was to press up against the guy ahead as they pretended to pass by and say how good it felt and make sexual remarks. Alberto and I were favorite targets of this prank. This also happened in between songs, when the smokers would retreat to the stairway and light up.

The homosexual joking also took place in the choir loft in back of the singers. The singers who remained seated were not always aware of what was going on behind them, since when they were not singing they were gossiping and looking forward. In between songs one of the guys liked to tease me that he knew I had a big crush on him and wanted to have sex. One morning as he was going through his routine, two of his friends overheard what he was saying and teased him about which role he would play with me—*activo* or *pasivo*. "Oh", he replied, "that's easy. I have a nice ass so that's what he would want." He then turned, bent over, and mooned us—quickly pulling his shorts down and up again.

I got upset over what appeared to me to be an increase in the level of homosexual horseplay and attributed it to my being there. Alberto was amused when I told him about my concern. He said, "Don't flatter yourself, it's going on whether you're here or not. Once many years ago I used to occasionally have sex with some of the guys in the bell tower."

The Barrio Today

I still maintain contact with my friends in the barrio. During my last brief trip there in the spring of 1994, I was only able to visit with two of my youngest respondents. In their mid-teens at the beginning of my study, in 1994 they were in their mid-twenties and employed part time. They told me they had thought about moving to California but were reluctant to go because they did not want to leave their family and friends and their barrio. Both also have *novias* and plan to marry and continue to live in the same neighborhood.

Although the friendship network I studied has changed with time, judging from what the young men told me the joking, games, and fun continue, and the barrio remains an immense source of daily pleasure for the people I know. I hope to be able to keep in touch with them and events in the barrio during the years that lie ahead. It will be fascinating to see how change in Mexico at large may affect the behavior of people I have come to know so well.

PART TWO | *Four Profiles*

These brief biographical sketches of four men from Guadalajara whom I have known for many years—Arturo, José, Federico, and Pedro—will provide the reader with a sense of what life may be like for individuals discovering their homosexuality at different ages while living within the confines of a large Mexican family in the second largest city in Mexico. Although these men followed different paths growing up, all of them have found acceptance within themselves and with their families and friends. Their lifelong patterns of behavior are quite different, yet each of them was able to cope over time with his adult homosexuality and each has had meaningful love affairs.

These sketches are not presented with the idea that these four individuals are representative of all Mexican men who have sex with men. The four men I selected do, however, have different sexual role preferences—two started their sex lives as *pasivos*, two as *activos*—and thus I hope these profiles will allow the reader to see how their attitudes and behaviors, particularly in adolescence, seem to have been affected differently by the sexual roles they preferred to play at various times in their lives.

The men profiled were first informants and then long-term friends. They knew about my research from the beginning and always encouraged me to continue. They also knew that at some point in time I would write profiles of them, and they gave me permission to do so. I have used only first names to protect their privacy. For two of them—Arturo and Federico—I have used pseudonyms, at their request. I have also used pseudonyms for all the other people that appear in the profiles.

FOUR | *Arturo*

I first saw Arturo in the spring of 1970 at the Baños Guadalajara. Like all public baths in the city it is a "straight" establishment, but unlike most its clientele are both straight and gay. Arturo stood out from the rest of the clients that Saturday afternoon because of his youth (he was twenty) and his handsome face, like that of a Spanish matador. He also presented a striking contrast to his friend Ramón who, although the same age as Arturo, was much taller, skinny, and not blessed with the same good looks. They were both effeminate, but watching them walk along the edge of the small rooftop swimming pool, I could discern that Arturo—with a husky deep voice and an angular trim body—had a more masculine way about him than Ramón. I was hoping they would come sit next to me so I could start a conversation and perhaps enlist them in my study. No such luck. Arturo was flirting with a middle-aged, very macho man several people over from me who had a large dark mustache and a wedding band on his left ring finger. He gave Arturo a come-on look so they immediately sat down beside him.

I next saw Arturo a few weeks later on a Friday night in a lower-class "straight" cantina at the southern edge of Guadalajara's *zona roja*. He was sitting at the bar talking to a man who looked similar to the one he had been flirting with at the Baños Guadalajara. He was not the same man but was obviously the type Arturo liked.

I had come to the cantina with a respondent named Enrique to check out information that it was becoming a popular location for homosexual cruising. We sat down at a table at the far end of the bar so we could get the best view of what was going on. Luckily, Enrique knew Arturo, so later on in the evening he introduced us. After a relatively brief time together, I invited him to come with us to another bar. Arturo liked the idea and agreed.

We left the cantina through a side door and headed for my car. About halfway there Arturo started running and shouted at us to hurry up. I looked back to see two men leaving the front door of the cantina. They were running toward us, angry and shouting obscenities at Arturo. We hurriedly got into my car and I drove away just in time. A beer bottle bounced off the back window of my car. Arturo explained later that he had led the mustachioed man to believe that he was going to have sex with him at a nearby cheap hotel. He had not told him the deal was off.

Arturo became a close friend and important source of information about effeminate homosexual Mexican men. His most intimate circle of seven friends—about the same age, effeminate, and homosexual—also became important respondents for my study. With my encouragement, they used my apartment as a base of operations and felt free to come and go as they pleased. As leader of the circle Arturo made it clear to them, however, that I was his "husband" and he was therefore in charge of their visits and behavior at my apartment. When we went out together as a group, he always sat in the front righthand seat of my car.

During the year that followed, Arturo and his friends visited me weekly. They lived at home, but because of family suspicions or knowledge about their homosexuality, most did not feel free to take their effeminate friends home. My apartment was thus a refuge where they could be themselves and camp and carry on. My car was also important to them as a means of getting around the city when the buses stopped running at midnight. Their weekday parental curfew was usually between 10–11 P.M. On weekends they could stay out later but were always expected to return home before the sun came up. Only occasionally were any of them willing to endure their parents' ire for violating curfew.

As I got to know Arturo and his friends better, they provided me with more detailed information about their private sex lives and started bringing some of their macho boyfriends to my apartment. They also invited me to go cruising with them in parks, bars, public bath houses, movie houses, and on certain boulevards in search of new boyfriends.

And I finally got invited to some of their most intimate parties. In all these events Arturo was the star and in charge.

During that year I also met part of Arturo's family and became a friend of his sister, Lucia. Lucia and Arturo were very close. She was five years older than Arturo and, after separating from her husband, decided to return home with her five children. She moved back into her parents' small three-room house, already crowded with five family members (mother, father, grandmother, and two brothers). Arturo liked living with his family but longed for more space and privacy.

By the time he was sixteen, all of Arturo's family knew about his homosexuality. His mother had accidentally come upon him getting fucked in the bushes with a neighborhood teenaged boy. His mother reproached him. Ashamed and angry over being caught, he moved out and went to live with a twenty-six-year-old male sex partner and his wife. While living with them, he became worried about causing problems. Meanwhile, he had reestablished contact with his family. They made it clear that they would welcome his return. After being away only five months, he went back home.

Shortly after he came back Lucia asked Arturo, "Do you only like men?" He had replied, "Yes, I think that's the way I'll always be." They had a long quiet talk. Arturo knew then that he had a strong ally and would always be able to share his secret life with her. His brothers continued to reproach him about his sexual orientation but not in heavy-handed ways. "When they make fun of me and my friends," he told me, "I just don't listen . . . It no longer bothers me that much."

Arturo was very close to his mother and worried a lot about her; she was not well. She had spent a good portion of her adult life bearing children, eighteen in all, but only eight had survived to adulthood: five sons and three daughters. Arturo was her youngest and favorite child. Disclosure of his homosexuality initially alienated and saddened her, but like Lucia she came to accept him the way he was. His father never said anything at all, pretending not to know his son's preferences.

In the fall of 1970 Arturo's mother died. It was a time of great sadness for the family, and the relationship between Arturo and Lucia became even closer. Just a few months before her mother's death, Lucia had begun a good assembly-line job in a toy factory. Now, with the mother gone, there was no one at home to look after her children. The problem was temporarily solved when Arturo lost his part-time factory job a few weeks later. He and his sister decided she would continue to work and he would stay at home and take care of her children and do the cooking, cleaning, washing, and ironing. This arrangement continued until Arturo moved to Los Angeles in the summer of 1972.

Arturo's Early Sex-Life History

Arturo remembers with great pleasure the sex play he had with boys in his neighborhood around the age of eight or nine. It was clandestine and consisted mostly of their fondling each other's genitals. He and a neighbor were once caught by the boy's mother and scolded. It frightened him but did not prevent him from continuing sex play with other boys (girls were never included).

His first complete homosexual experience occurred prior to puberty at the age of twelve with an eighteen-year-old neighbor. He remembers the anal penetration hurting; but he also remembers that he liked it because "it felt good." He had sex with the neighbor just one more time. Both encounters, Arturo remembers, were carried out stealthily.

During the next two years he had similar homosexual experiences with two, maybe three, more neighbors about the same age (sixteen to eighteen). As was the case with the first partner, the sexual encounters were secretly initiated by the older adolescents. Arturo, however, had made it clear beforehand that he was available and willing to be anally penetrated.

He would have liked to have had more male sexual partners but was afraid of being labeled a *puto*. He lived in a tough neighborhood and had already had to fight to retain his masculine status. He never thought of himself as macho, just "regular masculine." But when challenged he was not afraid to fight and would square off and box like a man. Although short, he had a boxer's physique and was strong. In most fights he could usually hold his own. He decided, however, that he should look elsewhere for sexual partners.

Arturo first "came" through masturbation when he was fourteen years old. He enjoyed this sexual pleasure but wanted to have more anal sex with men. The problem was that he was afraid of the unknown and did not know how to initiate homosexual encounters outside his own neighborhood.

A whole new world opened up to Arturo at the age of sixteen when a casual acquaintance he met in downtown Guadalajara introduced him to Bar Poncho, the only completely gay bar in the city at that time. He quickly learned that he could get exactly the kind of sex partners he wanted there at no cost and that there seemed to be an endless supply available. Moreover, he could come and go as he wished without "burning" his reputation. And he no longer needed to worry about being hassled by the boys in his neighborhood.

Since he had finished all the schooling he was to have (six years) and was not working, he started going to Bar Poncho two or three times a week. He found the majority of his sex partners there during his first year of intense homosexual activity. He also found some cruising on downtown streets and in certain movie theaters. And he began friendships with other young men he met downtown who considered themselves to be homosexual (*de ambiente*).

Arturo estimates that he had sex with at least thirty to forty different men that first year. The majority were "regular masculine" middle-class men from twenty-two to forty-five years old who usually picked up the tab and knew where to go to have sex. A few were from the upper class—none from the lower. It was important that they be masculine looking, have a dark mustache, and be mainly interested in the insertive role in anal sex. Foreplay usually consisted of full body contact and French kissing. The major event, however, was always anal sex, and Arturo was willing to play only the anal-receptive role. He told me he immediately lost interest "if they put their legs up in the air and also wanted to be fucked." He wanted "to have sex with men . . . not *locas*."

Arturo was not then particularly interested in establishing long-term sexual relationships, so most of his homosexual encounters were for one time only. During that year, however, he did have short affairs with two different men in their mid-twenties. One was single, the other married.

The single man had an apartment where he and Arturo could meet when they wanted for sex, usually once or twice a week. They had good sex together, but the relationship ended after only four months because of the man's jealousy. He lost interest when he discovered that Arturo was having sex with other men.

Arturo and the married man initially carried out their sexual encounters in private individual steamrooms of public bathhouses. When Arturo told the married man about his family problems, the man invited him to rent an extra room in his house. The rent was only a ploy to allay the wife's suspicions. They continued their sexual activities in Arturo's room late at night, but he was fearful that they might wake her up. The man told Arturo not to worry, that she slept soundly and he could easily satisfy them both sexually.

The man was very relaxed about sex and was willing to do anything with Arturo that he would do with a woman. There was plenty of foreplay—kissing and hugging—followed by good anal sex. Arturo had to be careful, however, never to touch the married man's rear end. It was the only thing that would make him angry.

After being there five months, Arturo moved out and terminated their sexual relationship because he felt sure from some of the wife's remarks that she knew what was going on. He did not want to create problems between them. He had patched things up with his family, so it had become all right for him to go home. He lived with his family until he moved to Los Angeles at twenty-two years of age in mid-1972.

Late Teens and Early Twenties Sex Life

During his late teens and early twenties, Arturo established a network of friends of approximately his own age who were both homosexual and effeminate. Out of this network came the core group of seven close friends who became inseparable. For all of them it was a time of increasing feminization and heightened sexuality.

Their social life at that time consisted mostly of weekend get-togethers downtown in parks or at Sombrillas—a popular outdoor restaurant in a main plaza—in the daytime, and at Bar Poncho and other bars and cantinas in the evenings. Occasionally, a few of them would go to Baños Guadalajara. Cruising for "husbands" and "one-nighters" was carried on in all these locations.

They also had access to some private spaces—small rooms in poor neighborhoods rented from time to time by network friends—where they could party and be in drag any day of the week if they chose. Arturo said that people living in the vicinity of these rooms "didn't pay much attention . . . even with all the noise and *locas* coming and going." When eighteen years old, he spent almost two weeks in drag while staying in and operating out of one of these rooms. He dressed in men's clothes only when he returned home to sleep at night. He did not want his family to see him in drag and still had "to be serious . . . not *loca*," going through his own neighborhood on his way home because of groups of hoodlums who might gang up on him.

Until his twentieth year, Arturo's sexual practices remained roughly the same. He continued to prefer playing the anal-receptive role with masculine-appearing middle-class men—many of whom he believed were married. He always let them take the lead as to the extent and kind of foreplay, and was generally willing, with only a few exceptions, to do what they wanted. He liked smooching but did not care too much for oral sex. He would go down on a partner if he was insistent, however, and did not resist if the partner in turn wanted to go down on him. He related his distaste for oral sex to his mother's constant admonition when he was a boy "to not put dirty things in [his] mouth." Anal sex for him was thus "okay."

Arturo's major sexual turnoff still was when a partner wanted to be anal receptive. Nothing annoyed him more than spending a lot of time cruising, catching a macho-appearing guy, and then finding out when they were in bed or in the bushes that he was "a *loca*." When there were doubts, he tried beforehand to find out if his potential partner "was *activo* . . . and so not get disappointed."

From seventeen to nineteen years of age, Arturo remembers having homosexual encounters with about seventy-five different men. Most of these encounters took place when he was nineteen—and were one-time only with some fifty different men. They had been fewer in number (only five) the previous year because he had had a five-month affair with a wealthy young man his own age. He became despondent when the young man withdrew from the relationship. Arturo attributes his intense sexual activity the following year—almost a different sexual partner each week—to getting over the breakup. "I was looking for something," he said.

Arturo continued his sexual activity at about the same level over the next two years but with some additions to his sexual repertoire. During his twentieth year he began to enjoy oral sex as foreplay more and more, especially going down on his partners. And in an interview that year, he told me he had tried some new things: "The first time I fucked a guy was early this year . . . did it three more times with different guys but didn't like it much. It's weird when a macho guy turns over like that and lets you give it to him." With some hesitancy, Arturo, blushing, also told me he was "doing *beso negro* [literally, the "dark kiss," but used here to mean rimming]. It's dirty, isn't it? Bad! But, when you're drunk you do many things . . . some macho guys will even let you do it to them." After telling me this, he felt the need to reassure me that he only did it once in awhile because most of his sex partners never attracted him that way. It appeared to be on the edge of perversion for him.

Social Gatherings and Parties

Arturo and his friends spent a lot of the time they were together playing cards and gossiping in campy ways about past activities. There were never any sexual tensions in their socialization because sexual attraction between them was out of the question. Arturo summed it up this way: "We're all *locas* looking for husbands, what would we do together in bed?" And there was an unspoken rule between them that they would not steal each other's husbands.

Occasionally, on weekends when they had enough money, they would spend a Saturday or Sunday at one of the *balnearios* (combination swimming and picnic areas) located on the outskirts of Guadalajara. Although they would not turn down an attractive man who made himself sexually available, these outings were mostly a time for relaxing, eating, drinking, and looking—not cruising. Oftentimes they would connect with other *locas*. This increased their enjoyment and sometimes added to their network of friends.

Parties were another means of enjoyment for Arturo and his friends. Lovers and relatives were sometimes invited, but usually the invitees were other *locas* and homosexual friends. The settings for the parties frequently surprised me; the endings were almost never predictable. Drinking and intoxication for almost everyone was the general practice at these gatherings.

The following excerpts from my journal provide a good illustration of the way their parties often turned out. The three described were held some weeks apart in the fall of 1970 in the same location: the "sleeping room" of Arturo's friend Fernando. To me it seemed like a strange place to have a party that Arturo had headlined beforehand as "a fiesta of *locas*." Located in a very poor neighborhood on the outskirts of Guadalajara, Fernando's sleeping room sat at the rear of a small lot behind his grandmother's two-room adobe house. It was separated from her house by a small packed-earth patio and had little privacy since the household had no indoor plumbing and the only running water and toilet were outside the back of his room. His family had to pass through his sleeping room to bathe and use the toilet.

Tuesday Evening (September 15, 1970)

Federico and two Franciscos (F/W and F/P) [part of Arturo's inner friendship circle] dropped by for a visit. Federico suggested we go to a Mexican Independence Day party that would be interesting for my study. I told him Arturo had already invited me and that I was waiting for him and Ramón to come guide me there. We waited. At 9:30 Federico insisted that we go—that Arturo and Ramón would surely be there.

The party was at Fernando's house. It's not clear whether his mother and father also live there, but his grandmother, two younger brothers (ages eight and twelve?) and younger sister (age seven–eight) were there. A lady was standing at the door when we arrived talking to two other women. Federico wouldn't get out of the car. The women made him nervous he said, so he sent F/W to see what was going on. F/W said there were lots of guys inside. Federico sent him back to get Fernando. Fernando came out and insisted we go inside. I moved the car so Federico could get into the house with the women's back to him.

The party was under way when we got inside—some fifteen young men were present, with about five couples dancing. Fernando was the host. The friends I had met with him last Saturday night were there: the small bespectacled taxi driver, the slightly feminine guy (Mario) who was after me, and the very thin rather dark-skinned handsome Indian type. A tall and extremely effeminate queen in drag (Gina) I've seen often at Bar Poncho on Saturday nights was there with his small queenly friend. Also present: Roberto (Jesus's ex-lover), Martino (in drag), and another guy in drag who passed as a girl until I learned otherwise. All present at the fiesta were in their twenties or younger and all were from the lower-income class (with maybe one or two exceptions). Two guys, deeply in love, stuck together all evening. They looked to be about seventeen to eighteen years old. From time to time later on in the evening they would lie on the bed and kiss. Several guests disappeared outside in back to use the toilet and maybe have quick sex.

After we had been at the party for awhile, Arturo and Ramón came in. They had been told, I'm sure, I was inside. I was lying on the bed next to F/P who was being pestered by a guy he didn't like. Ramón came over after I greeted them both at a distance. I told him we had waited. Arturo was clearly annoyed at me for not waiting. Ramón quickly sat on my lap and said it was okay. He got up and then Arturo did the same. I danced a lot with Ramón, only once with Arturo, and a few times with the two Franciscos. Mario had just started dancing with me when Arturo quickly came over and objected. He told the guy he would be in trouble if he kept on. The guy moved away, frightened by Arturo's threat. He told me he didn't want any trouble. Arturo took me aside and told me the guy wanted to have sex with me. It seemed to me that Arturo's objection was mostly based on the possible loss of face he would have should I stray. In the eyes of his social network I'm still his husband.

Then there was the contest for queen, with some grumbling about votes being bought. Manuel led the pitch for Gina, Arturo supported Martino, and two other contestants dropped out. Gina won! Her supporters put a red cloak on her and, complete with crown and scepter, she sat on a chair with her court. They tried to get macho Roberto to sit next to her but he refused. Martino sat on my lap afterward and, annoyed over Gina's using her own money to win, told "her" as she approached, that they "were" (i.e., no longer) friends.

The queen was drunk. When an older effeminate guy (late twenties) was about to start a fight she hit him on the head with her scepter hard enough for the fake glass jewels to bring blood. F/W also came in for an attack of sorts when the queen banged him with her crown. He promptly retaliated by grabbing the crown and hitting her back on the head with it, and then threw it on the ground and stepped on it. Someone suggested the affair should be in *ALARMA!* [the tabloid newspaper that often features homosexual men in the most unfavorable light possible].

We left shortly afterward, saying goodnight to the grandmother as we passed through her house.

Saturday Evening (October 24, 1970)

Both Franciscos, Federico, Victor, and an effeminate friend of the group (name?) arrived about 8 P.M. We played cards until about 9:30 and then left for Fernando's party. Arturo and Ramón said they would meet us there. We ran into Fernando some blocks from his house talking to a young boy from the neighborhood. He said he was waiting for someone to arrive on the bus, that we should go on to the party.

We could hear the music from the party as we got out of my car. I wondered what the neighbors standing and sitting in front of their small houses thought as they saw us going inside. Just as we were driving up, we saw Arturo, Fortino, and Ramón approaching the house from a different direction. I didn't recognize Arturo at first. He was in drag.

The party was in the same room as before. Fernando's grandmother, elder sister and brother-in-law (with baby in arms), and his younger brother and sister were in the front room. The grandmother looked quizzically at us as we filed by and mumbled greetings. The others said nothing. A blanket, not used at the previous party, more or less covered the wide entrance to Fernando's room. It presumably prevented people in the front house from having a complete view of the goings-on at the party.

Arturo seemed self-conscious about being in drag—partly probably because of my presence. He had all the eye makeup, dress, high-heeled shoes, and stockings of a female but no lipstick or wig (his hair was fixed like his sister's). But his angular male physique made him look comical compared to the other contestant in drag who had soft lines, a wig, and—with a little more care—could have passed for a rather unattractive female.

At its peak the party numbered about eighteen. There were no females present. Only Arturo and the other contestant were in drag. The party consisted of dancing, drinking, joking, a little conversation, and a lot of petting. The dancing took place both in the courtyard and in Fernando's room. Since the relatives had a full view of the little courtyard, the petting took place only in the room. Several couples were lying on Fernando's large bed embracing and kissing. Several couples were kissing as they danced. At one point in the evening I noticed Fernando's youngest brother standing at the foot of the bed watching the couples and fondling his genitals. Another time I saw his elder sister pass through the room to use the toilet in back.

Although there was a lot of petting, it did not lead to sexual intercourse at the party. The host was the only person accused of having sex. He had spent a long time out in back with a fifteen-year-old neighbor boy. The party started breaking up about 1 A.M. It was a warm night, the room was hot from all the people dancing, and there was nothing more to drink. Suddenly, no one was interested any longer in having the queen of Guadalajara contest. Arturo was clearly miffed. He had gotten up in drag for nothing. As a gesture of goodwill, Fernando announced that the contest would be held at next Saturday night's party.

Arturo and the other guy in drag changed into their male clothes. Arturo was wearing transparent silk panties underneath his dress. We left the party together in my car—five in back, four in front. Arturo and Ramón got into the front seat, forcing all the others to squeeze past them to get in back. Arturo was still in control.

Saturday Evening (November 7, 1970)

Arturo, Ramón, Fortino, and the two Franciscos came early this evening to get ready for another party at Fernando's. We had several rounds of vodka and soft drinks. With the rest of the bottle in tow we set off for Fernando's fiesta. We stopped at a liquor store to buy a cheap bottle of brandy. En route, there was lots of camping and calling of *papacito* to handsome young guys standing on street corners.

The party was not going very well when we arrived. We soon changed that since Arturo, Ramón, and Fortino—already drunk from the vodka at my house—livened things up fast. I danced with Paco, a butch friend of Fernando's. His hands are rough so he must do some kind of hard labor.

Once again the party consisted mostly of dancing, talking, and joking, but this time it was somewhat different: there was no smooching and Fernando's two sister's came in and danced, and his brother-in-law looked in from time to time. Other new people at the fiesta: Flavio (an older man, about forty-five, with a Volkswagen) and two well-dressed friends.

The party went on for some time in a friendly fashion with some regional folk-dancing by Jorge and José (from LA). Then, from across the room, I heard Ramón say to Arturo, "Chinga tu madre [fuck your mother]." Arturo didn't like it at all and got very upset that his best friend would say that to him, even in jest, so soon after his mother's death. Arturo's friends tried to calm him down.

Shortly thereafter, while I was out in back talking to Paco, Fernando's hefty older sister came in and started arguing with Arturo. (She and her husband must live with the grandmother in the front house.) On my return inside, José (LA) told me the argument was over red high-heeled shoes that Arturo had used as part of his drag outfit at the last party and had left behind in Fernando's room. Arturo had borrowed them from his sister Lucia. Now he wanted them back and knew that Fernando's sister had them. Fernando in turn accused Arturo of having a watch he had lost two years ago and of being responsible for the loss of a radio and a wig at the last party. At this point, Ramón joined the argument to defend Arturo.

As the quarrel became more heated, José (LA) started urging everyone to leave and go downtown to Bar Pancho. When we got to the street in front of the house, Arturo and Fernando started a fistfight, with Ramón and Fernando's sister in a side scuffle. I warmed up my car while the fighting carried on. Finally, it broke up and Arturo and Ramón got into the car. As we pulled away, my rear windshield survived another hit as someone smashed a beer bottle on the edge of it. I dropped all the guys off at their houses. Arturo didn't get his sister's shoes back.

Arturo continued socializing with his intimate circle of seven friends in Guadalajara until he moved to Los Angeles in the summer of 1972. In the spring of 1971, however, he had also started spending a lot of time with a relatively older new friend, Luis, who at the age of twenty-seven had recently found an American lover, Richard, and moved into his apartment. Arturo later told me that Luis and Richard helped fill the void in his life caused by my leaving Guadalajara that spring. Their apartment also provided a place for him and his close friends to hang out.

Arturo's friendship with Luis and Richard brought about a major change in his thinking about life and his future. They provided the final motivation he needed to cross the border and start a new life in Los Angeles—and to think seriously about finding an American lover. Three of his seven close friends, including Ramón, decided to cross the border with him in July 1972. Richard and Luis were already living in Los Angeles. Richard had moved there the previous spring and Luis had managed to get safely across the border and join him by early summer.

A Long Sojourn in Los Angeles

During the year prior to crossing the border, Arturo and Ramón had visited Tijuana to learn how best to get across cheaply and safely. Arturo and Luis also spent time together that year learning some English with Richard's help. Neither Arturo nor any of his three friends had relatives living in California—and I was by then working in South Vietnam and Washington, until the fall of 1973—so they knew they would be on their own when they got to Los Angeles. In early July they finally put together what they believed to be enough money to tide them over until they had income from work, so they took the bus to Tijuana. After two aborted attempts, they crossed the frontier and arrived safely in Los Angeles in mid-July 1972.

Arturo and his three friends lived together in a cheap apartment in south Los Angeles for close to six months. It was a tense time for all of them. Mexican immigrants were just starting to move into black neighborhoods in large numbers so there was considerable friction between the two ethnic groups. Early one morning, while waiting in the dark to catch a bus to kitchen jobs in a restaurant in downtown Los Angeles, Arturo and Ramón were robbed at gunpoint by two young black men. They were shaken by the experience but determined to stay and learn better how to protect themselves in a city far more dangerous than Guadalajara.

Arturo had not worked steadily for over a year, so in the beginning he had to learn to discipline himself to keep at it, particularly since the hours were long and the job was boring. Many times he felt like quitting. It was also a new experience for him to live away from his family in another country, and to live with his friends for a long period of time. He was homesick and especially missed his sister Lucia and her children.

Luis and Richard turned out to be a disappointment. They were going through an adjustment period of their own, so even on his few days off Arturo found he was not as welcome as before. They always invited him to come back for another visit but seemed distant and only rarely asked him to spend the night. He felt offended by their behavior and hated the hour-long bus ride back alone to his apartment through a dangerous part of the city. He no longer felt he could count on them for anything.

Knowing that he now had to rely only on himself to be successful in Los Angeles, Arturo concentrated on learning English. He decided that speaking English fluently would help him find a more interesting and better-paying job, and an Anglo lover. He wanted both as soon as possible.

He tried to get his friends to understand the importance of speaking and understanding English. When not working, however, they were far more interested in going to Latino gay bars and partying. If they learned English at all, it was going to be slowly. Arturo loved his friends but he began to see that in order to succeed he was going to have to move away from them eventually.

One of the first changes he made was to shift from Latino to Anglo gay bars. In the beginning it was reassuring to go to Latino bars and have Spanish-speaking sex partners. He and his friends rapidly learned that, just as in Mexico, men were available as sex partners in some of the bars and cantinas in Mexican neighborhoods. And there were more Latino gay bars in Los Angeles than in Guadalajara. In no time, they made many new Mexican homosexual friends and got invited to their parties. Thus, they swiftly got back into social networks that made them feel at home.

In the beginning, Arturo's friends went with him to Anglo gay bars, but they did not enjoy them as much as he did so he began going alone. He used his English more as a result and this improved his chances of being approached by Anglo men. Normally not a shy person, he still found it almost impossible to approach them with his limited English.

After several frustrating encounters with Anglo men, Arturo finally found exactly what he had been yearning for: Charlie, a handsome man of Hungarian extraction in his late twenties who was looking for a long-term relationship. It was not love at first sight for either of them, but both desperately wanted the stability of living with someone they could depend on, and to whom they were at least sexually attracted and reasonably compatible.

Charlie was a recovering drug user and alcoholic. He had been a successful, well-paid musician back in the Midwest and had left to get away from cocaine and booze. He had also left to get away from his middle-class family who he felt sure would never accept his homosexuality. Southern California offered him a new profession and freedom to pursue his own sexuality. Arturo was the first man he had met with whom he felt sure he could be happy sharing his life. In his eyes, the fact that Arturo was Mexican was a plus, not a minus. In actuality, Charlie could easily pass for a Mexican. He had the looks that Arturo always liked in a man: a big mustache and dark brown hair and eyes.

Because of work commitments and distance, Arturo and Charlie initially saw each other only on weekends. They lived and worked far apart. Arturo did not introduce Charlie right away to his friends because he feared they might not like him, or be jealous and try to break them up. In addition, Charlie did not speak Spanish, and Arturo's friends were still unable to hold a conversation in English. Arturo finally invited Charlie to come to his apartment. Much to his relief and surprise everything went well. Arturo's friends were quite happy that he had a lover with a big car who was willing to take them sightseeing in Los Angeles.

After three months of courtship, Charlie proposed to Arturo that they rent an apartment close to downtown Los Angeles and live together. Arturo accepted but said he wanted to give his friends enough notice so they could find someone to take his place and help pay the rent. Their combined income was not enough to keep the apartment without him.

Another month passed before Arturo and Charlie found an apartment and started living together. It was a stressful time for Arturo because he had never lived with a lover before, he could hold only a limited conversation in English, and his friends were not happy that he was leaving them so soon. And then there was the additional problem of sexual compatibility. Charlie had never practiced anal sex and adamantly refused to even try it. And, although he enjoyed oral sex, Arturo had never had to go for any length of time without anal sex.

Much later, however, Arturo told me that within a month he knew he had found what he was looking for: Charlie was the right choice and together he felt sure they would be able to overcome the obstacles that appeared to threaten their relationship. "Since crossing the border," he also told me, "it's the first time I'm relaxed . . . Now I'm living with someone that can help me stay out of trouble with immigration . . . someone that knows Los Angeles."

After moving in with Charlie, Arturo immediately began to spend all his free time studying English. He had a good ear for sound and a good memory, so his ability to understand and speak the language improved rapidly. Because he was having such a hard time learning Spanish, Charlie marveled at the speed with which Arturo increased his English vocabulary. Charlie gave up trying to speak Spanish. Ultimately, his failure helped Arturo learn English even faster since he had to speak it daily with Charlie.

Arturo's friends visited him and Charlie often for several months and then their visits tapered off. Although they liked Charlie, they were unable to talk to him. And he soon grew tired of listening to them and Arturo chatter in Spanish as they played cards and camped most of the time they were there. Arturo urged Charlie to use their visits as a time to learn Spanish. Charlie countered by saying that since they were now living in the United States, they all should learn English and he would help them.

About this time an unexpected problem surfaced—Arturo's effeminacy. Charlie was a loner who had never moved in a gay circle of friends. He felt strongly that a man should act like a man even if he was homosexual. He was very masculine and the thought that someone might see him as feminine made him uncomfortable. He was willing, however, to make a compromise: when they were out together in public, Arturo would act as masculine as possible. At other times, inside their apartment or when out with his Mexican friends, he was free to act as he pleased.

Arturo accepted this restraint on his behavior—after all, it was not that different from the way he had to act in Guadalajara—but he no longer felt comfortable having his effeminate friends party at his apartment. As a result, he helped organize parties elsewhere and eventually established a pattern of having a weekly night out alone—usually Friday or Saturday—with his friends.

During his first year of living with Charlie, Arturo also realized he was going to have to deal with another part of his past: he was (to put it in his words) *"muy puta"*—that is, he was used to having many different sex partners. Monogamy was a state that he had experienced only a few times in his life and for relatively short periods of time. Changing to this new state was not going to be easy.

By then Arturo had learned as well about Charlie's jealousy. When Arturo started going out with his Mexican friends on weekends, for example, Charlie's insistence on going with him ruined their parties. Arturo confronted him about this—reminding him that he was bored at the parties and that almost as soon as they got there wanted to go home. When Arturo suggested that he go to the parties alone, however, Charlie's immediate response was that Arturo would just use the occasion to whore around.

Eventually Charlie tired of the parties and tried to get Arturo to stop going and do something else. Again, a compromise was reached: they started bowling together one night a week and, holding his ground, Arturo continued to go to Mexican parties, but alone. Additionally, Arturo started working on masculinizing himself with the same intensity that he learned English. This pleased Charlie immensely.

The next big step that Arturo took was to look for more interesting work. With Charlie's assistance, he got a much better paying job as a bilingual clerk in a home improvement store that was just beginning to attract Spanish-speaking customers. He worked hard to learn all there was to know about the section he was assigned to and within a couple of months felt secure and happy in his new job. Charlie, meanwhile, continued to earn good money as manager of a variety store.

In the spring of 1973, Arturo bought his first automobile and paid the way for his sister Lucia and her children to come legally for a visit. How proud he felt that spring when he drove his own car to pick them up at the Los Angeles airport!

Arturo's car and Lucia's visit cemented his relationship with Charlie in ways that were never expected. The car represented Charlie's trust in Arturo since it could not have been bought without his financial help. Charlie's immediate rapport with Lucia and her children was unexpected since they were unable to speak one another's language. Arturo thought at best they might just be able to tolerate each other and had prepared himself to make an annual visit to his family in Guadalajara alone. He was especially pleased that they appeared to have a genuine liking for each other and that Charlie understood that he had a close and loving relationship with his family despite his homosexuality. Charlie was estranged from his family and only occasionally visited them where they lived in the Midwest.

I first met Charlie in the spring of 1973 when I returned to Los Angeles from Vietnam for a brief visit en route to Washington. Arturo was nervous about my meeting Charlie because of our close relationship in Guadalajara. Before my first visit he called me to talk about how much I should reveal about his past. He said it was okay to tell Charlie about my research, but because he was jealous no mention should be made of my role as his fictive husband in his homosexual friendship network. The visit went well.

On my return from Washington in the fall of 1973, Arturo, Charlie, and I established a close lifelong friendship. We met often, and I became a confidant to Charlie as well as Arturo. As the years passed, I talked with them together and separately about the most intimate aspects of their lives and relationship. At times I was just a friend, at other times a marriage counselor, and at still other times an arbiter helping resolve disputes related to their cultural differences.

During the first few years of their relationship, Arturo and Charlie spent the Christmas holidays together. Arturo's longing to be with his family was partially met by annual visits by Lucia and her children. He wanted to go home for the holidays, but because of his illegal immigrant status he worried about getting safely back across the border. Finally, the lure of being with his family at Christmas overpowered his worry about getting back, and Arturo took his first trip home in late December 1976. Charlie spent that Christmas with his family in the Midwest.

Arturo spent a wonderful two weeks with his family and then returned safely across the border. Charlie did not have such a happy reunion with his family. Although they had met Arturo during a brief visit to California, and told Charlie they liked him, he could feel their disapproval of his homosexuality. He also worried about Arturo getting caught at the border.

One of the first things Charlie did when he returned to California was to find out how to get Arturo a green card—the document that would legitimize his being and working in the United States. I do not know how he managed it, but when Arturo returned to Guadalajara for the Christmas holidays in December 1977 he had a green card. He was thus able to enter California legally on his return in early January 1978.

That Christmas changed the lives of Arturo and Charlie in another important way: for the first time they spent the holidays together with Arturo's family in Guadalajara. Arturo was opposed to their going together because he thought Charlie, as a result of not speaking Spanish, would become quickly bored with his family and thus ruin his reunion with them. He was afraid that Charlie might also try to pressure him to return sooner than he wanted to Los Angeles.

Arturo's worries about Charlie proved to be baseless. Lucia and her children paved the way for his visit. And to Arturo's utter astonishment, his family accepted Charlie right away as his lifelong "partner" (and, unspoken, "husband") and treated him as a member of the family. Despite the language barrier, Charlie and his "in-laws"—as he later described them—got along fine. The onerous task for Arturo was the endless role of translator.

Charlie's major pleasure with Arturo's family was the acceptance and love they gave him that first Christmas. He was surprised at the openness of Arturo's brothers and, after they had had a few drinks, the way they joked with him at fiestas in front of the rest of the family. On his return he told me: "They would tease me about being Arturo's husband . . . and things like that. When they got a little drunk at parties they'd ask me to dance and pinch my ass . . . I'm not kidding . . . Hector once playfully grabbed me and danced me around the room. I got upset at first. But then I remember your saying that they kid around a lot so I started kidding back and did some pinching on my own."

Although their relationship reached the breaking point several times during the next nine years, Arturo and Charlie were able to patch things up each time and continue to live together. Every Christmas during those years Charlie accompanied Arturo to Guadalajara for the family reunion. Charlie's love for Arturo's family and Guadalajara grew deeper each year. Alienated from his own family in the Midwest, Charlie told Arturo that he could be very happy living near his family, that they should start thinking about moving to Guadalajara permanently.

Arturo liked the idea of being back with his family, but he was reluctant to give up a good job and lose the financial security they had in Los Angeles. His response to Charlie was: How would they support themselves in Guadalajara?

Arturo actually had another problem that had troubled him from the beginning of their relationship—sexual incompatibility. It had never been openly and honestly resolved between them. Because of it, he was not sure he wanted to spend the rest of his life with Charlie in Los Angeles or Guadalajara. He discussed the problem with me a number of times. In a fall 1985 interview, I asked him to describe how his sexual behaviors had changed since he had been living with Charlie. The following are excerpts from his response:

You know a lot about this already. Remember when you saw me at the Silver Platter [a Latino gay bar near downtown Los Angeles] that Saturday night? I was embarrassed—you know how I am. I'd just had sex with a soccer coach . . . the guy from Hermosillo. I just made it for last call before going home. Charlie thinks I'm at my usual weekend party. I was . . . I left early to meet the coach . . . he's good sex. You know, José, it's like I told you before . . . the need builds up inside me . . . I have to get fucked. I think and think about it and have to find somebody. I can't tell Charlie about this. He says he'll leave me if I cheat on him. We make good sex . . . he knows that . . . but sucking isn't enough for me.

Arturo's sexual incompatibility with Charlie was irresolvable. Charlie had tried the anal-insertive role with Arturo but he just did not like it. Arturo liked oral sex, but it could not provide the release he needed and got only from being receptive in anal intercourse. He described it as being "twice [*el doble*] the pleasure coming while getting fucked."

Arturo had privately resolved the problem early on in their relationship by going back to his old ways. He focused his homosexual cruising once again on macho Mexican men. Saturday nights out with his Mexican friends gave him a good alibi for Charlie and the time to carry out his clandestine homosexual encounters. He always carefully hid this activity from Charlie, and his Mexican friends knew that it must never be discussed in English when Charlie was present. This is also why Arturo would be embarrassed when, during the years he lived in California, I occasionally caught him cruising at Latino bars—straight and gay—near downtown Los Angeles.

Return to Guadalajara

Arturo finally decided he could never leave Charlie. They had something going—love, friendship, family ties—that transcended his sexual needs. He told Charlie in the spring of 1986 that he would move back to Guadalajara with him if that was what Charlie still wanted to do, but they must first decide how they would be able to earn enough money to live comfortably. He did not want to live poor again.

Charlie came up with a realistic plan: they would use half their life savings to pay cash to buy a small two-story apartment house in Guadalajara before moving there. It would be located in a lower-middle-class neighborhood close to where Arturo's family lived and would have some space on the ground floor that could be converted into a shop or restaurant. Luckily, business zoning laws in Mexico are much more relaxed than in the United States.

Arturo and Charlie packed up their belongings and moved to Guadalajara in the spring of 1987. The biggest trauma for Arturo was giving up the security of a job he had held for close to thirteen years. It was softened by the store's owner when he said he would give him his job back if things did not work out in Mexico. But Arturo was still nervous about leaving California.

The second-floor apartment they moved into in Guadalajara was small compared to the little house they had rented in Los Angeles, but at least they did not have to pay rent. It was the first time they had ever lived in a place they owned. Another good thing was that when they opened their restaurant below, they could just walk downstairs to work.

Arturo's family was happy to have him back home for good and pitched in to help him and Charlie set up house and their American-style restaurant. When I visited them six months later, they were happily settled and the restaurant was up and running successfully. Arturo campily told me that Charlie was the cook and accountant; he was the *mesera* (i.e., the waitress). Several family members provided labor free or at low cost when the restaurant was crowded on weekends.

Shortly after moving back to Guadalajara, Arturo reestablished contact with his homosexual friendship network and started going out alone again on Saturday nights. On those nights Charlie entertained himself with his large video collection of American movies. Sometimes, he also invited members of Arturo's family to watch television or movies with him. He liked having them around and had finally learned enough conversational Spanish to make their visits more interesting.

Arturo never completely returned to his old ways in Guadalajara. He targeted the same kind of sex partners but no longer had the time or inclination for cruising bars, baths, or streets several days a week downtown. So he looked for macho men around his own age—or a little younger—in just a few favored locations (two "hot" movie theaters and a gay bar), who wanted to get together for sex two or three times a month and who understood that they had to carry out their liaisons discreetly because he lived with a jealous American lover. One great advantage Arturo had over past times in Mexico was an automobile. It made his clandestine affairs much easier to carry out.

Although Charlie never told me directly that he knew about Arturo's outside affairs, he made it clear that he felt free to have "some extracurricular activities" of his own. His way of handling it was to go up in the mountains near Guadalajara to a lakeside camping area ostensibly to fish. Arturo did not like roughing it in the countryside so it was easy for Charlie to get away alone. Charlie had a drinking problem that he handled most of the time by abstaining from alcohol. The fishing trip allowed him to "tie one on." And while drinking with some of the Mexican men, he soon found that late in the evening, when they were all drunk, a few would make themselves available for sex. He told me, "It was dark, so easy to sneak 'em into my van for a little hanky panky. Most were there with wives and kids . . . seemed happy to have me suck 'em off. You know, Arturo thought I went up to the lake just to fish and get drunk."

Although Charlie was pretty sure that Arturo had had sexual relations with other men during the years they had been together, surprisingly, Charlie was the one who got caught in the act. Both privately told me about the incident, which had happened before they opened the restaurant. Arturo was on his usual Saturday night outing. Charlie had stayed home and invited Arturo's eighteen-year-old nephew, Gilberto, to come over to see a movie video with him. Relaxing his rule about alcohol, Charlie drank some beer with Gilberto while watching the movie. When the movie ended, Gilberto asked to see one of the porn videos. Charlie told me what happened while they watched the film:

"You won't believe me—Arturo didn't—I didn't deliberately get Gilberto hot. He knew about our porn films . . . said he was old enough . . . well, to be honest, we had played around before on the couch watching TV. He started horsing around again when I got up to get the film. He sat close on the couch while we watched it . . .

and got a hard-on. I felt it . . . then he pulled down his pants. I was going down on him when Arturo came through the front door and yelled at us. He really laid out Gilberto [in Spanish] . . . I couldn't understand what he was saying."

Since the incident took place relatively early in the evening, around ten-thirty, it never entered Charlie's mind that Arturo might return and catch him in the act. Arturo almost never came back from his Saturday night adventures until the wee hours of Sunday morning.

This Saturday night was an exception. Arturo had returned early because he had been stood up by a favorite regular sex partner, could not find any of his old friends, and did not know of any fiestas to go to. He went to Bar Pancho but no one there interested him sexually. So he called it quits and returned home. Already out of sorts, Arturo got really angry on catching Charlie and Gilberto having sex. He vented most of his anger on his nephew and berated him for having sex with his "husband." Clearly caught in a double standard, Arturo was nevertheless jealous of his nephew and wanted to believe that he had unfairly tempted Charlie. Arturo's position was that Gilberto knew what he was doing: "He planned it . . . that's why he wanted to see the sexy movie . . . he was hot . . . then Charlie got hot too." Arturo also scolded Charlie for succumbing to Gilberto's desire, but he carefully did not push it too far, fearing a harsh counterattack.

It was a humbling experience for Arturo to learn that Charlie might also be looking for other sex partners. Charlie was still quite handsome, but it had never occurred to Arturo that his partner needed anyone else sexually. Arturo thought he met all of Charlie's sexual needs: he still liked having sex with him and did anything Charlie wanted to do when he wanted to do it. Now he could no longer take it for granted that Charlie was the good American husband who stayed home watching TV or movies with no interest in a little dalliance. He had to reevaluate him as a sex object for other men, especially younger men in his own neighborhood.

The incident eventually blew over, but for some time Arturo monitored Charlie's interaction with young men in the neighborhood. Charlie later told me he could have made out "like a bandit" with some neighborhood queens, but he found his men "by the lake" more exciting. To defuse Arturo's concern about his nephew, he always invited other family members to come watch films with him on Saturday nights. For awhile, Arturo spent Saturday nights at home or came home early.

He eventually reverted to his old pattern of Saturday nights out, however, with late returns on Sunday mornings.

The Final Years

Despite their infidelities, Arturo and Charlie spent three happy years together following their move to Guadalajara. Relations with Arturo's family were exceptionally good. Their restaurant—quite popular in the neighborhood—provided sufficient income. And through a satisfactory accommodation, they continued to enjoy their diverse sex lives in an unspoken "open relationship."

Charlie's major concern during these years was his relations with his family in the Midwest. He had visited them several times but they never came to see him in Mexico. He was disappointed and unhappy about their not coming for a visit and by their inability to accept his sexual orientation, but he continued to be nourished by the love and respect he received from his Mexican family. Equally important were the very special feelings he and Arturo continued to have for each other. They enjoyed each other's company and planned to spend the rest of their lives together.

After moving to Guadalajara Arturo began to worry about Charlie's health. Charlie was gaining weight, never exercised, smoked, and drank enormous cups of caffeinated coffee. Moreover, since he was the only one with operational know-how, the setting up and running of the restaurant put him constantly under stress. Although Arturo never mentioned it, Charlie also knew that his partner was concerned about financial failure.

In the fall of 1989, at the age of forty-five, Charlie had his first heart attack. He assured Arturo it was not a major one so there was nothing to worry about. He also told him he knew what he had been doing wrong and could take care of it: fewer cigarettes, less coffee, and more exercise. Arturo knew, however, that he did not do any of these things and did not regularly take the medications prescribed by the doctor. Nothing seemed to motivate Charlie to follow the right course.

Although he did very little to help himself, Charlie appeared to be recovering quite well from his heart attack. Then, suddenly after lunch one day in late January 1990, he told Arturo he felt like he was having another episode with his heart. At Arturo's urging he went to see their doctor that afternoon.

Charlie came back early in the evening, furious that he had waited such a long time and still had not been seen by the doctor. He was supposed to go back early the next morning. The pain persisted throughout the evening. Arturo tried to get him to go to hospital emergency, but Charlie refused, saying he would rather wait and go in the morning—it might not even be necessary by then. Arturo's sister, Lucia, came over after supper and also urged him to go to the hospital. He told her he was not that bad off and went to bed. Arturo and Lucia were concerned about his physical condition but decided there was nothing they could do but hope for the best.

Sometime during the night Charlie died. Arturo told me he had slept little that night because of Charlie's condition, but even though he was right next to him all night long he had heard or felt nothing that would have led him to believe anything was wrong. After Arturo became fully awake, he called to him. When he got no response he gave him a little push. When there was no physical response, he realized he was gone. He ran downstairs and called the paramedics and then Lucia.

Arturo and his family were devastated by the loss. Charlie, in his own way, had become one of them. They mourned him as they would have any other family member. His death, however, presented some unique problems: Where should the funeral services be held? What should be done with his body—bury it in Mexico or the Midwest? Arturo called Charlie's sister in Illinois to give her the bad news and ask her to let him know what the family wanted to do. He told her that Charlie had mentioned on several occasions that in the event of his death he wanted to be buried in Guadalajara.

Arturo and Lucia were shocked by the callousness of Charlie's family. They were not only quite willing to have the burial in Mexico but made no plans to attend the services. According to Arturo, this would be unthinkable for a Mexican family. Differences in religion was not the problem, since both Charlie and Arturo were Roman Catholic. Arturo knew that the major issue was Charlie's homosexuality.

Given that Charlie was to be buried in Guadalajara, the next question to be resolved was where? The closeness of the family to Charlie is illustrated by the choice they made: the family tomb. Only one brother objected and he was overruled. Religious services were held in the neighborhood Catholic church, and the body was interred with a small plaque bearing his name affixed to the top of the tomb. None of Charlie's family came to Guadalajara for the funeral.

It took Arturo a long time to get over Charlie's sudden death. He mourned the loss of his lover. He also worried about his finances.

Should he stay in Guadalajara or return to Los Angeles and try to get his old job back? Lucia turned out to be the crucial factor. He decided he needed her company and wanted to continue to live near his family.

As he became adjusted to his loss, Arturo began to think about ways to make a living other than running a small restaurant. It was too time-consuming, and he did not have the right temperament or skills to run it without Charlie. It also tied him down and he wanted a freer life—to visit with friends and cruise the streets, parks, and theaters again.

In March 1990 he closed the restaurant and sold one of the buildings he owned. He invested the money received in a neighborhood market that provided him just enough money to live on. He hired two nephews to work there part time and thus relieve him from daily responsibilities.

In April he decided to take a vacation in Los Angeles, his first visit back since leaving three years previously with Charlie. He needed to get away, to just rest and relax with friends and to recover his health. He had lost weight and felt depressed most of the time. Lucia told him to stay in Los Angeles as long as he wanted. Her two sons would make sure everything went well at the neighborhood market.

Arturo stayed two weeks with me that spring. I was delighted to see and be with him again. It gave us a chance to reminisce and catch up on all that had happened since Charlie's death. We also spent time visiting his close friends who had moved with him to Los Angeles and were still living there. He liked being in Los Angeles again but was looking forward to returning home. On the last day of his visit, he told me, "I'm going to find another lover . . . it won't be the same as Charlie but I'm used to having someone around. If I'm lucky, José, maybe I'll have many lovers."

When he returned to Guadalajara, Arturo moved to a new apartment in his old neighborhood. Lucia had remarried, but they still spent a lot of time together. And he reestablished closer contact with his old circle of friends. Their routines were not exactly the same as before, but it was reassuring for Arturo to slip back into familiar old ways now that he had a lot more time on his hands.

By the spring of 1991, Arturo had had a succession of several younger male lovers. He told me—while I was visiting him that spring in Guadalajara—how exasperating it was to have to deal with sex partners in their early twenties, half his age. The problem, he said, was that "they are not serious." Now that he was relatively affluent, he was experiencing the same things he had put older men through when younger. The fact that he liked only very masculine men created further complications.

I asked Arturo how these men differed from the ones he had been seeing during the years he and Charlie were together. He replied, "Well, José, I'm still seeing some . . . but they're married so it's just sex . . . we can't really be lovers. That's why I'm looking for someone younger to live with me. I'm making sex with many different guys . . . looking for a lover . . . so there are many more of them [sex partners] now . . . more time to go out and look. There's two hot movie theaters and a new bar near the old bus station where young machos go. Did you know Baños Guadalajara is still open? It hasn't changed since we used to go there. I go with Francisco sometimes."

Although discouraged about not finding another long-term lover, Arturo was quite happy with the way he had organized his life. His sex life was satisfactory. He had a nice car, and the neighborhood market was providing enough income. And his family was there with love and support when he needed it. He also knew he had given his family a lot in return and that they recognized how he and Charlie had made their lives more financially secure. Lucia was his favorite sibling, but he had helped all his brothers and sisters and their children.

Before I left Guadalajara that spring I asked Arturo about his health. He had lost additional weight since I had last seen him at my house in Los Angeles, and he talked about having persistent diarrhea. He said he felt "okay," that the diarrhea was probably from his bad habit of "eating street vendor's food." I then asked him if he had been tested for the AIDS virus. He said he had not—and did not want to know. I told him why it was important to be tested, and that if he was HIV positive he should immediately come to Los Angeles for a medical assessment. He could stay with me.

Shortly after I returned home from Guadalajara, Arturo called with the news that he was infected with HIV (the AIDS virus). He came to Los Angeles and stayed a little over a month while getting a medical workup and initial treatment. The prognosis was not good. All the medical markers indicated he had probably been infected for five to seven years, and that his immune system had already been heavily impacted by HIV. As soon as his diarrhea got under control, he returned home. I helped him get access to the best medical doctor for the treatment of AIDS in Guadalajara.

Arturo and I kept in close contact by telephone. Two of my Mexican friends living in California, who were also HIV positive, met him while visiting their families in Guadalajara and kept him supplied with zidovudine (AZT)—a costly medication for treatment of AIDS and difficult to obtain in Mexico. They also kept me posted on how he was doing.

Arturo's health stabilized over the next year and a half, and he finally found a "live in" lover who was both dependable and good sex. Accepting that he probably did not have many more years to live, he decided to enjoy himself, his lover, his friends, and his family as much as possible. He had breakfast with Lucia every weekday morning so they could gossip about the family and neighbors and make a plan for the day—lunch with his father, a short trip to nearby towns on market day, a visit to the movies, and so on. Since his lover and friends were not available during the week, he generally spent weekends with them. They went often to *balnearios* (combination swimming and picnic areas) located on the outskirts of Guadalajara and to festivals at nearby towns. Lucia rarely went with them because she did not enjoy the company of his lover.

Arturo's Death from AIDS

"Pneumocystis carinii" pneumonia (PCP) is an often lethal infection for people with impaired immune systems as Arturo had been told in the spring of 1991 by staff of the Early Intervention Program at the Orange County (California) Health Care Agency. He had been given a medical prescription for a daily dose of Bactrim, the drug used to prevent this type of pneumonia. When he returned to Guadalajara, he continued to take AZT but discontinued the Bactrim due to severe reactions to it. Toward the end of 1991, because he felt good physically, he also stopped seeing the AIDS medical specialist in Guadalajara. He objected to what he felt were the doctor's high fees.

Arturo continued to do relatively well physically until the summer of 1992. Then, suddenly, he began to feel poorly. By the end of July he was feeling bad enough to plan on returning to Los Angeles for further treatment. Realizing that he was too ill to travel, Lucia intervened and took him to a local hospital. He was diagnosed as having PCP and treated accordingly. I talked with him several times by telephone while he was in the hospital. He did not understand the gravity of his condition and believed that he would make it through. At the end of the second week he was no longer able to breathe and went into a coma. He died a few days later.

Lucia and I later talked at length in Guadalajara about Arturo's life and death, and his good relationship with his family. Except for one older brother, Arturo's homosexuality was accepted by the family as part of his being. Charlie was accepted the same way and held in high esteem because of what they conceived to be his good influence on Arturo. Charlie's generosity and willingness to accept the good-humored homosexual joking by Arturo's brothers further cemented his acceptance into the family. Now, just in their early forties, both were gone.

The family made one last loving gesture to Arturo and Charlie. Arturo was buried in the family tomb and a small plaque bearing his name was placed on top of the tomb next to Charlie's. The family has thus made them lovers forever.

FIVE | *José*

In late summer 1970, Arturo, Ramón, Fortino, Arnaldo, and I were sunning ourselves on a warm Saturday afternoon at the edge of a large swimming pool in Parque Agua Azul, near downtown Guadalajara, when we realized that three very young men were cruising us. One of them was José. Fortino knew him so he motioned for him and his friends Alfonso and Oscar to come over and join us. They did and spent the rest of the afternoon with us playing and camping around the pool.

Late in the afternoon I invited everyone to come back to my apartment for sandwiches and *lotería*—a popular bingolike card game. While I was in the kitchen, José came in laughing yet worried that I might be upset because his friends Oscar and Alfonso had pulled Arnaldo into my guest bedroom and closed the door. He said Oscar was "always hot" (*siempre caliente*) so he knew what they were doing. I assured him it was okay, that Arnaldo was a trustworthy old friend and often stayed overnight with me. I teased José, suggesting that he probably wished he was also in the bedroom with Arnaldo. José blushed, came over and gave me a hug, then, returning the teasing, whispered in my ear that while it was true he wished he was in the bedroom with "gorgeous, handsome" Arnaldo, he also liked older men.

José and his friends turned out to be the youngest circle of friends I studied. They were fifteen years old when we met on that lovely sunny summer afternoon. When they learned about my study, they were eager to be part of it and provided me weekly accounts of what it was like to be effeminate and homosexual in the lower-middle-class neighborhoods of Guadalajara. I kept in touch occasionally with all three long after my study ended. I reestablished a close friendship with José, however, in the spring of 1982—when he was twenty-seven— and we initiated a small-scale study of courtship and sexual behavior in his old neighborhood. During the past ten years I have also come to know and be accepted as a good friend of his large extended family, with whom he still lives.

José was born in the fall of 1954 of relatively poor parents in an old lower-middle-class neighborhood of Guadalajara that has been continuously occupied since the city was founded by Spaniards in the sixteenth century. Located a short distance from the center of the city, the neighborhood is mainly made up of four- to five-room single-story Spanish-style adobe brick houses that adjoin sidewalks and have interior courtyards. Neighborhood youth socialize on the sidewalks in front of houses each evening while buses, trucks, and cars rumble through the narrow streets. Many old customs are still followed. Families, for instance, continue to give "sweet fifteen parties" for their daughters, and boys serenade their girlfriends. Parents also worry about the virginity of their daughters and supervise as much of their behavior as possible, given the times.

Along with his mother, father, five brothers and five sisters, José has lived most of his life in the house where he was born. During his late teens and early twenties he lived on and off in the United States for five years, but moved back permanently to live with his family in Guadalajara in 1978.

The house they lived in all these years was rented. José's father wanted to buy it, but every time he saved enough money to make an offer, the owner raised the price. Finally, after deciding he would never find an affordable place in the old neighborhood, his father moved the family in early 1984 to an unfinished house in a newly developed settlement on the outskirts of Guadalajara.

The move overwhelmed José's mother. She not only had to leave the house where all her children had been raised, but in the new settlement she felt isolated from downtown and her old neighborhood friends and could no longer walk to market or a movie. In addition, the street in front of the new house, which was still under construction, was unpaved so dust blown in by wind and cars quickly covered every surface. She became tense and nervous as a result of all the changes, and shortly after moving suffered a mild stroke. Through care and resolute support by José and her other children, however, she made a partial recovery and gradually accepted her new situation. Now she tries to focus on how nice it is to be away from the pollution and noise of the inner city. And she welcomes the visits of her married children and grandchildren, who return every Sunday to spend at least part of the day.

José was also devastated by the move. The old neighborhood was his extended family. He had come back to Mexico from New York not only to be with his family but to live in and be a part of the neighborhood as well. It brought him close to everything he wanted in life: his family, friends, sex partners, social outings, and acceptance as a singer. He was luckier than his mother because he could still spend as much time as he wanted in the old neighborhood. Yet, at the same time, he knew he would eventually become an outsider, that his life had been permanently changed by the move.

José is a trim, nice-looking man, of small stature (about five feet, six inches) with a slightly oriental look around his eyes—"a Japanese ancestor," he will swiftly tell you. He is quick to laugh and joke about everything and himself, and with the least pretense will burst into song. Most people judge him to be much younger than he is. He dresses in a very flashy, sometimes feminine way with skintight pants and blousy shirts. He believes his only obviously femimine trait, however, to be his manner of walking. "I wiggle my bottom a lot when I walk," he says. In conversation he speaks in a masculine way with a deep resonant voice.

José's Early Sex-Life History

José's earliest homosexual experiences occurred before puberty, between four and thirteen years of age, with neighborhood youths who were between fourteen and eighteen. He remembers "sucking off" three teenage neighborhood brothers when he was four and being anally penetrated by a sixteen-year-old neighbor when he was six. He further remembers his initial anal experiences as being frightening and painful, and feeling disgusted with himself afterward for having allowed the older boy to do it to him.

Before reaching puberty at thirteen, he was penetrated anally by several other neighborhood youths, but only a few times. He gradually became comfortable with the anal-passive role and no longer felt repulsed by it. But he does not remember having a strong sexual role preference. He believes he ended up playing the passive role because he was sexually excited by the older neighborhood youths who would only play the active role.

Reflecting on his masculinity, José reports that he has "always been in the middle, neither macho nor feminine." As a boy, he liked playing with both girls' and boys' toys, but as a teenager he mostly liked playing male sports. He acknowledges, however, that in his neighborhood he was probably viewed by many of his friends as being "slightly feminine." And when he was sixteen, his cousin of the same age told him that he "acted like a homosexual," which meant, José said, that he "was acting feminine."

José's first ejaculation occurred when he masturbated with some older neighborhood boys at the age of thirteen. He remembers his early mutual masturbatory experiences with considerable pleasure and little guilt.

During the first two years following the onset of puberty, José became actively involved in homosexual behavior. He established a pattern of weekly sexual encounters, generally with very masculine neighborhood youths whose ages ranged from fourteen to nineteen. When I first interviewed him at age fifteen, he remembered having homosexual experiences with fourteen different youths the first year, ten different ones the second year. Although on occasion he performed fellatio on some, it was only preliminary to the anal intercourse that he and his sex partners enjoyed most. He continued to play only the anal-receptive role. During those two years, casual social contacts with neighborhood youths led to most of José's homosexual encounters. He almost never went out deliberately looking for sexual partners in his neighborhood, but rather had sexual encounters with the same youth three or four times.

When he was fifteen years old, José told me that only a first cousin knew about his homosexual behavior, and that the rest of his family neither knew nor suspected anything. He worried a lot about their finding out. To cover himself, he had girlfriends in the neighborhood and made a point of introducing them to his family and friends. If his parents found out about his homosexuality, he said, "I would leave home at once and never return because I wouldn't be able to face the shame."

Two years later, when he was seventeen, José's family found out. News about his homosexual contacts with neighborhood youths had finally reached his older brothers, and one of them told his parents. José's father was very angry with him, so José decided to leave forever. Although distraught about his homosexuality, his mother was not angry with him and did not want him to leave. He left to live with a friend, believing he would never return. Not long after leaving, however, he learned through relatives that the family's furor over his homosexuality had subsided. He therefore decided to return home, hoping somehow he would be accepted by his family.

After being back home a while, his relationship with his mother, older sister, and six younger siblings returned to normal. He remained estranged from his three older brothers, however, and for several years his father and second oldest brother almost never spoke to him. His homosexuality was not mentioned by anyone. José started seeking sexual contacts with males living outside his neighborhood.

A few months later, accepting that he had never had any real sexual interest in women and had no intention of getting married and having children, José decided that he was what he had known himself to be for a long time, a homosexual, and so should learn more about the "homosexual world." He envisioned it as a place where he could be as feminine or as masculine as he wanted, where he could be around people like himself and thus not have to put up false fronts. José remembers this period of time as his "coming out of the closet" (*salir del closet*) and establishing a "homosexual identity" (*los de ambiente*).

After coming out, José started socializing with several young "queens" he had met in Bar Pancho—Guadalajara's only gay bar at the time—and adopted a feminine nickname, "La Chepa." Every Friday and Saturday night over the next several months, he was either camping and carrying on with his friends at the bar, in a nearby park, or at private parties. During this time he said he was "*muy loca y muy puta*" (extremely effeminate and very promiscuous). And when he sobered up, he did not always remember who or how many men he had sex with nor what he did. He soon reached the point where he was dissatisfied with the life he was leading and what he had become.

When José reached his eighteenth birthday at the end of 1972, he decided to find some means of quickly escaping from his newfound life. Finding an older North American lover and moving to the United States appeared to offer him his best chance. Good news had filtered back about people he knew—like Arturo, Fortino, and Ramón—who had moved successfully to Los Angeles and had found jobs and lovers.

José started cruising the best locations for finding North American gay men in Guadalajara—downtown parks in the afternoons and Bar Pancho in the evenings. He spent several discouraging months socializing with several different North American men. Finally, in the spring of 1973 he met and started a sexual relationship with Karl, a German man in his early thirties visiting Guadalajara as a tourist from New York where he had recently taken residence. Karl was looking for a companion and, after knowing José for several weeks, invited him to come to New York for a visit the following summer.

José accepted Karl's invitation but made it clear from the beginning of their relationship that, although he would initially need money to get to New York, he would find a job there and support himself as much as possible. José's great advantage was that, even though he had almost no job experience, he had been studying English for over a year and could already understand enough to carry on a reasonably good conversation. He had a good ear for the language.

Late Teens and Early Twenties Sex Life

José ended up spending most of his late teens and early twenties with Karl in the United States—on and off for five years—much of it in New York City. Initially, they led a rather quiet life together. With Karl's help, José got a job in a delicatessen that provided enough income for him to buy a nice used car and save some money. And Karl's friends liked José so they were able to socialize together as a couple despite age and cultural differences. They spent many long weekends visiting Karl's friends in southern states. Karl loved traveling and spending time with his rich friends living outside New York City.

According to José, he and Karl also had a satisfactory sexual relationship. It was something new for José to have just one sex partner for any length of time and to focus as much on oral as anal sex, but he was having to make so many different adjustments in his life that it was comforting to have a nice place and lover to come home to. Besides, there was no sense of neighborhood where he and Karl lived, so even if he had wanted to find someone else to have sex with, it would have been difficult and, José felt, probably dangerous (José's main concern was being ripped off by Anglo male hustlers or being a target for queer-bashing). While they were living together, neither José nor Karl were much interested in the gay scene in New York City. Outside a few excursions from time to time, they knew very little about it.

Although José enjoyed many aspects of his new life in the United

States, he missed his family and neighbors. During his first three years in New York, he returned to Guadalajara every Christmas and on several other occasions to assuage his homesickness. Karl often traveled with him and became acquainted with his family. They knew the foreigner was José's lover but were nevertheless hospitable, and no one confronted José about his homosexual relationship. The conspiracy of silence continued.

In the fall of 1975, when he was almost twenty-one, José had a serious falling out with Karl. Although they were sexually compatible, José found Karl to be possessive and jealous of the younger friends he had made while working—straight as well as gay. Differences in age, social backgrounds, and interests contributed to the breakup of their relationship. José returned to Guadalajara in October 1975—he believed at the time for good—and moved back in with his family and got a job.

José Meets Juan

José was happy to be back home and easily resumed his old lifestyle and friendships. Not long after his return, he started a relationship with a sixteen-year-old neighborhood youth named Juan that continued on and off for many years and became the most consuming and passionate affair of his life. José told me how he met Juan while socializing with neighborhood friends:

> I came down here and met this kid. He used to hang out with the guys in the pool hall. He was like the tail . . . followed them around wherever they went. And I thought this kid was kind of lost. When I met him I knew only one brother of his. Then all of a sudden he got attached to me . . . he liked me. When I came home at night from work he used to be waiting for me at my door or across the street on a park bench . . . just waiting to go with me wherever.

According to José, his intentions toward Juan in the beginning were just for friendship since he had never had sexual relations with anyone younger than himself. He continues the story:

> Then somebody bought Juan a bike . . . he used to wait for me with his bicycle. He liked to ride around the park . . . and most of the time he was the only one driving the bicycle. All of a sudden one time he asked me to drive the bicycle and he would rest. [That is,

José would steer and pedal while Juan rode standing in back of him with both feet on the hub caps of the back wheel.] By this time each one of us were without any bad meaning or things like that . . . at least myself I never thought . . . of trying to make him. But after he wanted me to drive the bicycle he started to put his crotch on my back . . . to lean on me. And after leaning on me . . . before he used to put his hands on my shoulders . . . then he was putting his hands on my chest instead of on my shoulders. And every time he put his crotch on my back he would start getting hot and bothered. And my God, I started getting a little bit excited too but very very afraid of letting him know it.

They continued their bicycle riding arrangement for several weeks, and then José told Juan he had better "stop *that*" and cool himself. But Juan kept doing it anyway and told José finally, "Well, *panchito* wants something." José was afraid to ask what "*panchito*" wanted because he was sure it had to do with sex—in his neighborhood *panchito* was a euphemism for penis—and he was still unsure whether he wanted to have sex with Juan. José explained:

I was quite afraid because he was such a nice kid . . . quite cute, very honest. I really did like him so I didn't want to do anything wrong to him. So after . . . going over and over on that . . . I got my nerve and asked him what does *panchito* want? And he says *panchito* wants to . . . no, wants you to suck him, right? Boy! Again I felt shy . . . so I told him you better wait a little . . . we'll do it . . . in a nice way. Wait, I'll tell you when. And I'm gonna ask a friend of mine if we can borrow his apartment.

Juan kept asking José, "When, when, when?"—for several weeks, while José fended him off. It was now late December and José knew that Karl had come to Guadalajara from New York for the holidays and was looking for him. But since he was not sure he wanted to get involved with Karl again, José invited Juan instead of Karl to come spend Christmas Eve with him at his house. José describes what happened when Juan arrived:

So this friend of mine was in the living room playing the guitar and I was singing . . . a special song which talks about December and you are leaving me now. I don't know how to say this but I was feeling really quite bad. I was remembering Karl and I kind of started to feel like my tears were gonna pop out . . . and I just ran to the park outside of my house . . . right to one of the branches and I was crying. So Juan came . . . and tried to console me. He asked me: "What's happening, José?" "Nothing!" I said. So I just told him I felt kind of down. Then he started to feel down also and I had to console him because it so happened that his mother had to leave his father . . . bad treatment or something like that. And he was always feeling lonely. Then we went back to my house and I knew he needed someone too.

Shortly after Christmas José and Karl met and decided to live together again. José moved into the apartment Karl had rented in Guadalajara for the holidays. Juan, who did not know about this relationship, became angry and jealous when he learned about it.

José remembers being surprised at the level of his anger:

He got quite mad, really . . . I was surprised he got that mad and called me all kinds of names . . . and he even said, "What is this, does he have a bigger one than I do? What is he giving you?" I just told him, "Listen, I might like you and you might be important to me . . . but he is the cathedral." He got so *mad* that he didn't talk to me for about a week. After that he came back again . . . and never said, never apologized because I didn't want him to apologize for anything.

In early January, Karl returned to New York with José's promise that he would follow in a couple of months. José and Juan resumed their friendship and saw each other often during these months. José, however, still had mixed feelings and successfully avoided having sex with Juan before returning to New York. Before leaving Guadalajara, he promised Juan that he would keep in touch, and when he returned for a visit he would take care of his *panchito* as promised.

José Returns to New York

In late February 1976, José returned to New York to join Karl and resume their relationship. They both worked hard to patch things up. José got his job and car back and was happy to take up his old work and social routines and be able to save some money again. Karl encouraged him to spend more time with his friends than before and tried to be less bossy. José, for his part, was more attentive to Karl and was grateful to him for making it so easy to return.

Although José enjoyed being back in New York, things were not quite the same as before. His relations with Karl were good but now Juan was often in his thoughts. Shortly after arriving in New York, he received a long letter from Juan. José responded right away and encouraged him to keep writing, so they embarked on an active correspondence. José remembers some of the highlights:

He used to write me kind of funny letters, love letters as a matter of fact . . . writing that I miss you very much, I really care for you, I wish you were here with me. And they kept going that way until one time he put a heart on the letter with an arrow through it . . . I felt so nice. Then in the next one he drew a heart with two guys kissing. And you can imagine by this time he wasn't just telling me that he was missing me, he was saying he loved me. I wish I had kept his letters. I burnt them all because Karl knew about Juan.

José now had a double allegiance going—one to Karl in New York, the other to Juan in Guadalajara. This did not trouble him much because it was more or less accepted in Mexico that a man might have both a wife and a mistress. He knew many married men in his old neighborhood in Guadalajara who had something going on the side. Why should there be a problem if, while living with Karl, he "secretly had an affair with Juan by mail"?

All went smoothly with Karl and José for the rest of the year. They both looked forward to returning to Guadalajara together at year's end for the holidays. Luckily for José, Karl arranged for a one-month stay in a furnished apartment, so they went south in late November and returned shortly after Christmas.

Christmas 1976 in Guadalajara

After settling in their apartment in Guadalajara, José decided to be open with Karl about spending time alone with Juan as well as his family. He told him he had not had sex with Juan but could not promise that nothing would happen this visit. Karl's response was that he might be out doing a little shopping himself. This was a signal to José that they now had a sexually open relationship.

The apartment was located only a short bus ride away from José's family's neighborhood. He spent the second day after arriving with his family, then after supper went out looking for Juan. Several of his neighborhood friends teased him about his interest in finding Juan. "Are you looking for a husband?" they asked. José kidded them back, saying, "I'm always looking for one . . . any of you volunteering?" They told him that Juan knew he was back and to just wait with them because he would be arriving shortly.

Juan appeared not on his bike but on foot. He greeted José as he would have any other returning neighborhood friend, calmly, matter of fact; but José told me he could see around his eyes the excitement Juan felt about his return. José told him he was back for at least a month and would be staying with his friend Karl in an apartment near downtown rather than with his family, and that he was welcome to come visit anytime. They exchanged banter with the guys for awhile and then moved away to walk alone through the little neighborhood park and talk about what they could do together during José's visit in Guadalajara.

During his stay, José generally spent the days either with his family or with Karl, and most evenings with neighborhood friends and Juan. Karl knew he could tag along, but he went only occasionally with José to visit his family and only rarely with him to visit his neighborhood male friends because Karl felt out of place and was soon bored by their endless banter—only part of which he could understand.

José's first sexual encounter with Juan occurred one evening after a work-party session with Juan's brother and three other guys from the neighborhood. They had gone over earlier in the evening to the vacant house of one of the men to fix up some things before his family moved in. José picks up the story here:

> We went to Mario's house supposedly to put up a TV antenna. And all of a sudden we wanted to take a shower and so all of us went into the bathroom to take a shower. My god, that was fun and games because everybody got naked and went into the bathroom. They all knew about me . . . they didn't care because we were comrades. The guy that was in the shower was splashing . . . and the guys waiting were trying not to get wet and were pushing against each other. Two of the guys got a little erect but we were just enjoying ourselves and laughing.

Nothing sexual happened between the guys in the shower, but it was the first time José and Juan had been naked together. Juan, now seventeen, decided that this was going to be the night for José to make good his promise.

After they showered, Juan's brother drove everyone to José's apartment. Karl was not there, so they all came in and the partying continued. When the other guys suddenly decided to leave, Juan wanted to stay, so he told his brother that he would go back to the neighborhood with José later. José recounts the rest of the events that evening:

Juan wanted to stay with me. So he and I were alone. Then all of a sudden Karl came in and sometimes he's too much . . . he takes people as sex objects. He saw that Juan was there and came over to me and said, "Oh boy, you are going to have him . . . or you had him already." This thing wasn't in my mind at all . . . and I was even feeling embarrassed for Karl saying that to me. Then I told Karl to leave because he was making Juan feel so embarrassed . . . he was telling him, "Oh, oh! Juan, you are going to . . . uhh . . ." You know, oh my God, I felt so bad.

After Karl left I told Juan, "Listen, I'm just gonna change and we'll be leaving in a little bit." Meanwhile, I gave him my photo albums to look at. All of a sudden, he calls me . . . "Hey, José, come on Pepé, come on, see this photo." And I went to him and I was looking at the photo album and I say "Which one? which one?" And he says, "Here! here!" What he wanted me to see was his "*panchito*"—he already had a hard-on. And I didn't know . . . and I was still saying, "which one?" So he says, "*Panchito*." "Oh, oh, Juan, are you going to go there again. No!" "You promised." "Come on, Juan, I never promised. I told you that if we have a chance we'll do it but I never promised." "Ah, come on," he said. "I told you if there was a chance." "OK," he said, "now is the chance . . . and we fuck." Then I go, "Well, listen, we'll talk about it . . . I think not fucking." "No," he says, "I want to fuck you."

So I told Juan, "Listen, Juan, as you know, that is one of the dirtiest parts in our body. As this is going to be your first time, I wouldn't like you to have a bad impression." So he says "OK!" . . . then I told him to lay on the bed with his face up. He lay on the bed. I open his shirt and pull his pants down almost to his knees. And he was so tense, I mean, with a big hard-on. It was a rock! So . . . I was licking his body from his chest . . . because he would get very afraid for me to go a little bit higher so I started on his chest and worked on his sides and navel . . . he was just arching himself, pulling his loins all the way up . . . he wasn't touching the mattress anymore. And then I would get him excited because I was going there, but all of a sudden I would go around and down on his thighs. My God, he was all tense, he was all of himself a rock. So when I went to the right point and down on him he just shot, I mean, he didn't give me two seconds . . . he just shot.

José and Juan dressed and went down the street to catch a bus back to the neighborhood. While they were waiting for the bus, Juan said to José, "Please don't say anything about this to any of our friends." José replied, "Well, you know Juan, that is quite nice to hear from you because I ask you the same thing—for me it would not be so bad because the guys know me, how I am, but for you it would be the bad thing." They continued to see each other until José returned to New York, but they had no further sexual encounters.

Final Year with Karl

After the holidays, José returned to New York with Karl for what turned out to be their final year together. They had been able to patch up many of their differences, but José became increasingly resentful of Karl's continued need to be in control. José was emotionally attached to Karl and most of the time still loved being with him. At times, however, he felt like Karl wanted to own him. Now in his early twenties, José could no longer allow Karl to believe he could organize his life and tell him what to do and how to behave. He wanted to be free to make his own decisions about the course of his life, right or wrong.

As the year passed, bickering between José and Karl increased. It did not relate to infidelity directly, since neither of them were having sex with other men in New York; or to their sex life, which, though not particularly exciting according to José, continued to be satisfactory for both. But it did relate partly to José's long-distance affair with Juan. José continued to get love letters from Juan, and Karl knew that at times José longed to be with him in Guadalajara. Karl would remind José of this sometimes in the course of arguments over petty domestic problems. This would prolong the argument since José knew that he did have those feelings from time to time. He would remind Karl that he had in fact made a choice as to where he wanted to be, New York, and who he wanted to live with, Karl.

José and Karl returned to Guadalajara for the Christmas holidays in 1977. Neither of them wanted to admit that they were once again at the breaking point, that their affair was at an end. The trip to Mexico was an attempt to smooth things over. Karl hoped he could buy another year by letting José have another brief fling with Juan. José had mixed feelings. He wanted to continue a comfortable, certain life with Karl in New York. Yet part of him wanted to be with his family in Guadalajara and continue his romance with Juan even though he knew it would last at most only a few more years because Juan, now eighteen, had already written José about having a neighborhood girlfriend.

The stay in Guadalajara went reasonably well. José made a special effort to go often with Karl on the kind of social outings he enjoyed most in Mexico—shopping, lunch in Tlaquepaque, drinks in the early evening at the mariachi plaza. Karl relaxed and urged José to do the same and spend as much time with his family, neighborhood friends, and Juan as he wanted.

As was his custom, José usually visited his family each evening and then went afterward to be with neighborhood friends. Juan was always there with the guys, waiting for him. José and Juan spent a lot of time together on this visit but mostly in the company of the guys or Juan's girlfriend. Juan liked going out with José and having his girlfriend tag along. According to José, by the end of his visit she had cut out—she had had enough of the threesome and Juan's infatuation with José. Although Juan did not appear to be too upset by her departure, José told me that Juan was nevertheless confused about wanting to be with both of them. By mutual agreement, José and Juan did not have any sexual encounters during this visit.

José and Karl returned to New York after the holidays, both hoping that they could live together and continue a relationship that had given them so many pleasures in the past. But by early summer, tensions returned and José decided he wanted to be on his own and moved into a small apartment near where he worked.

After leaving Karl, José's homesickness for Guadalajara came back and worsened. Although part of him wanted to stay on and go it alone for a while, he did not stay much longer. Within a couple of months, he moved back home. José explains:

Even though I had a lot of gay and straight friends, a nice apartment, car . . . I was lonely. I'm sure it sounds crazy . . . to give all that up to come back to a poor family and share a small bedroom with two younger brothers. But my lover and I had broken up . . . and I really missed being with my family. Also, Juan and a neigh-

borhood of straight young guys were waiting for me . . . available
. . . most know I'm gay.

Final Return to Guadalajara

On returning to Guadalajara, José found his family (except for his
father and second oldest brother) delighted to have him home for good.
He easily slipped back into family life, reestablishing a close bond with
his mother and warm relationships with his sisters and their husbands.
Whenever he and one of his brothers-in-law got together, they privately joked about his sexual availability. He was careful, however, not
to say or do anything that would antagonize his father. They rarely
spoke to one another.

After returning home, José's presentation of self to family and neighbors differed from before. He was still careful—to put it in his words—
to "act like a regular guy," but he never denied his sexual orientation
to anyone and was no longer ashamed of being homosexual. This did
not mean that he stopped participating in the homosexual joking that
went on almost daily among the men and boys in his neighborhood,
and he did not mind at times being the target of jokes from any quarter,
but he now insisted that he be treated with the respect (*respeto*) due
anybody his age.

Through a New York connection, José found a good job in a well-
known restaurant as a singing waiter. He enjoyed the combination of
singing and waiting on tables and for the first time in his life had a
certain celebrity. The work gave him much-needed income and independence, and his father was pleased to have additional money coming
into the family.

Because of his many trips back to Guadalajara during his five-year
residence in New York, José easily reintegrated himself into his old
neighborhood friendship networks. He resumed his old pattern of
spending most of his free time socializing with neighborhood friends
and covertly having homosexual encounters with some of them.

And José still had a romance going with Juan. They spent as much
time together as possible and started having sex again occasionally,
even though Juan was now dating girls and José was having sex with
other guys in the neighborhood. They had an understanding, each
being free to have other relationships. José told me how this understanding came about after his final return to Guadalajara: "The thing
is, unfortunately, since I broke with Karl I don't want to feel that
emotionally attached to a person . . . although I feel it . . . but I don't

want to give them the sense that they own me, or that I own them. So, Juan knows I have had many other guys. And sometimes he tells me about his girlfriends."

After his return, José learned that Juan had been subjected to a lot of ribbing by their friends in the neighborhood and was being called "the blond faggot" (*el huero maricón*) because he had been hanging around with José so much. But this did not deter Juan from continuing their affair. José explains:

I heard about that because sometimes the guys rejected him. I felt quite bad about that. When I came back I brought him a sleeping bag. All the guys were going "oh boy, no, *el huero maricón*." They still kept on calling him that . . . they were teasing him. He was feeling embarrassed also. But you know being around me he did not give a damn . . . I mean I have never been able to take it away from him. Sometimes he was so irresponsible and wanted to do things his own way that he was all the time laughing and laughing and I used to call him clown. So he used to hang around me and ask me about things, advice and things like that.

José continued his affair with Juan for several years after he returned to Guadalajara. Although Juan became more interested in girls and marriage as time passed, he maintained his attachment to José and always managed to find a way to get together with him in the company of their friends in the neighborhood or alone. It was a wonderful time for José. He and Juan enjoyed just being together, touching, hugging, kissing—and talking about their lives and what lay ahead. José said that when they did have sex, from time to time, it was usually initiated by Juan, and he was often surprised how passionate Juan became while beginning and having anal sex.

José describes at length one of these occasions that started when he, Juan, and a bunch of neighborhood guys went to the patio of his house to celebrate New Year's Eve and ended with him and Juan having wild sex in a hotel room:

We were first running around with the cars all over my neighborhood. And then they felt like stopping at my house . . . because in my house every year they build a big fire in the patio and put sleeping bags around, and everyone is drinking or playing guitars, singing, eating, whatever . . . having a good time. All of us went in there and then all of a sudden I find out that Juan was not in the house. So

I say, wow, and go out of doors and see him in his car. I ask him, "What is going on with you?" He says, "I feel like being alone. Why don't you come into the car with me?" "Come on, Juan," I said, "come with the guys." Then I saw he wanted to be alone . . . so I got into the car. He had a bottle of brandy and some glasses . . . so we were drinking and drinking. Then I see the guys coming out of the house . . . and they just said good-bye to us. So we waved good-bye. And they left.

Juan turned to me and said, "Pepé, I want to be with you tonight . . . tell your mother that you are going to my house." I said OK. I went into my house and told my mother and I was surprised, I mean, my mother was never like that and she very easily said OK, go, but take care, tell Juan not to drink too much because he is not going to be able to drive. I was surprised my mother agreed so easily . . . and even my father said to take care.

I asked Juan, "Where are we going?" He says, "Well, I want to be with you, never mind where I'm taking you." "Oh, OK." "We are gonna go to a hotel." "What? Juan I'm sorry, if you're counting on me, I don't have any money right now." He says, "I'm not asking you for anything." He got mad and I said, "Forget it, I never said anything." So he stopped first at a liquor store for another bottle, for more sodas, and a little ice, and then on to the hotel room.

Juan undressed and said I want to start with fucking you . . . so that night was quite marvelous . . . and he took a very long time . . . it hurt both of us . . . after we made it we were caressing each other because we made it like wild. I mean the bed . . . like half the mattress on the floor, with no pillows, no sheets, no blankets, no nothing. He didn't feel embarrassed with me anymore.

José's Late Twenties and Early Thirties

José lost his job as a singing waiter in late 1981 because of conflict with the restaurant's newly appointed manager. He felt the loss keenly since he not only loved the job but also needed the money, and good jobs are always hard to find. Furthermore, José now realized, at the age of twenty-six, that he did not want a job just as a waiter; he wanted to make money singing. He finally had to compromise. He took a day job as a waiter and in the evening hired out as a singer with a small music group he put together with talented musicians from his neighborhood.

Realizing José's distress over losing his job, Juan became even more attentive to José and, although their relationship was stormy at times, he started spending more time with him. In a summer 1982 interview, José told me how they were doing:

Well, many many things have gone by and sometimes we get kinda mad with each other . . . mostly I give up, my God, because he wins over me. We're getting together now about three or four times a month. It has increased a lot because now he doesn't feel embarrassed to ask me . . . even in front of the guys to say, "Come on, you know you're for me." The guys know he is number one . . . and sometimes tease me: "Be careful, José, you are starting" . . . you know like we will go some place and then I would be looking at a guy . . . then they will say, "Stop that, you know, don't be flirting because Juan will know." They also tease Juan . . . when I'm around the guys . . . they start hugging me and everything . . . and Juan comes all of a sudden and then he says to me, "Hey listen, I'm watch'n, I'm watch'n, be careful because you are not going to have it anymore." He teases me . . . and at the same time he makes the guys feel embarrassed and get away from me . . . because they do, they also respect Juan because they know that Juan and I are together.

In the same interview José also told me how he and Juan had expressed their feelings about each other in the past:

Sometimes we are mad at each other, and then when we make up again we both like to tell each other the truth. Like he would say, "Come on, José, don't be so stubborn. If I do something wrong, just tell me . . . but don't get mad and all of a sudden you just don't want to talk to me. I feel hurt when I see you around and you don't answer or answer me badly." So I said, "Juan, you know, you make me mad, really, I mean I want to eat myself! I want to eat myself!" And, so, we end up . . . this was about a year and a half ago, I told Juan, "The only thing I know is that at least I love you, and you know that I love you a lot . . . I also know that you love me, at least a little, but you love me because in many ways you show it to me." And then he says, "Yes, I have shown you . . . that I don't love you a little, I love you a lot." And he said that to me face to face. That feels quite nice, really, he has shown that to me in a very nice way.

Well that was about eight to nine months ago. We already knew how we felt, but only when we got mad and wanted to make up would he talk about it because he is very shy. And all this time he had a girlfriend, Carmen. I like the girl . . . she's not bad. But the thing is that Juan sometimes is just too much of a sweetheart . . . that I feel she takes advantage of him in some ways . . . and maybe, in many ways, people think I take advantage of Juan. I don't really think I do.

I met Juan, who was twenty-three at the time, at José's house several nights after the interview. He was slightly taller than José with sandy-colored hair, a trim muscular body, masculine, and very good-looking. He appeared to be well accepted by José's band members, who had just finished a practice session, and by José's family. He stopped by on the way home from his job with a steel company to say hello and leave José some music tapes and a message. José told me later that they planned to meet again later on in the week.

Juan got married about one year later to a neighbor whom José had known and liked all her life. He was glad that Juan broke up with Carmen. José and Juan's wife got along fine. According to José, she probably knew about their sexual relationship but was not particularly bothered by it. They occasionally went on social outings together as a threesome, and she made a special effort to make José feel welcome.

José knew, however, that things would never be quite the same now that Juan had to set up a new household and adjust to married life. He continued, nevertheless, to see him as before for several months. Then, gradually, each pulled away, and more and more time passed between their get-togethers. José, meanwhile, started spending more of his spare time in the neighborhood socializing with his friends and looking for additional sexual partners. To earn extra money, he also worked more with his band on weekends and rejoined the *estudiantina*, a music group mostly made up of neighborhood youth who sang for masses conducted in the local Catholic church.

José moved to Puerto Vallarta in the early spring of 1984 with the hope of finding a job in a restaurant catering to American tourists. Tips to English-speaking waiters in these restaurants were supposed to be quite good, and he had been led to believe by friends that there were many openings. There were none, so he took a job that paid only a little more than the one he had in Guadalajara and kept looking. After about five months, he gave up and returned home.

It was at this time, while José was away, that his family moved to the house his father had bought on the outskirts of Guadalajara. Already depressed over his failure to get a better-paying job in Puerto Vallarta, José came back to find his mother seriously ill and his family's new house located far away from his beloved old neighborhood. The need to help his mother recover from her stroke and to adjust to the new house did not leave José much time to dwell on his own problems. Equally important, because all the family recognized José's unique ability to help his mother, no pressure was put on him to go back to work right away, and his father and brothers started being civil to him in ways they had not been for years.

José returned often to his old neighborhood. It made him feel good to be there and to know that he could continue on with the things he had always done—practice with his band, sing masses with the *estudiantina*, and participate in horseplay with the neighborhood guys, who made it clear that he was always welcome back. He also resumed his homosexual liaisons in the old neighborhood.

José and Tomás

In early 1985, José started a new romance with Tomás, the fifteen-year-old brother of a close neighborhood friend. The initiation of their special relationship was similar to what had happened with Juan. Tomás, a tall wiry youth with a slightly pockmarked face but engaging smile, appeared to be always there waiting for José whenever he returned to the old neighborhood. He tagged along with him and the guys wherever they went. He was pushy and José often did not have a choice about having his company. Unlike Juan as a youth, Tomás already had an air of toughness about him and led rather than followed. But he also had a soft edge. He loved playing the guitar and singing, and that is what attracted him to José.

The neighborhood guys soon became aware that something was going on between José and Tomás. They teased José about having a new young husband now that Juan had married, but they were careful not to tease Tomás too much and watched what they said to him. Tomás had a sharp tongue and would verbally attack anyone who went too far. From the beginning of their relationship, José counseled Tomás that he should take care about his reputation, that some of the guys in the neighborhood would assume they were having sex together. Tomás told José that he could handle it, and even if they were having sex it was his business, not theirs. Moreover, his brother never said anything to him about being with José too much.

Initially, José did not want to include sex in his relationship with

Tomás. He was content just to be a close good friend. He had all the sex he wanted with other guys in the neighborhood. These sexual encounters were clandestine and thus without the additional emotional element that was bound to become part of a sexual involvement with Tomás. José wanted to steer clear of another involved relationship. It was not to be.

Tomás did not push José into having sex with him, as had Juan, but as they became more intimate, he made it difficult for José not to respond sexually. They would often lie together on a bed, fully clothed, talking, learning the words of new songs, singing. Then, when there was sufficient privacy, they gradually started touching each other more and more—hugging, caressing, and, finally, kissing. One afternoon, when no one was in the house, they took a shower together. José said this was the beginning of their sexual relationship:

I think we both knew something was going to happen. When we got in the shower, I scrubbed him with soap, just like a baby. He pulled me close, and with the water pouring down our heads we hugged and kissed. Then he moved away a little and gently pushed my head down. I really liked the way he did it . . . so nice. I didn't feel ashamed after about sucking him off . . . I felt good. That's all that happened. When we got out of the shower, he didn't say anything, but while we were drying off he kissed me right on the mouth.

José and Tomás continued their love affair and occasional sex until the fall of 1987 when Tomás, a few months after his eighteenth birthday, married the girl who lived next door. During those three years, they had their ups and downs, which José attributed mostly to Tomás's young age. José wrote me in November 1986: "Tomás and I are having kind of a nice affair with a few problems but I know I have to be patient sometimes because he is still a kid and I'm not so mature myself so I'm going to play it as it comes." By the summer of 1987 things were not going so well. José wrote: "My affair with Tomás has ended. To tell you the truth, I don't even know why, for all of a sudden I didn't want to even speak to him anymore so I don't even say hello to him."

José did not want to admit it at the time, but the reality was—as he told me some months later—that Tomás was courting his bride-to-be, Maria. She had known José since she was a little girl, and the three of them spent some time together during her courtship with Tomás, so-cializing with friends in the neighborhood. Maria knew that Tomás and José had something close going, and suspected that it probably included sex. She accepted their past but did not plan to include José after she and Tomás got married. According to José, before her marriage she teasingly used to tell him: "I'm not going to share Tomás" (*no me voy a compartir*).

José made up with Tomás before the wedding. He wrote me in October 1987: "I have plenty of things to tell you ... Remember I told you in my last letter that Tomás and I were not talking to each other anymore? Well, that's over. We are friends again but nothing about the other no more." The "other" José referred to was sex. After Tomás got married, sex between them was supposed to end.

José wrote me in May 1988: "At last Tomás's child was born and he is so proud." Their friendship continued, and when I met them the following July in Guadalajara they told me they were still seeing each other but not as often as before. I invited them to spend the next Saturday evening with me in the large guest quarters of a friend's house where I was staying. They showed up with three young neighborhood friends, Tomás's older brother, and two guitars. Anticipating this might happen—you invite two but six show up—I had laid in a good supply of food and drink. My host was out of town and had given me permission to entertain friends. I was glad he had gone away because, except for Tomás's brother, who left at midnight, we partied until the sun came up. And nobody said anything when, shortly before daybreak, José and Tomás disappeared. They had gone to the bathroom to take a shower together.

José and Tomás remain friends to the present day. José, however, except for his music group, has gradually withdrawn from Tomás and his old friendship network. He still goes back to visit them from time to time but no longer feels the need, as he once did, to spend most of his free time in his old neighborhood.

Tomás and his wife had a second child but are now separated. He moved away and is living and working on the outskirts of Guadalajara. In a recent letter (April 1993), José wrote: "Tomás has been having some problems with his marriage and sees his wife not quite so often and does not have almost any sexual relations with her and he thinks she is not getting anything on her own." Tomás, according to José, is having sex with some of the ladies he knows at work. He has two gay friends at work as well, but José said he does not know whether Tomás has had sex with either one. José also mentioned that, like Juan, Tomás at present is just a friend. He has not had sex with him for over four years—the last time being a bash they had together in the fall of 1989.

Living at Home in the New Neighborhood

Except for a few relatively short periods of time, José has lived with his family since returning from New York in early 1978. Like most families in Mexico facing high unemployment rates, they continue to be supportive even though José has worked mostly part time for the past ten years. José's homosexuality is now a nonissue. His brothers and father no longer carp about his lack of interest in women and marriage and talk with him as with any other member of the family. His sisters and mother harass him only about his excessive use and dependence on alcohol. He is the favorite of his younger nephews and nieces, and on Sundays when the family comes together he spends endless hours playing with the children. All the family enjoy his wit, singing, and general cheerfulness around the house.

Since moving, José has established a large network of friends in the new neighborhood. His gregariousness, singing, and guitar playing make him very popular and get him invited to many parties, large and small. As was the case in the old neighborhood, he is paid to perform at some, like coming-out parties traditionally given for fifteen-year-old girls and twenty-fifth anniversary parties for married couples.

José quickly learned that he could use the same strategies to make out with young men in the new neighborhood. Because of the AIDS epidemic, however, he is a little more cautious about what he does sexually. He knows about the importance of using condoms, but he says that they are not easy to find and most of the guys he has sex with do not like using them—so he does more oral sex than before. José also believes that by limiting his sex to young, inexperienced guys in the neighborhood he lowers his risk of HIV infection as well.

José almost never goes to gay bars anymore. He was aware of the gay liberation movement from the time it started in Mexico in 1981, but has never been an active participant. Although he has picked up some sex partners at gay bars, the majority have always been guys from his neighborhood, none of whom think of themselves as being "gay." Some of his old neighborhood friends saw the first gay demonstration in the Umbrellas Plaza. They were curious and astonished, but not hostile. They questioned José as to what had brought it on and wanted to know what he thought about it and why he had not participated. He said he told them, "I'm in favor of gay rights . . . gay people have only a few places they can go and be together, like Pancho's place [Bar Pancho] where I've taken some of you. But the police close down gay bars and extort and arrest lots of gay people for nothing."

José made no reply to them about not actively participating in the gay liberation movement. Although he supports gay rights, he has never felt involved enough in the struggle to become an active participant. He prefers spending most of his free time socializing with straight rather than gay people. He recently told me that if he had wanted to live in a gay ghetto he would have stayed in New York.

José cannot conceive of life without being with and part of his family. They have always helped alleviate his major disappointments in life. Sex is important and pleasurable, he told me, but it can never supplant the greater pleasures he gets from the time spent with his large extended family. He does, at times, still enjoy camping and carrying on with gay friends in downtown Guadalajara. But he gets equal pleasure, he says, from verbal dueling about sex with guys in both the new and old neighborhoods.

SIX | *Federico*

In the fall of 1969, I often went to a restaurant in Guadalajara located next to the lobby of a small downtown hotel. Federico was a waiter in that restaurant. Because he spoke some English and helped customers select the best Mexican entrées, he was very popular with American tourists staying at the hotel. Initially, he was aloof with me. He warmed up when he learned I was studying Spanish and planned to live in Guadalajara for a couple of years. Gradually, as I got to know him better, I revealed that I was a graduate student embarking on a study of machismo and the various kinds of behaviors related to it. After some time, he cautiously started joking with me— half in English and half in Spanish—about Mexican men and their masculinity. One Saturday as I was getting ready to leave after lunch, he came over and quietly told me: "In your study you have to know about *hombres más o menos* [men who are not quite men] . . . Wait for me in the lobby tonight. When you see me leave, follow me to the plaza . . . I'll take you to some interesting places."

That night, after I caught up with Federico in the plaza, he apologized for meeting the way we did and explained that he had to be careful because the owner did not like waiters to socialize with customers outside the restaurant. Much more important was that Federico was apprehensive because he was not sure how I would react to the bars he planned to show me. I assured him that I wanted to go and that they would certainly be of interest to my study. I also made it clear that both heterosexual and homosexual behaviors of Mexican men were of major importance to my investigation.

Federico, who was twenty-seven at the time, gave me my first tour of lower-class drinking establishments in Guadalajara. Located in the *zona roja* near the center of the city, he pointed out the ones that were special because homosexual men used them as pickup places. By the time we got to the third bar, we were both feeling mellow and comfortable with each other. We entered and stood at the end of a long wooden bar and ordered beer. When we got our *cerveza*, Federico gave me a *salud* and then abruptly asked, "Do you like men?" I replied that I did. He said he did also and now that we knew about each other we could relax and enjoy ourselves more being together. To make sure I understood that he was not coming on to me sexually, he jokingly said a short time later that we should think of ourselves as "sisters . . . both looking for men."

The tour ended about 1 A.M. Sunday morning. Federico, apologizing for cutting off the tour so early, said he needed to return home so his parents would not worry. I offered to drive him home. He accepted but stopped me before reaching his house, explaining that it was better for him to walk since the unpaved streets were full of potholes and I might get lost trying to get back to the main road. He suggested we meet again, as before, for another tour the following Friday night.

Federico and I continued our weekend tours for several months. During our hours together, I gave him a detailed description of my proposed study and asked him to become a respondent. He was enthusiastic about the idea and accepted immediately, saying he would be happy to introduce me to his friends. On thinking about his participation, however, he did make one condition: never to let his workmates know about the study. Although he and the other waiters did a lot of homosexual joking together, he did not want them to know for sure that he was homosexual.

I soon learned that Federico was a loner. He had several homosexual friends but he knew them separate from each other. He would meet one or the other for drinks after work or run into them at bars he frequented. His general preference, however, was to cruise alone. When he occasionally went to gay parties, he could enjoy them only up to a point and would then start thinking about what he might be missing at the bus station, in the movie theaters, on the street, or in his favorite bars. Much as he liked socializing at parties, he was almost never attracted sexually to anyone. He wanted to have sex with "real men, not *locas*." And in his experience they were to be found and available mostly among the laboring class of Mexican men.

In Guadalajara Federico lived with his family—mother, father, three older sisters, and three younger brothers. He said that even though none of them knew for sure about his homosexuality, "They must suspect because I'm not married . . . when you get to my age and haven't married they think about it . . . but if you act masculine they can only suspect." I was invited to meet his family for the first time in the summer of 1974—five years after I met him. He never offered any apologies for not inviting me sooner, saying only that it would happen some day. The reason for the delay was clear on my first visit—a mentally retarded sister kept lovingly at home by the family. An additional factor, which was alleviated over time, may have been the crowded poor circumstances under which his family then lived.

To increase his annual income, Federico worked three to four months every year in Puerto Vallarta during the tourist season (November to February). Both wages and tips were much higher there than in Guadalajara, and there was always a seasonal need for skilled labor. Federico also liked getting away from the noise and demands made by his family and the freedom to spend more time meeting his sexual needs with the surplus of men available on the beaches of Puerto Vallarta. He met his family responsibilities, he said, by sending money home monthly. Besides, after some months living alone, he was always happy to be back with his family. He had spent one year working in Los Angeles in the early 1960s but returned to Mexico because he was homesick and missed his friends and cruising in Guadalajara.

Shortly after meeting Federico, I asked him how long he thought he would continue to live with his family. He replied:

I have no plans to move. I'm the oldest brother so it's my obligation to help my family . . . that's why I must always take care to have a job. My father's not well, only working part time. I could move away if I wanted to . . . it's exciting to live alone, but then I get lonely and miss my family. I get along good with my sisters and brothers. Now that I'm older there's no problem about my coming and going anytime.

Federico liked both his parents but had a closer relationship with his mother. Many years later he told me that his father spent too much

time worrying about his retarded sister and was thus somewhat re-
moved from the rest of the family. Of his siblings, Federico was closest
to his older sister. They maintained close contact even after she moved
to southern California.

One of Federico's major objectives in life was to improve the house
in which he and his family lived. He and his oldest sister had helped
his father buy the house. Now he set out to enlarge and improve it
with some modern amenities. After all, he planned to live there most
of the time for the rest of his life. He was rather comfortable with
himself. By his reckoning, he had done quite well with only eight years
of schooling. He had no interest in trying to move to a higher station
in life or to live and work in California. He was happy with his life in
Mexico and liked working as a waiter in first-class restaurants. Mexican
men were another major attraction. He knew the homosexual scene in
Mexico and could usually find all the sexual partners he needed.

Federico's Early Sex-Life History

From his earliest memories onward, Federico remembers himself as
masculine. When I first met him he was good-looking, of medium
height and build, and masculine in appearance and bearing. His angular
face was set off by a carefully trimmed mustache. He later told me he
could act feminine when he wanted to, but that it was strictly a performance and not part of his nature. It was something, he said, that he
did for fun after he became comfortable moving in the homosexual
world of Guadalajara.

He remembered clearly his first sexual experience with another person. When he was about six or seven, a young man probably in his
mid-twenties offered to buy him something at a nearby neighborhood
store. He got Federico to walk a few blocks with him toward the store
and then lured him into a small room where Federico was used sexually.
Federico says, "He must have done it between my legs . . . I don't
remember any pain. I never told my parents or anyone about it." He
never saw the young man again.

Federico's second sexual experience before puberty occurred at the
age of nine with a fifteen-year-old youth who worked with him in a
neighborhood store. The youth befriended Federico, who was nervous
and excited about taking his first part-time job. They joked a lot together. Eventually, the jokes turned to Federico's approaching puberty.
One day during siesta when the store was closed and nobody was

around, the youth, pointing to his erect penis under his pants, told him he would soon be able to get a hard-on too. Federico said that he then

took me upstairs to a storeroom and had me masturbate him . . . it was exciting. We did it almost every day during siesta for maybe six months. One day he tried to fuck me. I didn't like that. I resisted. He kept promising it would make my cock grow longer. Luckily, before he put it in me, the door opened. The owner looked in and saw what we were doing. He called us *putos* and left. The young guy got up and ran away. I was scared, but I stayed because I didn't think I'd done anything wrong.

There were no repercussions. The owner never mentioned the incident to Federico's family and kept him on as an employee. The young man never returned to work.

I asked Federico about the long-term effects of these two incidents. Did he find it difficult to talk about them? Had they influenced the way he behaved sexually? He replied that he almost never thought about them. When he did, it never upset him. In fact, he remembered both young men as being handsome and masculine and could still get sexually excited thinking about the times he had masturbated the fifteen-year-old youth. The depressed feelings he had in his late teens about his homosexual behaviors had more to do with significant others' negative attitudes about homosexuality.

Late Teens and Early Twenties Sex Life

Federico's third homosexual encounter happened when he was fourteen, the year he began puberty. He had been looking forward to the time he would have pubic hair and be able to get an erection and ejaculate the way the "young man" did some five years previously. He was overjoyed when it finally occurred during a homosexual encounter a few months afterward in the balcony of a downtown movie theater with an effeminate man in his late twenties. Although the balcony was almost empty, the man sat down right next to him. Federico sensed that the man was interested in doing something other than watching the movie:

He put his hand on my leg. When I didn't say anything he moved his hand on my crotch and played with my dick until it got hard. He

leaned over, pulled it out, and sucked me off. He never said a word
. . . got up and left. I was watching the movie while he did it. He
came back after the movie ended and asked me to go downstairs to
the bathroom. I didn't know what to expect. He took me in a stall,
pulled his pants down, and asked me to fuck him. I'd never done
anything like that before. I said to myself, why not? So I pushed my
dick in . . . that's all I did . . . and he masturbated. He cleaned me
afterward. We never talked. I never saw him again.

Three or four months later he was in the balcony of another theater
watching a movie when a young man wearing a ranchero's hat played
with his ear with a peso banknote. Nothing further happened because
Federico's sister was sitting next to him on the other side. The incident
made him feel uneasy, however, because he would have liked something to happen. He began to worry about the possibility that he was
homosexual, and that his family might learn about his homosexual
activities. He knew how his family felt about homosexuality: they
disapproved.

During the next two years, Federico explored his heterosexuality.
He started dating girls when he turned fifteen. As he grew older and
matured physically, he noticed more and more neighborhood girls flirting with him. His sisters also began teasing him about his good looks
and physique—developed by lifting weights—and offered to fix him
up with some girlfriends. He enjoyed their teasing and accepted their
offer.

Federico dated many neighborhood girls, taking them to movies,
parties, and downtown parks. He felt flattered by their attention and
excited about the possibilities of eventually having sex with them. He
developed *novia* relationships with two girls about his age, but they
proceeded no further than lots of talking and petting in the park. He
wanted more.

He had his first heterosexual relationship when he was sixteen, with
a twenty-two-year-old maid who worked part time for a nearby family.
They had met at a neighborhood bus stop. For the first time in his life,
a woman had come on to him sexually. He courted her. In the beginning they met at the bus stop and then in a downtown park. Later,
they decided they wanted more than petting in the park so they pooled
money and moved their rendezvous to a cheap downtown hotel room
where anonymous sex was possible and acceptable. No one at the hotel
worried about his being under age. They met weekly for social outings

and sex for close to three months. Their relationship ended, according to Federico, because he "wanted her to go down on him. That was too *raro* [kinky] for her."

Federico's sexual relationship with the maid turned out to be his longest one with a woman. In the thirteen years that followed he had sporadic sexual encounters with six different women, the last one being with a twenty-five-year-old cousin when he was twenty-nine. Although he still enjoyed having sex with women during his twenties, none was that important to him sexually, since at the age of seventeen he had already gone back to having many sexual encounters with men. The sex happened mostly as the result of women pursuing him, not the reverse. There was also an element, he thinks, of trying to prove to himself in those years that he was not really homosexual.

When his affair with the maid ended, Federico started cruising for men around his own age. His next sexual partner was a slightly effeminate young man he met on Avenida Juárez in downtown Guadalajara. Just one year older than Federico, who was seventeen at the time, the youth had come from a neighboring village to work in the city. The village was too far away to commute, so he lived in a small one-room apartment near downtown. When their affair started, he and Federico were thus able to get together for sex whenever they wanted. Another bit of good luck: they were compatible sexually. Fresh from his heterosexual conquest, Federico was interested in playing the macho role and the young man was interested only in being anal receptive. The young man also wanted to please Federico so he would go down on him whenever he wanted oral sex.

Federico and the young man were having a wonderful affair, meeting three to four times a week for sex. Then toward the end of the third month, much to Federico's dismay, the young man professed that he had fallen madly in love with him. Federico loved being with him but did not love him. It was a one-sided affair. Federico had meanwhile taken on a new job as usher in a downtown movie house and had learned a great deal more about men who came to look for sexual partners rather than to watch the movie. He could not resist cruising some of them. He was wise enough, however, to make dates and carry out most of his sexual encounters elsewhere. He was pleased to find that private sections of a nearby public bath were cheaper and easier to go to than the hotel rooms he had used in the past.

When the young man learned about Federico's sexual encounters with other men, he became jealous and possessive. He could not understand Federico's need for additional sex and insisted that they have a monogamous relationship. As it became clear to him that Federico was going to continue having other sexual partners, the relationship was over. Federico was sorry to lose him. He missed the social outings and good sex they had together, but was happy to be free again. He was ready to move on.

Federico was fascinated by all the new men he suddenly had access to through his job as usher and by their intense interest in anal sex. He still liked being sucked off best. He was willing, however, "to fuck them too if that's what they wanted." "But," he said, "I didn't let no one fuck me then." During his seventeenth year he could remember having sex with at least eighteen different men he had met in the theater balcony. Most encounters were carried out in private steamrooms in the nearby Baños Nilo. The main thing he wrestled with after each sexual encounter was feeling depressed. None of his family or neighborhood friends knew he was having all these homosexual encounters. He worried about what they would do and say if they found out about them. He kept promising himself to find another female sex partner.

Federico maintained roughly the same cruising pattern and number of sexual partners through his early twenties. In his late teens, however, a major change had occurred in what he was willing to do sexually. He started allowing selected young men to penetrate him anally. He had met a handsome, masculine young man who would only give and not receive in anal sex, and decided that he might as well try it out. It took a while to get used to, but he discovered that he actually came to enjoy the experience.

Another important change that took place during this time was a gradual lessening of the depressed feelings that surfaced when he finished having sex with men. Incorporating the anal-receptive role in his sexual repertoire had briefly increased the intensity of these depressions. But he rationalized that, after all, it really did not make much difference what he did sexually with men: it was either right or wrong. After agonizing some weeks about his sexual behavior, he decided that as long as he was discreet and a good person, nothing he did sexually was wrong. In his mind, the real issue was that his behavior should not reflect badly on his family or friends. Knowing this, he said, put him at peace with himself and helped guide his behavior. As will be seen, however, his coping strategy did not preclude his becoming involved in a lot of risky sexual behaviors.

Even though Federico learned to cope with his homosexuality, he still struggled with an ongoing need to prove his masculinity. One result of this was that in his nineteenth year (1962) he had two more sexual encounters with women. He met both while working at the movie theater. One was a twenty-two-year-old coworker. He had sex with her just once in a small private room in back of the movie screen. The second was a thirty-two-year-old customer who had come on to him in the balcony. Their weekly sexual liaison was also carried out in the room behind the screen and lasted for three months. Federico was touched by the gifts she brought him. The affair ended when they both started worrying about being caught in the act by one of Federico's coworkers; and she did not want to move their liaison to a hotel room.

Federico had another brief heterosexual affair three years later when he was twenty-two with his youngest sister's girlfriend. He had been dating her on and off for several years. They were close to the same age and enjoyed one another's company. Occasionally, she teased him as to who he was more interested in sexually, her or the young men in the neighborhood. Federico decided to prove to her that he did like having sex with women. He was pleased that she seemed to enjoy their sexual encounters as much as he did. Their affair lasted only a few months. It ended late that year (1965) when he went to Los Angeles to take a job his oldest sister had found for him as a waiter in a classy Mexican restaurant.

He stayed in Los Angeles only a little less than a year, however, and then returned to Guadalajara. The only good things he remembers from that sojourn are being with his sister and learning a new trade as a waiter. The worst event occurred as a result of his not knowing about the Los Angeles Police Department's undercover vice operations and California's laws dealing with homosexuality. He had continued his usual pattern of cruising for men in the balconies of movie theaters. His luck ran out. He was entrapped by an LAPD vice squad officer in the balcony of a popular Latino movie theater in downtown Los Angeles. He spent five days in jail and paid a fine. It was a frightening and degrading experience. Through the help of a gay Mexican friend in Los Angeles, he concealed the arrest from his employer and sister. He nevertheless returned to Mexico as soon as he got out of jail. He knew undercover vice squad officers arrested men in movie theaters in Guadalajara too, but he knew how to read the landscape there better and had never been entrapped. In any event, one could usually negotiate a settlement with Mexican police officers and thus never have to appear in court. Additionally, he knew that one rarely went to jail for this kind of offense.

Two years after returning to Mexico, in 1967, Federico had what he considers to be one of the most eventful years of his life. He turned twenty-four the spring of that year and was the most comfortable he had ever been with himself and his homosexual practices. And for the first time in his life he not only had a job he loved going to—he had moved from being a waiter in a small neighborhood restaurant to a much higher-paying position as a waiter in a luxury hotel restaurant— but also had sufficient income through salary and tips to make him feel financially secure. He also discovered he had a special talent as a waiter and would eventually be able—with some training—to elevate himself to headwaiter.

It was also a memorable year because he had long affairs with two handsome young men. The first was with a twenty-four-year-old, very masculine (*"muy varonil"*) military student he had met at a party. Federico recalled that

in the beginning he was quite shy and didn't know much about sex
. . . just wanted me to jack him off. Little by little I taught him all
the things I liked better. I wanted him to be *activo* so he did that.
Anyway he would have been upset with me if I'd tried to fuck him.
He didn't even like me to kiss him. Later on we'd kiss and hug.
He'd lie right on top of me and press his cock on mine and jack us
off together.

They met for sex in a private room in a public *baños* almost every week for a year. Their affair ended when the young man was posted to military duty in the state of Sonora. Federico ran into him in Guadalajara two years later, but the man had married and was no longer interested in resuming their affair.

The second affair was with a man two years younger who worked as a clerk at the same hotel; it was carried out concurrently with the first one. Federico did not plan it that way, but he liked them both and since he was usually able to be with the military cadet only once a week he had plenty of time left over. The clerk was also *muy varonil* but considerably more experienced sexually than the cadet. From the beginning, he made it clear that he was *activo* and so if they were to have sex together Federico would have to be *pasivo*. This was fine with Federico since he had grown to enjoy being receptive as much as insertive—and he saw the clerk as being more macho than himself. This was important because Federico had strong feelings against letting any effeminate man penetrate him anally.

Federico's sexual affair with the clerk lasted four years, the longest one he has had to date. For the first year it was also a mutual love affair. Federico remembers:

It was the first time, maybe the only time, I've ever fallen in love with a man. Two months after we had been going together I moved him into my aunt's house. She had a spare room and he could afford to pay something. I knew he was a good person [*muy serio*]. We had a passionate relationship . . . kissing, good sex, jealousy. Both of us liked to make sex often . . . at least three times a week. We did it everywhere . . . *baños*, hotels, in the woods. Our love affair ended after about a year . . . I don't know why . . . but the sex didn't. We made a lot of sex for about two years . . . then it got less and less . . . and ended about four years from the day we met.

Their sexual affair ended finally when the clerk decided to take a job in a new hotel built in his hometown, Mazatlán. Both decided their affair had run its course.

Enjoyment of the Hunt

Even when he had two affairs going on at the same time, Federico never stopped looking for other sex partners. He enjoyed the excitement and dangers of hunting. At the end of the hunt was sex, and that was important and enjoyable, but when he had sex with any one individual for too long it became repetitive. He was thus always ready to embark on a search for yet another sex partner.

Although he has not methodically kept count of the number of different men he has had sex with, Federico has always loved to speculate about how many there have been at various points in his life. We invariably played this game whenever we got together. He would fill me in as to whom and where he had been cruising, his success rate, and what kind of changes had taken place in his sexual behavior since we last met. He knew I was also interested in hearing about his latest juiciest adventures, and he enjoyed reliving them by giving me detailed accounts of the best ones.

Federico was twenty-seven when he gave me the first accounting of the number of different men he had had sex with up to that point in time: "About two hundred." I taught him how to estimate the number by figuring his success rate by the week; an average of one a week would mean a total of fifty-two a year, and so on. I also pointed out he should not count the same person twice even if their homosexual encounters were spaced far apart in time. He replied that would not be much of a problem for him since for any one year he had had sex more than once with only a few men and, because of their importance, he could easily remember who they were.

Federico slowed down in his thirties and forties—instead of one new sexual partner a week, it was more like two different ones a month—so by the time he was fifty, in early 1993, he reckoned the total number of different men to be around seven hundred. He was always awed by the total when he summed them up: "Could I have had sex with *that* many different men?" But there was also an element of pride in giving his "guesstimate" that he had had such good luck in finding men. And, of course, at this writing the hunt goes on.

Regardless of how often Federico went out hunting in the past, his pattern of cruising has remained remarkably stable over time. His major strategy has always been to look for younger masculine men in their late teens or early twenties who are either "horny" or in situations where they are waiting for something to happen. He looks for horny men on downtown streets, in movie theater balconies, in the general section of public baths, and in bars and cantinas. He looks for men waiting at central bus stations for the departure of their buses—often for hours—with the hope that he can talk at least some of them into going to the private section of public baths where he can usually get them aroused for sex.

After locating a sexual target, Federico tries to ensure success and minimize risk by making prospective partners demonstrate some interest in having a homosexual encounter. With horny men, this usually means he will make the first eye contact and verbal come-on. The prospective partner then has to take the next step and make it clear that he is also interested and available. The final steps differ somewhat according to where he meets them, but they mostly center around what they would do sexually, where they would do it, and what it would cost each of them.

Bus station men are another matter. They require a lot more time and a completely different approach. Federico is willing to spend the additional time because of the added excitement of cruising and having sex with these generally sexually naive men. His opening verbal gambit with prospective partners is that he has come to the bus station to meet relatives, who have not arrived as planned, so he now has to wait and see if they will be on the next bus—always at least two hours away. If the prospects also have a long wait, he then invites them to have a drink with him in a nearby cafe across the street, which just happens to be next door to a public bath. Gradually, Federico moves the conversation to joking about women and sex. If there is an enthusiastic response, he continues with a few jokes about feminine men and what they do sexually and drops a few hints as to his availability. By the time they finish their drinks, Federico usually knows enough about the prospective partner either to say good-bye and return to the bus station or to take him to steam and bathe in a private room in the public bath next door. Once they are in the private steamroom, Federico claims he is rarely disappointed.

Federico's riskiest hunting occurred on long-distance bus rides at night returning from cities and towns located three to five hours from Guadalajara—the finale of day-long outings to moderately sized urban areas located in states adjoining Jalisco. These outings invariably included late afternoon cruising for men in movie theaters and public baths, and then, en route back to Guadalajara, having sex in the back of the bus late at night when most passengers were sleeping. Appropriate bus routes for this type of sexual activity must have long distances between towns to ensure uninterrupted stretches of darkness and privacy.

I questioned Federico about the risk of discovery in "back-of-the-bus sex." He told me how he minimized the risk of being caught:

You have to understand, José, these are second-class buses making late-night trips. They're never full so the back two rows are usually empty. It's uncomfortable to sleep there because you have to sit straight up . . . the backs don't recline . . . so people sit in front where it's comfortable. I like to sit in the next to last row, then when someone is interested we just move into back corner seats and make sex. It's dark, people are sleeping, nobody can see us. Some young guys know this goes on and sit in back looking . . . sometimes even playing with themselves. I've had 'em sit next to me, open their fly, pull it out and show me. They want you to go down on them.

He also told me he usually tried to find a prospective sex partner before getting on the bus by either verbal or eye contact. Federico would then take his seat in back and if the guy was interested he would sit next to him or just across the aisle. This further lowers risk since it reduces the chance that there will be any misunderstanding about having sex.

Recently, I asked Federico if he continued to make his monthly one-day outings. He grinned, and said, "I just had a good one to Durango. Who could I have safer sex with than these guys from small towns? They never have much sex anywhere else. Nothing has changed . . . I still follow my old routines."

Settling Down

During the twenty-three years I have known Federico, he has often talked about settling down and finding a person to live with permanently. When he was younger, he thought that person would most likely be a woman—a wife and children would be a wonderful hedge against the loneliness of old age. As the reality set in that he really had a strong sexual preference for men, he began talking about having longer-term relationships with men. The AIDS epidemic further motivated him to try hard to find more permanent male partners since he had to worry not only about becoming HIV infected but also about the supply of young *mayates* he targeted becoming smaller. "They too," he told me in 1987, "are worried about getting infected by *putos*."

But since his attempts over the years at maintaining these longer relationships have not been particularly successful, Federico has now given up hope of finding a more permanent partner and says he is no longer interested in having any kind of lover. He is content most of the year just being with his family in Guadalajara. Working and living in Puerto Vallarta part of the year provides a nice break. "I enjoy being there," he says, "because I have more freedom, time to cruise, and sex." He hastily added, however, "I'm always happy to get back to my house in Guadalajara. It's more convenient, cooler . . . and there are many places to fish for men in a big city so I can still find sex. The main problem is they cost me more because I have to take them to the *baños* for sex." Federico also mentioned to me recently that the decline in the number of *mayates* available—due to their concern about HIV infection—had been reversed by their need in current hard economic times for money. "It's harder," he says, "for me to make out at fifty, but I think my chances are getting better . . . there's more guys out there making themselves available than last year."

The Future

In my most recent conversations with Federico in Guadalajara in the spring of 1993, he was full of hope about his future. He has a job, owns a house, makes enough money to live comfortably, and continues to have good relations with his family. He worries about the Mexican economy and tourists since his job depends on both, but believes he will be able to work and have a job for many more years. He also feels lucky that two family members live and work in California and are considerate enough to help pay some of his mother's expenses. In emergencies he can also borrow money from them.

He was saddened to learn about Arturo's death from AIDS. They were not close friends, but they knew and liked each other and occasionally their paths would cross while cruising the same movie theaters and bars. He wanted to know how Arturo got infected with HIV—did it happen in Los Angeles or Guadalajara? I told him that it probably happened eight or nine years ago while he was living in Los Angeles. I asked Federico if he had been tested. He said he had not and could not see how he could have gotten infected since the men he targeted were young, sexually inexperienced, and mostly came from small towns. Somewhat annoyed with my question, he went on to say, "You know where I go to look for men, they're places where there are many country people [*campesinos*] . . . who I like to have sex with. I don't like gay discos or snobbish queens who go there. Anyway, when I do anal sex I most always use condoms." Arturo is the only person Federico knew who has died of AIDS.

Several years ago Federico took up painting as a hobby. He mostly paints rustic landscapes. As he has gotten older, he told me, he gets a lot of pleasure just staying home and painting. His sisters in Los Angeles have sold some of his paintings to their friends, and some of his American customers at the restaurant have bought a few. He is quite excited about the possibility that should he lose his job he now has another way to make money, perhaps enough to live on.

On my last trip to Guadalajara in late spring 1993, Federico invited me and a mutual friend to have lunch at his house. Since he had not returned from the store when we arrived, his mother and favorite aunt greeted us at the door. While waiting, it was pleasant to sit in his small living room and see his many paintings hanging on the walls. When Federico returned, it was satisfying to see how well he looked and how at ease he appeared to be with himself and his family.

| *Pedro and*

Gay Liberation

Pedro and I first met in January 1986 as a result of an investigation I was just starting of gay liberation in Guadalajara. Clark Taylor, an American anthropologist who did pioneering research on homosexuality in Mexico City in 1974–75, had been telling me about the gay liberation movement in Mexico City for several years and encouraged me to study the movement in Guadalajara. He suggested I start by interviewing Pedro, an acknowledged gay leader. Sergio Jaime, a Mexican psychiatrist and friend, arranged for me to meet Pedro at his office in the headquarters of the gay organization, Grupo Orgullo Homosexual Liberación (GOHL).

GOHL headquarters was then located in a two-story rented villa within walking distance of the center of the city. The second floor of the villa had been carved up into offices, meeting rooms, and a small living space for Pedro and his friend Jorge, an ex-lover and fellow activist in the gay liberation movement. It was spartan living for both of them with just one room, a hot plate for cooking, and a bathroom. And sometimes noisy living too, since on weekends the downstairs was turned into a gay disco called Boops, the major source of income for GOHL. Disco music from Boops was played at such high volume it could be heard blocks away.

Our first meeting was during the siesta hour on a weekday. Pedro met me at the front door of the villa and took me to the head of the stairway and seated me at a small desk. From where he sat he could see the front door, which had been left slightly ajar. Pedro explained that for reasons of security it was necessary to monitor who came into GOHL headquarters. Threats of violence had been made against him and GOHL, and though at that time none had been carried out, he said that one had to take such threats seriously.

After we introduced ourselves, I briefly described my interest in learning about the gay liberation movement in Guadalajara. I had been told that since he led the movement, he was the best person to contact first for information on its history. I also recounted how long I had been studying homosexuality in Guadalajara—eighteen years then— and had obviously been remiss in not knowing more about gay liberation in Mexico.

Pedro expressed surprise that I had been studying homosexuality in his city for so long and wondered why he had not heard about my research before. I explained I had published articles only in English in scholarly journals in the United States and had been unable to get any of them published in Mexican journals. He pressed me for further information, but I was anxious to hear his story and told him I would talk about my work another time.

Pedro spent the next two hours talking about gay liberation in Guadalajara: how and why it got started, who participated in it, the reaction of the people and civil authorities, and the accommodations that had been made with the mayor and police in favor of gay rights. It was a highly personal history, emotionally told, because Pedro was so much a part of it and because the movement was still in a fragile phase in which everything that had been gained could yet be lost.

One of the remarkable things about Pedro as a gay leader is that he does not in any way fit the cultural stereotype of how a homosexual man is supposed to look. Pedro is a brawny, handsome man, slightly taller than average (about five feet, ten inches) with long curly black hair, a square jaw, and large moustache. He speaks in a masculine way with a deep resonant voice. Based on his physical appearance, most Mexicans would be surprised to learn that he is gay.

When I first interviewed Pedro, he was twenty-nine and had been actively involved in the gay liberation movement for four and a half years. For close to four of those years he was its acknowledged leader. They were difficult years and his gay activism was personally costly. The notoriety associated with his leadership position had alienated him from most of his family. He lost his job teaching school, so he had no income. And, at times, he became physically and mentally exhausted by his leadership role. In the summer of 1982 he had run for the National Chamber of Deputies as a member of a far left political party—the only one in Mexico then that was supportive of gay rights. His candidacy led to further strains with his family and more conservative friends.

Born in the fall of 1956 of relatively prosperous parents in an upper-middle-class neighborhood of Guadalajara, Pedro is one of the few respondents in my study to come from this social strata. His father is a well-known lawyer who retired several years ago. Pedro has a college degree in economics and professional experience as a secondary school teacher. His sister and most of his brothers (he has four) have attended college as well.

Pedro's education and upper-middle-class roots have greatly facilitated his role as gay leader in meeting and bringing about accommodations with government officials. Equally important, however, is his presence and charisma. Although I have never seen him march down Avenida Juárez—Guadalajara's main downtown boulevard—in a gay demonstration, I can imagine quite well the impact it must have had on people viewing the parade. A couple of years ago (1992) during a public meeting in Guadalajara during International AIDS Day, I was seated next to Pedro when he stood up to protest to the large audience that no gay speakers had been included in the program. In a loud voice that could be clearly heard across the auditorium, he introduced himself: "My name is Pedro. I am a homosexual . . ." There was an audible gasp from many of those present and a scowl on the faces of the Jalisco State Minister of Health and his aides.

When I met Pedro, his life was totally dedicated to gay liberation and GOHL. A man of enormous energy, he single-mindedly focused on improving the lot of Mexican men who have sex with men. Although from the affluent privileged class, he already understood the special needs of those men who were less well off. And though very masculine, he also understood the particular needs of effeminate men who were most often the targets of harassment and arrest by the police.

I learned early on in our friendship that the best way to have uninterrupted conversations with Pedro was to spend the day with him at a spa on nearby Lake Chapala—San Juan Cosela. During those visits over several years, he related rich details about the history of GOHL and the ongoing progress and problems of the gay movement in meeting its major objectives. Equally important was the personal information he gave me, past and present, about his sex life and lovers, his particular problems in regard to the nonacceptance of homosexuality by his family and society, his coming to terms with his sexual orientation, and his use of his own personal anger and anguish about prejudice and harassment to try to bring about societal changes that would better the lives of people with similar homosexual orientations and problems.

As we got to know each other better, our friendship deepened and Pedro invited me to stay with him when I visited Guadalajara. I gratefully accepted and stayed with him on month-long visits in 1988 and 1989. He and Jorge had moved from their cramped quarters in the GOHL villa to a small remodeled house located in a modest neighborhood of the city. These visits made it possible for me to spend even more time with Pedro than before. We continued our conversations at the lakeside spa, plus by living at his house I was able to see him in action as a gay leader and sit in on conversations and meetings he had with members of GOHL and other gay organizations. I was also able to spend time socializing with Pedro's close friends and current lovers, and I met his mother and sister and two of his brothers. Like most Mexicans, Pedro's family continues to be a major force in his life.

Pedro's Early Sex Life

Pedro believes he entered puberty during his twelfth year, the age when he first remembers masturbating. Before then, he says he did not have sexual experiences of any consequence other than the usual kind of sex play resulting from a child's curiosity about the bodies of other boys and girls. He remembers himself as always being masculine and interested in playing boy's games, but he also remembers that since kindergarten he knew somehow that he was different from others his age:

I knew already I had a deep, deep attraction—I don't think sexual but, yes, pleasurable—to be with other boys. Clearly, in my mind I didn't think myself to be a homosexual then but neither did I think myself odd [raro] feeling that. Yet, I didn't sufficiently swallow the heterosexist education that was subsequently given me, and that made me feel different and like something apart.

Before puberty, Pedro did not have any physical sexual contacts with persons older than himself, male or female.

Pedro's first sexual experience with another person occurred when he was thirteen. A thirty-year-old woman had invited him and some of his friends to spend the night at her small vacation house in the countryside. He was pleased to find that she was interested in him sexually and that he finally had a chance to have sex with a woman. He enjoyed it and would have liked to meet her again, but it turned out to be just a one-time encounter. She had no further interest in their meeting again for sex.

During his early teens Pedro was preoccupied with his schoolwork, family, and friends. Over those years, masturbation was his solitary source of sexual pleasure. He knew it was considered a sin in the eyes of the church but not a big one. His friends masturbated too, and none of them worried about it either. Nevertheless, he was still not quite comfortable enough with himself to even attempt doing it with them—either in pairs or in "circle jerks."

Late Teens and Early Twenties Sex Life

Pedro describes the seven-year period of his life from late teens to early twenties (seventeen to twenty-three) as a time of looking for what was happening inside him. He felt a certain disquiet over his sexual orientation. He was interested in having sex with women, yet a part of him wanted to also explore male bodies. Unlike masturbation, violating societal rules about homosexuality was unthinkable. He masturbated with almost no guilt. The thought of having sex with another male, however, loaded him with guilt.

Pedro thinks that during these years, like most Mexicans who suppress their homosexual feelings, he felt anguished and frustrated:

I was going through life with a heterosexual mask, knowing that deep down I had incomprehensible desires and emotions that, in some way, should give a man pleasure. This caused me such distress, and was such a threat to my emotional equilibrium, that I felt repressed and spiritually low. I was living a life like that of any straight person. But, in my case, I was an anguished straight person [*buga angustiado*] because I did not understand what was going on inside me.

Seeing himself as an ordinary masculine person, Pedro was thus unable to face the trauma of physically acting out his inner sexual longings with other males. He once confessed to a priest, for example, that he masturbated. But, he remembers, "clearly I never told him that the fantasies which stimulated my masturbation were homosexual. I simply told him I masturbated, and he almost laughed. So I then told him I masturbated obsessively. But I thought to myself what really was obsessive was my inability to touch and explore another man's body."

As time passed, Pedro gradually began to learn about the homosexual world and how he might be related to it; much of what he learned made him feel bad about himself. Referring to what he had read about homosexuality, he remembers:

That was my first contact, I identified myself with what was being said in books—even though many things I read were venomous. For example, they say in encyclopedias that the homosexual is sick, dirty [*lugarcete comun*], you understand; and specifically that homosexuality is a perversion. And in medical books they give all kinds of explanations that make you feel bad.

Pedro was twenty when he had his second sexual encounter. Again, it was with an older woman—this time a twenty-six-year-old woman he met where he was going to college. She was very attractive, interesting, and fun to be with. They had sex a few times, then their relationship reverted to friendship alone. Neither one was interested in a long-term serious courtship that would lead to marriage.

Over the next two years, Pedro's thoughts turned more and more to acting out his desire to have sex with men. Finally, in the summer of 1979 when he was twenty-two, he had his first homosexual encounter. Late one night, when walking near the oldest gay bar in Guadalajara (Bar Pancho), he was approached by an older Anglo-American man named Jim—a bisexual fifty-three-old professor from the United States who combined work with vacations in Mexico every summer. Pedro accepted Jim's invitation to join him for a drink in the bar of a nearby hotel. After a few drinks, Jim took Pedro to his room upstairs and introduced him to oral sex. Pedro found it exhilarating and wanted to meet Jim again the next day. Jim wanted to meet Pedro as well, but unfortunately he had to return home to Ohio early the next morning. Their brief encounter, however, was the beginning of sexual affairs for Pedro and Jim that lasted through the next three summers. It was also the beginning of a tumultuous year for Pedro when the encounter plus additional events led to his coming out to himself and out of the closet (*salir del closet*).

Pedro's sexual encounter with Jim took place just a few months before his twenty-third birthday. They corresponded and their letters soon turned into affirmations of love and desire to meet again when Jim returned to Guadalajara the following summer. Pedro's awareness of what he had done sexually and what he was planning to do frightened him. A few months after his twenty-third birthday, he went through a "homosexual panic":

I thought myself very bad, and many times I was at the point of suicide. I don't know if I really might have killed myself, but many times I thought about it and believed it was the only alternative. This caused me problems with many friends. I felt they thought me to be different, homosexual, and really sick. It made me separate from them. I felt myself inferior and thought I was the only one these things happened to.

Some weeks before I left the closet, I went into a terrible panic. A panic that overwhelmed me above all, I was hysterical, psychotic. One morning I woke up yelling . . . in a cold sweat, stiff, eyes rolling. My family came into my room and asked me: What happened? What's going on? There were no medical explanations. And no other kind of explanation other than the strong anguish I felt over being what, at that moment, I did not want to be; and that I was rejecting . . . a product of the education I had received.

I had an enormous fear that they might discover me . . . that my family or a friend might *know* something about me. Many times in the few family reunions I used to go to, talk would always turn to the subject of the *joto*, the homosexual, or something related, and I was forced to conceal myself. Everyone was saying bad things about homosexuals. I used to stay quiet then, distressed.

Pedro overcame his bad feelings about being homosexual, just as he had overcome his feelings of being "an anguished straight person," a heterosexual who "did not understand what was going on inside me." It came about in part as a result of telling a heterosexual childhood friend of his dilemma of being a "homosexual." His friend gave him some positive articles to read about gay people. Referring to them, Pedro recalls: "I remember reading in *El Viejo Topo* some articles by Carlo Forti, and others in *Sábado de Uno Más Uno*, that were truly revelatory. I was able to identify myself and know more of myself.

They were excellent and permitted me to know my homosexuality from a political point of view. I knew I didn't have to reject myself just for being gay."

Pedro still had another problem to surmount: coming out sexually. Although at some level he could accept being gay, he found it difficult to even think about playing the feminine receptive (*pasivo*) role in anal intercourse. Oral sex did not present this dilemma to him, and he was thankful that in his first homosexual encounter it was with a masculine man who was interested only in oral sex.

In finally coming out to himself, Pedro started looking for homosexual encounters in the street (*el ligue en la calle*). He had been looking only halfheartedly when Jim approached and picked him up. Now he undertook serious cruising. He remembers his first attempts to find sexual partners as excruciating experiences. He knew the special signals, "intense looks, lustful ones that say something." And he knew where to go to find them. "I knew that things happened in the center of Guadalajara . . . that here in this city the zone most open for an encounter is the street; there are few places for gay people here."

He describes the very first time he set out to look for a sexual companion:

The first time I tried to make it with someone was horrible. I crossed Avenida Juárez and in a dark side street found a *chavo* [a young man], very feminine for sure. I saw him and said to myself: fuck my prejudices, fuck my education, fuck everything. I want to go to bed with a man now, and I'm going to do it.

He, she, was a *loquita* [a little queen]; and I was standing close to her. But it was difficult for me to approach. With every step I took, I was feeling more flushed in my head and felt it growing. I was very nervous because I didn't know what to say to the *chavo*. I didn't know how to begin the conversation. The only thing I could think to say was, "Hey, carnal." I thought the word *carnal* was also used between homosexuals. He turned around. I looked at him, but couldn't say another word. My jawbone was paralyzed. I wanted to say something strong, to express how I felt, but I couldn't. My brain thought I was saying things; but I couldn't hear anything. No sound left my mouth. A horrible sensation. For fractions of seconds, of course, but they seemed like long ones. I felt bad, my head was going around. And then what I did was to go running. I was running desperately, like a *loca* [a queen]!

Pedro persisted and after a few tries scored with a slightly effeminate eighteen-year-old in Parque de la Revolución, a park near the center of Guadalajara and long known as a favorite meeting place for men looking for sexual encounters with other men. Having made the breakthrough, the park became Pedro's major cruising ground. Pedro estimates that in his twenty-third year he picked up and had sexual intercourse with fifty to one hundred young men between the ages of sixteen to nineteen. He is not sure of the exact number but remembers that he went cruising just about every week and made out with at least one or two a week. He practiced receptive and insertive oral sex in practically all the sexual encounters, and insertive anal sex only in some. He could not yet bring himself to even try the anal-receptive sex role with all its feminine cultural implications. The psychological dissonance that would result from playing the *pasivo* role was more than he could handle at that time.

Pedro Comes Out to His Family

Pedro's final coming out was to his family, who he believed was not aware of his homosexuality—or, at least, if they did know or suspect, never mentioned it. This situation changed dramatically during the latter part of Pedro's twenty-third year when one of his younger brothers came home unexpectedly and found him having sex with a boyfriend and told both his father and eldest brother about the incident. A family crisis ensued, with lots of bitter remarks, tears, and rejection. But because by then Pedro had completely accepted himself as gay, he felt ready to confront his family. He first explained the situation to his father, then later to his brothers and sister as a group. Pedro, his father, and his brothers and sister, however, decided to keep his homosexuality a secret from his mother, who was in Mexico City at the time. She did not learn of Pedro's homosexuality for another two years.

Pedro had decided not to tell his mother because she and his father were estranged and he did not want to burden her further. He felt very protective toward his mother then because his father treated her in a chauvinistic way. Pedro deeply resented the way his father treated his mother, and he often upbraided him about it. In the fall of 1981, just one month before Pedro's twenty-fifth birthday, his father asked him to leave. Pedro claims, ironically, it had nothing to do with his homosexuality.

One of Pedro's younger brothers, who had gotten into some legal difficulties and become estranged from his father, joined him and they rented an apartment together. A short time later, their mother moved in with them on a temporary basis.

It was at this time that Pedro's mother discovered his homosexuality. In a later taped conversation with her ("Mother," 1984) for GOHL's new magazine *Crisálida,* she recalled to Pedro how she had had "small indications" that left her wondering and uneasy:

> some telephone calls, some friends of yours who came to the house, who I saw [being like] homosexual. Then I thought to myself . . . why do they visit my son? . . . Why do they call by telephone? Why? I wanted to cloud it over, it was not like you . . . not you. And I was rebelling and saying to myself, no! I looked for explanations . . . you were very sociable, you had all kinds of friends. When I finally realized, it was a tremendous shock for me.

Later in the taped conversation, Pedro asked his mother, "What feelings or emotions did you experience when you discovered that a very beloved son of yours was a homosexual? Do you remember that day? Can you describe it?" She replied:

> Yes, son . . . I am never going to forget that day. Can you imagine . . . among my family I had discovered a homosexual . . . a son of mine . . . very dear, very special as you are . . . was homosexual. Given what I thought about homosexuality all of my life, you must know how it shocked me and took me a long time to get over . . . a shock that included much rejection of you, very nearly . . . like . . . blaming you insofar as you might hurt me personally with this. And later I thought of you even as a cynic in the way you treated me. I don't know, son . . . I wished . . . maybe to attack you, beat you. How was it possible that you could be so bad, I thought to myself . . . because for me this was homosexuality. I was going through a terrible personal crisis when I discovered it. Then, this came to give me yet more pain.

At the end of the interview, Pedro's mother explained her eventual acceptance of her son's homosexuality: "At first I was very hard with you . . . severe. Later, little by little I began to understand you, I was . . . grasping it . . . I was understanding all that you had also suffered before."

Pedro and Gay Liberation

Pedro's twenty-fourth year (which ended in the fall of 1981) turned out to be one of his most eventful years. By the end of 1980, he had worked through his most difficult personal problems related to his homosexuality and had turned his anger outward with the hope that he and others like him might bring about some changes in the way homosexual people were viewed and treated by ordinary citizens and officials in Guadalajara. The use of the word *gay* to identify oneself or others as homosexual was relatively new in Mexico and just beginning to be popularized by the press (see Murray and Arboleda 1987). *De ambiente* was still in wide usage by insiders to discreetly identify men actively seeking other men for sexual encounters, and the press usually used pejorative terms like *mujercito* (meaning "girl boy," a derogatory term coined by tabloid journalists for effeminate males), *maricón*, or *puto* as labels for homosexual men. Pedro liked the neutrality and internationality of the word *gay* and immediately assumed a "gay identity."

Early in 1981, Pedro learned about the Homosexual Liberation Movement (Movimiento de Liberación Homosexual) in Mexico City and set about to meet some gay-identified men and women in Guadalajara who would be interested in bettering the condition of homosexual men and women in their city. By summer 1981 he and some of the gay people he had met founded the first gay liberation movement in Guadalajara. They started regular meetings to plan a fight against police repression and to help obtain civil rights for homosexual people in the city.

The movement consumed most of Pedro's life and thoughts in 1981 and for many years thereafter. Through interviews with many different kinds of men involved in homosexual encounters and his own personal experiences in Parque de la Revolución, he learned a lot about the strategies used by law enforcement officers to suppress homosexuality and at the same time increase their income through extortion by threat of arrest and after an arrest. He learned everything he could about the behaviors of the different types of homosexually behaving men as well. All this information helped him formulate an action plan for the group, and he became its acknowledged leader. By the end of 1981 the group numbered around forty, representing all social classes although about half were "street people" from relatively poor families.

Pedro and Jorge

Another major event in Pedro's life occurred in 1981 when he met a young man named Jorge while cruising in Parque de la Revolución. Jorge, who was fourteen at the time, became Pedro's lover and lieutenant in the gay liberation movement. He knew far more than Pedro about the gay world when they met—especially about *locas*. He had been sexually active with men since he was eight years old.

Pedro fell passionately in love with Jorge, who was small, cuddly, bright, and very interested in gay liberation. As their relationship developed, Jorge became much more than a love object for Pedro. They had good sex together, but equally important to Pedro was the conviction they shared about the need for change and their willingness to work hard and put themselves at risk to bring it about. Jorge also provided Pedro with additional knowledge about homosexual behaviors related to his different family background and lower socioeconomic class.

Their love affair ended by mutual agreement after four years. Pedro blames himself for the breakup. Although he no longer had the time or interest to continue his weekly cruising in the park, he was not totally open with Jorge about his long-time summer sexual affair with Jim or his need from time to time to have ongoing sexual relationships with younger men. He terminated his relationship with Jim in the summer of 1982, but he continued having a few sexual affairs with other men. This led to the undoing of the sexual aspect of his relationship with Jorge, who found another lover. Pedro still loves Jorge deeply, however, and looks on him as a son. They continue to live together along with Jorge's new lover. Pedro cannot conceive of life without having Jorge working by his side.

Pedro's Outing as a Gay Activist

Pedro's major coming out to the citizens and officials of Guadalajara occurred in two 1982 events. The first had to do with the national elections to be held in July 1982. A gay committee had been formed to promote the female presidential candidate of the newly recognized Revolutionary Workers' Party (PRT, Partido Revolución Trabajadores). The PRT was the only party sympathetic to gay causes, so Pedro agreed early in the year to run as the local candidate for the National Chamber of Deputies.

The second event took place on May 8, before the election, as a result of the arrest of seven flamboyant and effeminate homosexual men in a straight restaurant in early April 1982. The restaurant had become a popular meeting place and hangout for homosexual people. For some time the manager had tried to get homosexual patrons, especially the feminine ones, to stop congregating in and around his open-patio restaurant. Being unsuccessful, he called the police and the seven men were arrested. Since sex between consenting adults is not illegal anywhere in Mexico, arrests of homosexual people are usually made for immoral or scandalous behavior, or for disturbing the peace.

In response to the arrests, several militant members of the committee staged a peaceful demonstration in the restaurant on April 24. On being refused service, they pointed out to the restaurant's manager that it was a violation of the Federal Consumer Protection law to deny them service systematically just on the basis of their sexual orientation. Police were once again called. After being roughly handled and verbally abused, they were arrested and jailed. Because Pedro was the PRT candidate for the National Chamber of Deputies, the event was widely reported in the local press.

The committee then called for the first gay protest march ever held in Guadalajara, at 6 P.M., during the rush hour on May 8, 1982. On that day, despite the possible consequences for their personal lives, 120 courageous gay and lesbian demonstrators marched down Avenida Juárez from the Umbrellas Plaza to the site of the arrests. Bold banners announced their cause:

STOP POLICE HARASSMENT

LESBIANS AND HOMOSEXUALS ARE NEITHER SICK NOR CRIMINALS

STOP THE REPRESSION AGAINST LESBIANS AND HOMOSEXUALS

LESBIANS AND HOMOSEXUALS ARE EVERYWHERE

In the march, Pedro, with Jorge at his side, was unmistakably front and center.

The second gay protest march was held June 4 at the end of a week of campaigning for PRT candidates. Over 150 lesbian and gay demonstrators, some holding the bold banners, walked down Avenida Juárez during the evening rush hour from the Umbrellas Plaza to Revolution Park. At a meeting in the park, they denounced the maltreatment of the gay community by the police, press, robbers, and extortionists. They specifically accused Guadalajara patrol officers of arresting "homosexuals" and then getting payoffs to let them go free. Again, Pedro was in the forefront of the gay and lesbian marchers down Avenida Juárez during the rush hour.

When Pedro became a leader of the gay liberation movement and a candidate for the National Chamber of Deputies, he overcame the final barrier to acceptance by most of his family. The notoriety associated with these positions continued to alienate and disarm them for awhile. But believing in the cause he pursued, all except his oldest brother set aside their fears and prejudices about homosexuality and accepted and supported him as best they could in his role as a leader of the movement. That Pedro remained alienated from his father had more to do with domestic problems between his parents. His mother eventually became an activist in the gay liberation movement herself, and one of his younger brothers helped Pedro run GOHL's disco nightclub until it was closed by the mayor.

Pedro, Accommodation with Police, and AIDS

Pedro lost the July 1982 election, but the political experience he gained proved to be invaluable in the fight that was just beginning with the city administration to stop the police from harassing and arresting homosexual men when they congregated in certain parks, restaurants, and bars. Pedro was the principal negotiator in the talks with the mayor and police chief that followed the first two marches down Avenida Juárez. Before the talks started, however, Pedro had to deal with internal problems in the group. He wanted to present a united front in negotiations with city officials.

For the political campaign and protest marches the group had named itself the Committee of Lesbians and Homosexuals in Support of Rosario Ibarra (CLHARI), the female presidential candidate of the PRT. Some discord, however, had occurred within the gay liberation movement at this time. Political alignment with the PRT disturbed many members. And friction developed between the radical and openly gay members, many of whom were very effeminate, and those who wanted to be less open and stay in the closet with respect to their families and work. Part of the discord was resolved by renaming the organization Grupo Orgullo Homosexual de Liberación (Group Pride for Homosexual Liberation) and by establishing its absolute independence from PRT. Pedro became the acknowledged leader of GOHL.

Pedro finally met with newly installed government officials in Guadalajara early in 1983. As expected, he found them to be extremely homophobic and unwilling to talk in realistic terms about the oppression of gay people by police in the city. Pedro said the most important outcome of the meeting was that they had met with him, thereby establishing the existence and legitimacy of GOHL, the first gay organization in Guadalajara. Pedro had gotten considerable press coverage in his PRT campaign. He made sure this event was also well covered by the press.

The response of city officials was nevertheless dramatic. In March 1983 they persuaded the governor of Jalisco to close all gay bars in the city on the grounds that such establishments violated the moral codes of the people. Police repression not only continued but increased. Pedro knew what he had to do. He had learned from meetings with government officials that the thing that upset them most was a gay demonstration downtown. Before calling a demonstration, however, he decided to build a strong case for gay liberation in the press. During the next four months, he held several press conferences outlining the grievances of the gay community about the continuing harassment of its members by the police and setting forth the positive aspects of gay life in the city. Pedro also organized a "letter to the editor" campaign to newspapers. The media response was good—some of the city's most important newspapers published many letters and positive, objective articles about the gay community, and television news programs broadcast interviews of Pedro protesting the illegal police arrests and extortion activities.

By midsummer, Pedro decided the time had come for GOHL members and their friends to demonstrate again. In early August 1983 an attention-getting, noisy, disruptive meeting was held during the rush hour in downtown Guadalajara's cathedral plaza. Using a platform and loudspeakers, Pedro and other GOHL leaders demanded that police harassment be stopped and gay bars be reopened. If their demands were not met, they promised further demonstrations and marches.

Pedro resumed negotiations with the mayor and police chief, and a limited accord was reached. By December 1983 the gay bars reopened. And, gradually, harassment of homosexual men lessened so that by the autumn of 1984 Pedro said he had developed a direct link with the police chief to help adjudicate problems related to homosexual people arrested for a variety of offenses, some legitimate, some not.

Pedro also made a decision then that greatly affected his personal life. He felt sufficiently secure in his relations with city officials so that with the reopening of gay bars he decided the time had come for gay people to run their own bar in order to put most of the profits into projects that would benefit their community. Income from the bar would also enable Pedro and Jorge to eventually move into a small house. The bar-disco, named Boops, opened in December 1983. Located on the ground floor of the GOHL house, it was an immediate success.

But the establishment's success added another time-consuming chore to Pedro's already busy schedule. Since he was in charge of the disco, it just about used up every weekend—Friday, Saturday, and Sunday from the hour it opened, 8 P.M., to at least 3 A.M. each morning. In addition, GOHL was gearing up at that time for a fight against AIDS by providing its members and interested others—through meetings and its new newsletter (*Crisálida,* September 1983)—with information about the AIDS epidemic in the United States and about the importance of practicing safe sex. Pedro, meanwhile, had to continue various negotiations with the mayor and police chief over gay rights. It was an exhausting routine, but with the opening of the disco he at last had some money again. This was his first regular income since he had lost his job as a school teacher. And Pedro also got substantial help—not money but labor—from his mother and two younger brothers in support of the many different tasks he had to perform for GOHL.

Close to five years passed before Pedro could accumulate enough money to move himself and Jorge out of their GOHL lodgings in early 1988 into their own house. These were five difficult years for Pedro, with continued fighting with officialdom and more demonstrations for gay rights. In February and March 1986, for example, the civil authorities had the police close down the offices of gay liberation groups and the gay bars. Only after more demonstrations were they allowed to reopen. Yet Pedro knew by then that through his leadership GOHL had brought about significant improvements in the daily lives of homosexual men and women in Guadalajara. For the first time, in the summer of 1985 a homosexual man, a leader of gay liberation, could talk directly with the chief of police and negotiate with him at any time about the illegal actions of his officers. He knew as well that through his leadership GOHL had also been in the forefront of the fight against AIDS. In the summer of 1985, for example, GOHL sponsored a two-day presentation about AIDS by a member of the medical faculty at the University of Guadalajara Medical School; and in January and July

1986 GOHL sponsored lectures on HIV infection and AIDS by the director of the university's Institute of Infectious Diseases, Dr. Eduardo Vázquez-Valls.

Pedro had several love affairs during those turbulent five years (1983 to 1988). His lovers eventually left him because of his need to have open sexual relationships. Pedro liked having a principal lover but found it difficult to give up little sexual adventures on the side. A walk through Parque de la Revolución always lifted his spirits and the excitement of finding someone new never left him. Given the long hours he spent carrying out his many tasks for GOHL, one of the few ways he had to relax was to spend a day at the Lake Chapala spa with a lover and friends.

One of the first things Pedro did to the house that he and Jorge moved into was to make it secure. Anonymous threats of violence against Pedro and GOHL had been made for several years and one had finally been carried out in 1987—a small explosive device had been detonated by the front door of the GOHL house. Pedro's new house was therefore completely enclosed by barbed wire, and the entrance to the front courtyard was through a gate in a solid heavy metal fence.

Pedro and Jorge, nevertheless, enjoyed living in their first private house. They had separate bedrooms so Jorge's lover was now able to live with them part time. And when he wanted, Pedro could entertain his different lovers at the house. I stayed there for several weeks in the summer of 1988 and again in the fall of 1989. During my stay, it became obvious that although the house was private it was also used as an additional facility for GOHL business and housing—gay leaders from Mexico City and elsewhere usually met and stayed there when they came to Guadalajara.

Pedro, GOHL, and the 1988 National Elections

Pedro knew that a major test of the accommodations he had worked out between GOHL, the mayor of Guadalajara, and the police would take place with changes in government officials—both state and local—following the 1988 national elections. The tradition in Mexico is for elected officials at the beginning of their administrations to change at will such positions as chief of police. Pedro thus knew he would have to renegotiate everything with the newly elected mayor, Gabriel Covarrubias.

The change in government eventually affected Pedro's personal fortunes and set back not only gay rights but also the programs that

GOHL ran to help people with AIDS and prevent HIV infection through safe sex. Mayor Covarrubias, extremely moralistic and homophobic, immediately began a moral crusade and sought to represent only the interests of the city's far right religious extremists. Initially, he refused even to see Pedro. He agreed to talk only after Pedro and some other GOHL members camped out in his office and threatened a march. The new mayor, however, refused to carry on any of the accommodations made by his predecessor with respect to gay rights. He ordered the closure of all gay bars, including GOHL's disco Boops, and the police resumed their harassment of homosexual men, especially those who cross-dressed or were feminine appearing. Pedro, however, continued to hold talks with Mayor Covarrubias and, gradually, the mayor softened his positions somewhat and after several months allowed the reopening of all the gay bars, though not Boops. Police harassment continued but lessened, and Pedro could still intervene at times on behalf of gay arrestees. Gay rights were not where they had been before the new mayor took office, but some progress had been made in reestablishing an accommodation.

The closure of Boops had an immediate impact on GOHL and on Pedro. For GOHL the loss of income meant they had to give up their offices and meeting rooms in the large two-story house they could no longer afford to rent. For Pedro the loss of income meant he would eventually have to sell the house he was living in and use the money to try to reopen another gay disco to provide both GOHL and himself with income.

Pedro, AIDS, and ILGA

Pedro and Jorge lived on in their house for three more years. Pedro decided to stay on until 1991 for several reasons. The most important was that Pedro had learned that Jorge was infected with HIV. He was thus more determined than ever to make life as easy for Jorge as possible. He also became even more actively involved in the fight against AIDS. During these years Pedro, along with Francisco Galvan, a gay leader in Mexico City who died of AIDS in 1993, represented the nongovernmental organizations of Mexico that were running programs to prevent the spread of HIV or to assist in the treatment of persons with AIDS. A third reason was that Pedro had not been able to obtain a permit from the authorities to open another gay bar. He would not sell the house until he was certain the money could be plowed back into an income-producing bar for GOHL and himself.

Meanwhile, Pedro had been actively seeking money so that GOHL could resume some of its programs. One promising group was the International Lesbian and Gay Association (ILGA). Pedro asked ILGA if it gave financial assistance to needy gay organizations. It did not, but the association provided money for Pedro and Jorge to attend its next international conference in Europe. Pedro became very active in ILGA and invited it to hold its 1991 international conference in Guadalajara. ILGA accepted and expressed pleasure over being able to meet for the first time in a Third World country.

As the time for the ILGA conference drew closer, Pedro began to worry more and more about what effect it would have on the few concessions on gay rights he had gotten back in tough negotiations with Mayor Covarrubias. When I visited Pedro in the spring of 1991, he already realized he had made a serious error in trying to hold the conference in Guadalajara. It was too late, however, to withdraw the invitation to ILGA. Under pressure from influential extreme right-wing groups with objectives similar to the "Moral Majority" in the United States, the mayor knuckled under and helped prevent the ILGA conference from being held in Guadalajara. With great embarrassment to Pedro and GOHL, the conference was held in Acapulco. This was a major setback for gay rights and GOHL in Guadalajara, and Pedro was despondent for months over the outcome and his poor judgment in inviting ILGA and trying to hold an international gay conference in such a hostile environment. But on the national level it was not a complete disaster for gay rights since the federal government intervened and the city of Acapulco showed that opprobrium is not uniform in all Mexican cities.

Pedro and the Future

Pedro finally obtained permission to open a gay bar in late 1992. He sold his house and used the money to buy a small building in a location suitable for a gay bar. He opened the bar but it did not draw enough customers to survive. Since he and Jorge were temporarily living with Pedro's mother at the time, they moved into the bar while planning what to do next.

When I visited Pedro in May 1993, he and Jorge had moved to a small rented house and were getting ready to reopen the gay bar. During that visit, Pedro told me he had grown tired of his gay leadership role. He said he has been actively trying to recruit someone else for several years but without success. Now he wants to spend most of his time taking care of Jorge.

Pedro and Jorge reopened the bar in the spring of 1994 as *El Taller 2*, a Guadalajaran branch of one of the most popular gay discos in Mexico City. It has been doing relatively well. Pedro hopes the profits will be sufficient to supply him enough money to run his household and have adequate funds left over for GOHL to get their AIDS programs up and running full time again.

Although he now prefers to let other people take over the leadership of the gay liberation movement in Guadalajara, Pedro is still actively involved in helping maintain the hard-won accommodation that still exists between the government and gay people. Most of all, he wants to continue the fight for good HIV-prevention programs and better medical care for people with AIDS.

Conclusions

It is striking how little Mexican male homosexual behaviors appear to have changed during the twenty-five years of my field research. The methods for finding a sexual partner in Guadalajara are about the same in 1994 as they were when I first visited the city in 1969. Men interested in initiating homosexual encounters, for example, still cruise mainly in the same places—certain parks, streets, movie houses, bathhouses, straight bars, and gay bars; and even though there are more gay drinking establishments than before—four discos and two bars by my last count—they are still few in number for a city of close to five million.

Family relations have also remained much the same, with the majority of males continuing to live with their families until marrying in their late twenties. Because some young "straight" males—frustrated in their search for female sex partners—are still willing to have sex with another male as long as he plays the anal-receptive role, local neighborhoods remain fertile cruising grounds for certain homosexual men. However, in spite of gay liberation, the general public continues to view male homosexuality with considerable disapproval. The homosexually involved Mexican male, single and living with his family, must therefore still cope over time with the dissonance generated by his behavior and the family's negative view of the homosexual as a shameful being.

Although we saw examples in the profiles of how some Mexican men—like Pedro, Arturo, and José—are "out of the closet" to their family, concealment remains the major strategy today for most Mexican men who have sexual encounters with other men. And even when an individual's homosexuality is known by his family and friends, a conspiracy of silence is usually maintained so that his sexual orientation is brought up only by a select few in joking relationships and, except when with homosexual friends, he always presents as masculine a front as possible. Arturo and José's relations with their families are good examples of this strategy.

The various ways Mexican males cope with their homosexuality are still mostly related to categorizing behavior as acceptable or unacceptable insofar as it might result in exposing them to their families and friends. The verb *quemar* (literally, to burn or scorch) is generally used in conversation in Mexico to label behavior considered unacceptable. Reference is thus made to the fact that one's reputation may be burned or scorched by a revealing bit of behavior.

The two situations most feared by many Mexican males involved in homosexual encounters are (1) being seen in the company of, or acknowledged by, males judged effeminate and thus by implication homosexual, and (2) being seen going into or leaving a place where *maricónes* are known to congregate. In the early days of my study, I unwittingly put a number of informants in extremely tense situations by not understanding this apprehension and fear. For example, while walking down a main boulevard in Guadalajara early one evening with an informant who judged himself quite masculine, I stopped and engaged in a brief conversation with an effeminate informant coming from the opposite direction. Before I could make an introduction, the masculine informant quickly walked a short distance away to dissociate himself. This informant explained later that in such a public location he was afraid his relatives might see him talking to such an obvious "homosexual." He concluded by saying, "*El me quema!*" (literally, he [the feminine male] scorches my reputation).

The fear of being seen going into a place identified with homosexual men by relatives or neighbors causes many Mexican males even today to limit their attendance. Some of the "straight" guys I came to know quite well in my neighborhood study in Guadalajara would occasionally ask Alberto and me to take them to a gay disco, but they were willing to go only as a group and it was clear that for them it was just a lark. I remember late one night encountering two masculine young men from the neighborhood in Boop's. I knew they played around because Alberto and I both had had sex with them and suspected that they were finding male sexual partners outside the neighborhood. They were nevertheless embarrassed by being found there, said it was the first and only time they had been to Boop's, and made me promise I would not tell anyone in the neighborhood about seeing them in a gay disco.

Although, as we have seen, the closing of gay drinking establishments by law authorities in Guadalajara is a recurring pattern, the reluctance of many homosexually involved men to enter would by itself probably limit their number. It is difficult to imagine Guadalajara ever having as many exclusively homosexual establishments as are found in major cities in the United States.

Another aspect of male coping is activity carried out to divert attention from homosexual involvement. Social contacts with girlfriends and heterosexual intercourse with prostitutes may be maintained as a cover. And any masculine-type activity may be participated in on a routine basis to promote a heterosexual image. The Mexican custom of paying a great deal of attention to a passing girl by whistling or making remarks, for instance, may be as avidly carried out by a homosexually involved male as by a heterosexually involved one.

The level of activity required for family coping appears to depend for the most part on the individual's degree of involvement in homosexual encounters and on his relative effeminacy or masculinity. Individuals heavily involved in homosexual encounters structure their social life differently from less involved males. The greater the involvement, the greater the need for defenses and covering activities within the family. To sustain a large number of different sexual outlets, for example, they must spend proportionately more time hiding the activity from the family. Those males maintaining a relationship with only one partner also carry a proportionately heavier burden since they must create a cover for the time spent socializing with the lover.

Exclusively homosexual males, the available data suggest, spend most of their free time—that is, time away from family, work, and/or school—socializing with homosexual friends. Because a large majority continue to live with their families, however, social activity is limited by family functions and parental rules and regulations. For example, a common regulation is that he must return home to sleep each night, generally by a specific hour, or face the anger or scolding of parents. This may even include those males in their late twenties and thirties. It is still not unusual in Guadalajara, for instance, for one of two male lovers sharing an apartment to have to spend (or want to spend) part of his time living with his family.

Most of the above limitations continue to apply to individuals even though their homosexual behavior may have been revealed to all members of the family. As previously noted, a major coping strategy for both sides is to act as though the behavior is not taking place; in other words, there is a "conspiracy of silence" or "counterfeit secrecy." Homosexually involved individuals thus continue to act in such a way that they do not expose themselves to unknowing relatives, neighbors, or friends. They may maintain the fiction, for example, that some day they will marry and have children; and social occasions at the house may be organized as though their interests were heterosexual.

A Limited Gay Subculture

The gay liberation movement has brought about some important changes in Guadalajara during the twelve years since it began in the summer of 1981. Although the outcome has been uneven, GOHL has generally been able to reduce or at least control police harassment of homosexual people and institutions. In doing so, it has educated the press about the different types of police harassment and gay rights; and as a result it can now present a gay point of view to the public on television and in newspapers in ways not possible in the past.

Another major achievement of GOHL is its attempt, through education and condom distribution, to modify the behavior of significant numbers of men who have sex with men in the city toward safer anal sex practices, thus helping to prevent the spread of HIV. Its work on HIV prevention has also benefited similar programs, like Project Azomali, aimed at the heterosexual population in Guadalajara.

Still another achievement of GOHL is the sense of pride and belonging it has given many young homosexual men in Guadalajara who can now identify themselves as being gay. When funds are once again available, GOHL hopes to reestablish a "Gay Community Support Center." It is interesting to note that in a study of gay liberation groups in Mexico, Lumsden (1991) concluded that

> although the Guadalajara gay movement has had its share of personal and factional disputes, it has nevertheless developed the most effective gay organization in the country. The explanation can be attributed in great measure to the outstanding political skills of its leader, Pedro Preciado, who early on made a conscious decision to eschew abstract rhetorical denunciations of gay oppression. (p. 81)

Lumsden also notes that the lesbian counterpart to GOHL in Guadalajara, Grupo Lesbico Patlatonalli, is also "recognized to be the most effective lesbian organization in Mexico" (p. 81).

Finally, the gay liberation movements in Guadalajara and other parts of Mexico have created through a combined effort a gay rights lobby that can exert pressure on the Mexican government on issues of great concern to homosexual people in Mexico, such as providing good medical care for people with AIDS. Nongovernmental organizations (NGOs) dealing with AIDS care and prevention have received their greatest impetus from the leaders of gay liberation organizations.

However, insofar as I can determine, the gay liberation movement in Guadalajara has not brought about any significant changes in the size of the gay subculture. Guadalajara's gay scene has been enriched by gay liberation with annual gay pride weeks and festivities from time to time; by the increased availability of gay magazines (with nude male photographs), novels (like Zapata's hot and brilliant stories with realistic homosexual male protagonists), and newspapers published in Mexico City (*Del Otro Lado*) and Tijuana (*Frontera Gay*); and by networks of gay people in the city that can help homosexual individuals in need of social and psychological support.

Yet judging from the number of existing gay institutions in Guadalajara, the gay subculture is still quite small. There are only a few gay establishments and no exclusively gay bathhouses. Gay neighborhoods do not exist. And GOHL's informative news magazines (*Crisálida* and *Las Maracas*) and radio magazine (*Ruta 41*), the latter formerly broadcast on the University of Guadalajara's radio network, all folded some years ago; and their more recent and ambitious "Gay Cultural Information Bulletin for Latin America" (*Boletín Informativo para America Latina: Organo de Información y Cultura Gay*), which was produced by GOHL member Jorge Romero and partially subsidized by the International Gay and Lesbian Association, had to be discontinued for lack of funds.

Gay Liberation and Sexual Behavior

An interesting question is: what kind of impact has gay liberation had on the homosexual behaviors of men who have sex with men in Guadalajara and in the other areas I have studied in northwestern Mexico? If one considers the subpopulation of these men as a whole, I think the answer is that gay liberation has affected the homosexual behaviors of only a small part of it, mostly those males who identify themselves as being gay and see the world as polarized between being gay or *buga,* the *buga* world being composed of nongay people who hold traditional, stereotypical, views of Mexican male homosexuality (see Taylor 1978b, for an excellent description of how the *buga* world is viewed by Mexican gay men).

One *buga* stereotype of Mexican male homosexual behavior rejected by many gay-identified men is that the subpopulation of men who have sex with men can be easily divided into *activos* and *pasivos.* They believe this to be untrue and have thus created their own label for those men with no clear homosexual role preference: *internacional,* "imputing both variety and foreignness" (Taylor 1978b, 112). In some sense, then, it has become "politically correct" for Mexican gay men to move away from being a *"puro pasivo"* or *"puro activo"* (that is, only anal receptive or anal insertive) and to be more like their gay male counterparts in the United States who, according to common knowledge in the Mexican gay world, are not into role playing. Two of the things that always astounded my Mexican homosexual male informants when they went to California in the late 1970s and early 1980s and sampled the gay worlds of San Francisco and Los Angeles were that so many *norteamericanos* were interested only in oral sex, and that those also interested in anal sex were usually willing to be either top or bottom.

One may thus conclude that, as a result of political correctness, many gay-identified Mexican men who had a sexual role preference changed their sexual practices over time to include being both anal insertive and anal receptive. If this is true, one should expect to find an increase in the number of *internacionales,* but this increase would probably be limited mostly to that small segment of the subpopulation that identify themselves as gay.

Unfortunately, because a survey based on a random sample of the subpopulation has never been carried out with respect to its distribution by sexual orientation/identity (i.e., gay, homosexual, bisexual, or heterosexual) or its distribution by sexual role preference (*activo, pasivo* or *internacional*), there is no baseline data from which we can estimate the amount of change in any one group. Therefore, as elaborated further in my appendix on small-scale interview surveys, based on the judgment samples available at present (i.e., nonrandom samples selected on the basis of the researcher's knowledge of the population being studied), one can make only an educated guess about the percentage of homosexually behaving men who identify themselves as being gay, or the percentage of gay-identified men who by preference or practice are *internacional*.

Based on my study findings to date, *my best guess* is that the homosexual behaviors of a majority of the subpopulation of Mexican men who have sex with men—living in the geographical areas I have studied—have probably not been affected very much by the gay liberation movement. That is, a large majority of them still prefer and practice anal sex; and many (a large majority?) continue to have a preference for playing one sexual role over the other. The tripartite division of the subpopulation by sexual role preference or by practices into *activo*, *pasivo*, and *internacional* thus remains valid.

I am willing to concede, however, that as a result of gay liberation the total number of *internacionales* has increased, but neither I nor anyone else can do more than guess as to what percent they are of the total now or, for that matter, how large a group they were prior to gay liberation. At the end of my original study in 1971, I knew that Mexican men involved in homosexual encounters could be sorted into three sexual role preference groups. I also knew that many *activos* and *pasivos* changed their sexual repertoires during their lifetime—and the direction was most always toward playing both sexual roles. Since none of my informants back then knew of any term for the group, I used *ambos* (meaning both) as a label. I learned about the *internacional* term from "Arturo" and Clark Taylor in the late 1970s.

A relatively current view of the patterns of sexual practices in Mexico City, drawn from interviews with a nonprobability sample of "2,314 homosexual and bisexual men tested at the AIDS National Center" located on Flora Street, is given by Hernandez and his colleagues (1992):

> Our analyses have provided only limited confirmation of a pattern of behavior long described as existing in Mexico: that of homosexual males taking the "passive" role in anal sexual practices. . . . The data from Flora Street indicate that homosexual males practice solely receptive behavior more frequently than bisexual males, but that these individuals constitute a minority of the homosexual and bisexual males tested. The much more common pattern was that of "mixed" behavior, particularly among the homosexual males.

These findings are consistent with data collected in six Mexican cities (including Mexico City), which also indicated the less common nature of exclusively receptive or exclusively insertive behavior.   (page 892)

[*Note:* Both the Flora Street study, done in 1988–89, and the study done in 1988 for six Mexican cities are discussed in the appendix, which describes the small-scale interview surveys.]

The findings from the Flora Street study present another interesting view of a *segment* of the Mexican population of men who have sex with men. Given the highly selective nature of their sample, however, one cannot generalize from their data any more than I can generalize from my data onto the whole subpopulation of homosexually behaving men in Mexico. Thus, in the excerpt quoted above they should not have implied that their data could be used to say anything definitive about the distribution of the subpopulation by sexual role preference or practices.

Still another view of Mexican patterns of sexual practices—but in rural communities in northern Mexico—is described by Alonso and Koreck (1989). They note that their preliminary investigation in rural areas has led them "to concur with the results of Carrier's long-term research on sexuality in urban areas" (p. 113). They found that anal intercourse is the preferred sexual technique of men who have sex with men, and that in terms of sexual role preference they can be sorted into *machos* or *jotos:* "Though fellatio is often part of foreplay, in *macho-joto* sexual contact, anal intercourse is considered the culminating act. . . . The privileging of anal intercourse in *macho-joto* sex is partly motivated by an analogy between this type of erotic contact and relationship, and that which occurs between machos and women" (p. 109).

It is of special interest to note, however, that Alonso and Koreck did not find any evidence of there being a group of men who were playing both sexual roles in their homosexual relationships or that gay liberation had had any effect on male homosexual behaviors. They conclude that in the areas where they carried out their preliminary study, "where the population is largely composed of agriculturalists and rural workers, there were no 'internationals' " (p. 114). I suspect there are some homosexually behaving rural men in the areas they studied that had played both sexual roles in anal intercourse, but these men were just not prepared to admit it or to be interviewed. I also suspect they are few in number in rural Mexico. As was the case for my early study findings in Guadalajara before gay liberation, at present there is no native label for this category of rural men.

Homosexual Role Preference and AIDS

If we did not have an AIDS epidemic, questions concerning the tripartite distribution of Mexican men who have sex with men by their sexual role preference in anal intercourse would be only of academic interest. Three Greek epidemiologists (Trichopoulos, Sparos, and Petridou 1988), however, recently pointed out "the potential importance of role separation (active vs. passive) among male homosexuals as a population variable in models of the AIDS epidemic" (p. 965). They conjecture that since "receptive anal intercourse is by far the most important risk factor for HIV seroconversion" and "insertive anal intercourse may be no more conducive to HIV seroconversion than insertive vaginal intercourse," then

> if all male homosexuals were either active or passive, but never both the proportion of male homosexuals would not be critical to understanding the past or predicting the future spread of AIDS. Those practicing insertive anal intercourse would not be at increased risk because of the inherently low risk of their practice; those practicing receptive anal intercourse would not be at very high risk because of the low prevalence of HIV among their sexual partners, and they would not transmit the infection further.   (pp. 965–66)

They go on to note that although this polarity may not be completely realistic, "countries in south-eastern Europe, the Middle East, and, possibly, other parts of the world may provide various degrees of approximation to it." They further conclude that "the slower spread of AIDS in the eastern Mediterranean and Middle East may be accounted for not only by differences in classical AIDS variables such as promiscuity and intravenous drug abuse, but also by a more clear homosexual role separation" (p. 966).

Taking the Greek epidemiologists' theory a step further, two American social scientists (Wiley and Herschkorn 1989) explore the implications of homosexual role separation and AIDS epidemics with elementary mathematical models. They keep their models relatively simple by assuming that "the population in question is closed to births, deaths, and migrations, that the incubation period for AIDS has effectively an exponential distribution . . . , that the variation in rates of sexual activity across individuals is minimal, and that the probability of infection from the receptive to the insertive partner in unprotected anal intercourse is nil" (p. 435). They note that with perhaps the exception of the last one, "relaxation of these assumptions would not alter the qualitative implications of the models developed" (p. 435).

Wiley and Herschkorn conclude that given their assumptions, "as expected, role differentiation in anal intercourse and mixing preferences affect the course of an AIDS epidemic in crucial ways: if HIV can be transmitted sexually only from an infected insertive partner to a receptive partner in unprotected anal intercourse, an epidemic will be of smaller size in a population with a correspondingly smaller segment which takes both roles. In fact, with a small enough size dual-role subpopulation, an epidemic may not occur at all" (p. 447).

They also conclude that their "simple models imply that role separation with respect to sexual behavior should be considered carefully in the construction of models of HIV epidemics among homosexual men. This point is especially relevant when such models are applied to populations where ethnographic accounts indicate a rigid stratification according to roles in anal intercourse; it is also important where there is evidence of a trend from role separation toward more catholic preferences in sexual activity" (p. 448).

Three Dutch medical statisticians (Van Druten, Van Griensven, and Hendriks 1992) recently tested a "role separation mixing model" with data from an Amsterdam cohort study. The model "provides a framework to test the conjecture of Trichopoulos et al. (1988) and validate the theoretical results of Wiley and Herschkorn (1989)." It investigates the spread of HIV within and between four subgroups. The composition of the subgroups is "based on the preference for: (1) no anal intercourse; (2) anal insertive only; (3) anal receptive only; (4) both insertive and receptive." The model is based on the assumption that HIV is acquired through anal-receptive intercourse only—so subgroup 2 may pass the infection to members of subgroups 3 and 4, subgroup 4 to subgroup 3, and members of subgroup 4 may transmit it to each other.

They point out that an analysis of the Amsterdam HIV prevalence data ($N = 723$ homosexual men), linked to the role separation mixing model,

> shows that the spread of HIV is not only influenced by differences in rate of partner change, but also by role separation. The results indicate that there is a substantial difference in the risks attached to insertive and receptive anal intercourse. The most riskful practice is receptive

intercourse with an infected partner. The probability of HIV transmission from an infected insertive partner to a receptive susceptible is estimated between 1 and 5 percent (under the assumption of a closed cohort).

The difference in risk of insertive versus receptive intercourse is partly a finding and partly an assumption-driven conclusion. The part that is a finding is that more persons became infected in the subgroups 3 and 4 [receptive only and both receptive and insertive] than can be explained by change in sexual role behavior and loss to follow up.

(p. 494)

They conclude that their analysis, which is based on data, "clearly indicates that homosexual role separation could be an important factor in the spread of HIV" (p. 495). In discussing sexual mixing models, they also remind their readers that sexual mixing "is not random; it is graded by personal characteristics like age, lifestyle and the participation in sexual subcultures. And, the pool of possible sexual partners that an individual has access to is connected to both the individual lifecourse and the social and (sub)cultural environment." And that "in order to stimulate further research in this direction we need to know the sexual preferences of both the individual and the partner and preferably the reasons governing why sexual preferences change. Until now, reliable data on these aspects of sexual partnerships are lacking" (p. 497).

Bisexually Behaving Mexican Men

Of all the Mexican men who have sex with men, those we know and understand the least about are those men who from puberty to marriage have a significant number of sexual encounters with men as well as women. Over the years of my fieldwork, I have had the greatest difficulty getting access to and communicating with bisexually behaving men and learning about the things that motivate them to have male as well as female sex partners. Although, as previously explained, a certain acceptance of their homosexual encounters exists as long as they play the macho *activo* sexual role, most of the bisexually behaving men who have become informants have nevertheless been reluctant to let me know in detail what goes on in their lives. I should also point out that, so far as I know, no one has made a detailed study of Mexican male bisexuality anywhere in Mexico. Epidemiological surveys have confirmed my finding that many homosexually behaving Mexican men have had sexual intercourse with women, but the men interviewed in these surveys were not asked about the social and psychological circumstances of their bisexual behaviors.

One thing made clear by my study of these men over the past twenty-five years is that they should be conceptualized in terms of their bisexual behaviors and not be labeled simply as "bisexuals." Using bisexual as a noun to describe this segment of the subpopulation of men who have sex with men obscures the diversity of their lifestyles, motivations, and sexual behaviors. And judging from my data, not many of them identify themselves as "bisexual" anyway.

In my judgment, at any given point in time the largest portion of the bisexually behaving subset of Mexican men who have sex with men—in my area of study in Mexico—are probably single men at the peak of their sexual needs (thus aged from, say, puberty to late twenties) who identify themselves as being heterosexual. Their homosexual partners are usually relatives, neighbors, classmates, or workmates of the same age or much younger. Although some may play the *pasivo* sexual role and some may play both sexual roles with their homosexual partners, my data suggest that the majority prefer and play only the *activo* sexual role in their homosexual relationships. As previously discussed, most of these Mexican males target effeminate males as sexual partners in place of females who for a variety of reasons may be unattainable. They may talk to close friends about these relationships but are usually careful not to let anyone else know about them with certainty. Money is not the primary motive for these homosexual relationships.

Another significant portion of this bisexually behaving subset, but I think a minority of the total, is made up of young men who primarily have sex with men as their major source of income or to supplement their income. The former, who usually come from extremely poor families, are called *chichifo*. The latter, who come from lower-middle-class as well as lower-class families, are called *mayates*. Their clients generally come from middle- and upper-class families and run the gamut of sexual identities from gay to heterosexual. According to my male prostitute informants in Guadalajara, most of their clients are heterosexual married men, old rich "queens," or American tourists. Gomezjara, Barrera, and Perez (1978) present some additional interesting information about this subset of bisexually behaving men in their study of the sociology of prostitution in Mexico (pp. 80–104).

Two commonalities of the *mayates* and *chichifos* discussed thus far are their macho behavior and the preference for playing the *activo* sexual role. The major difference between the two groups of men is related to their motivations for having homosexual encounters—one group looking at their male sexual partners primarily as *free* female substitutes while they are single; the other, who may be single or married, as a means of making a living or supplementing family income. In my mini study of one neighborhood, I found that, because of changing financial needs, some men who start out having homosexual encounters just to satisfy their sexual needs start using them occasionally to make money as well. They were always apprehensive, however, about being called a *chichifo* (which may also connote they steal or extort money from their clients). They were embarrassed by anyone thinking they were really male hustlers. It was okay to joke with friends about who bought them the new expensive tennis shoes, but it was not okay for the friends in a serious manner to call them *chichifo*.

Time deals with the two groups of bisexually behaving men differently. When the single men marry, many no longer have need for female substitutes and so may discontinue their sexual encounters with men. As they age, whether single or married, the men motivated by money to have homosexual encounters find it increasingly difficult—as do all sex workers—to find customers. Another factor enters the picture over time: *sexual pleasure*. Whatever their original motivation(s) for having homosexual encounters, whether single or married, some bisexually behaving men find that as time passes they do in fact enjoy having sex with men as well as women. These men may thus continue their homosexual relationships for many years and change their lifestyles to make them more congruent with their acceptance of bisexuality. They may also change their sexual identities from heterosexual to bisexual and thus become part of what I conceptualize as still another group in the subset of men being discussed.

A third group of bisexually behaving men, probably a small minority of the subset, is composed mostly of men who early in their sex lives realize that their interest in homosexual encounters is more intense than that of their similarly involved male friends. They are as masculine as their male friends and start out playing only the *activo* sexual role, but they know they are different. Some develop romantic relationships, like the ones José had with his barrio boyfriends; but they nevertheless continue to think of themselves as being heterosexual, court women, and eventually get married. Yet even after marriage their homosexual encounters may continue for years. Others may develop romantic relationships with women and have sex with them, but never marry. Instead, they follow a path to heavier involvement in the homosexual world and, although their heterosexual encounters may continue, they see themselves as having either a bisexual or homosexual orientation. Over time, the true test of their sexual orientation in their own eyes may turn out to be the male-female ratio of their sexual partners. (It should be noted that I am not including in the subset under discussion those homosexually oriented males who have had only a few sexual contacts with females, usually in early adolescence.)

Future Work

My fieldwork in Guadalajara is ongoing. I am still in touch with José, Pedro, and Federico, and I maintain contact with Arturo's family through his sister Lucia. With Alberto's help I am also continuing my mini barrio study in Guadalajara. At present, I am focusing my research on the sex lives and motivations of three young male informants I met during the outset of my study in the barrio ten years ago when they were just fifteen years old. Playing the *pasivo* role, Alberto had homosexual encounters with all three until a few years ago. Now, at twenty-five, two are married and have children, the other has a *novia* and is contemplating marriage. In a recent letter describing what was going on in the barrio, Alberto wrote that he is sure all three are still having homosexual relationships—but less frequently, doing less talking and joking about it, and with younger men. Alberto also indirectly pointed out an important fact about homosexual male behavior in his barrio: as is the case with female prostitutes, one *pasivo* homosexual male can service a large number of *activo* bisexual males. He gave me a count of the number of young men he was having sex with in the barrio and then wrote that like a woman he could have multiple sexual encounters with many different *activo* men in a relatively short period of time.

Given the importance of male bisexuality as a possible route of HIV infection to female populations, I plan to continue my study of bisexually behaving men in Mexico. My three barrio informants let me know what is going on in their sexual lives and provide additional insights as to what motivates them to continue their bisexual behaviors and how they are able to cope with their bisexuality. Meanwhile, my *pasivo* homosexual informants like Alberto will continue to provide me a window through which I can catch glimpses of their bisexual male partners.

Another area of research I am pursuing at present is a study of the important role the family plays in the structure of Mexican homosexuality. Findings from my years of research in northwestern Mexico have made it clear that lifestyles followed by homosexually behaving Mexican men reflect their continuing close relationships with family members. The profiles of Arturo, José, Federico, and Pedro provide excellent illustrations of the powerful role the family plays in the organization of their social activities during the formative years of their lives. Little is known, however, about the different ways in which family members view and deal with their knowledge of these activities. The interview with Pedro's mother provides some important insights as to how a Mexican mother deals with her son's homosexuality. We need to know more about these significant others in the lives of homosexual men. They can help us better understand the role they play in the lives of their sons, brothers, and husbands who seek other men as sexual partners.

Afterword

Most of my Mexican friends had high hopes for an improved economic future after the trade agreement became effective January 1, 1994. By the end of the year, however, their financial situation had grown worse because of a major devaluation of the Mexican peso in late December 1994. During the spring of 1995 the peso's value declined further. And rising interest rates and double-digit inflation reduced their buying power as well.

The unstable political situation in Mexico in 1994 and early 1995 also caused concern. Then the unthinkable happened in the middle of February 1995: the ultraconservative National Action Party (PAN) won the governorship of the State of Jalisco and the office of mayor in Guadalajara. Expectations were that all gay bars would be closed and harassment of gay people by police would resume. The story, however, may have a happy ending. Unexpectedly, in mid April Pedro Preciado was able to meet separately with both the new governor and the mayor (the latter for over an hour), and he reports that both appear to be interested in working out a political accommodation with the gay community in Guadalajara.

Appendix: Small-Scale

Interview Surveys

First Small-Scale Survey: 1970–71

As the yearlong participant-observer phase of my initial field research neared completion in the fall of 1970, I prepared a set of questions for a small-scale interview survey to elicit information about the
sex lives of a select group of informants and the sociocultural settings
in which they occur. My observational data had led me to generate a
number of hypotheses that could be best tested by a more structured
examination of the sex lives and sociocultural settings of the different
types of Mexican males identified as having ongoing sexual encounters
with other men. Field research data indicated, for example, that Mexican males involved in homosexual encounters could be sorted into at
least three different classes of actors differentiated by their sexual practices—*activo, pasivo,* and *internacional* (both active and passive)—and
that the kind of lives they led, choices they made, and relationships
they had with their family, friends, and workmates were influenced in
important ways by both their gender identity and sex role played.

From the fall of 1970 to the spring of 1971, I interviewed face-to-
face a judgment sample (i.e., a nonrandom sample of men based on my
field research knowledge) of fifty-three respondents in Guadalajara. I
had become acquainted with most of them through social intermediaries
and contacts developed during the nine months of fieldwork that pre-

ceded the interview time period. As previously noted, I socialized with ten friendship circles and ten additional individuals, spending varying amounts of time with any one group or individual. These people formed the central pool from which I selected the respondents for interview. As the interviews progressed, respondents outside this pool were also selected.

At the end of the interview period in March 1971, the final list of prospective respondents numbered seventy. Of this total, fifty-three completed interviews; seven agreed to be interviewed but did not keep appointments (after three no-shows the prospective interviewee was dropped); and ten declined to be interviewed. Of those completing interviews, thirty-five belonged to one of the ten friendship circles studied; five were individually known prior to the interview; and thirteen were either slightly known or not known prior to the interview. I attempted to develop equal samples of each of the three groups identified by sexual practice: *activo, pasivo,* and *internacional.*

The respondents were interviewed in Spanish in my apartment. They were assured easy and private access since the apartment house was located near the center of Guadalajara and had commercial establishments on the ground floor. It took from three to five hours on the average to complete the structured interview. All but six completed the questionnaire in one session. Once started, none refused to complete his interview. Four, however, showed signs of extreme nervousness and resisted answering questions relating to their own homosexual practices. Their interviews are considered incomplete but usable in that sufficient information was obtained from the questions answered and from some of their sexual partners known by the author. It is important to note that additional information on all the respondents, differing in amount and quality, was obtained from their friends and/or sex partners during my one and a half years of fieldwork.

The questionnaire was divided into seven parts: vital statistics, relations with family and friends, physical characteristics, history of early sexual experiences, history of homosexual experiences, history of heterosexual experiences, and beliefs about societal attitudes toward homosexuality. Each part contained a mix of "forced-choice" (multiple choice) and "open-ended" questions. The part dealing with family also had the respondents rate their mother, father, and self on a "semantic differential" scale of thirteen bipolar adjectives—such as adequate-inadequate, strong-weak, dominant-submissive, and active-passive—according to their experiences remembered up to the age of seventeen.

The thirteen bipolar adjectives, as well as several additional questions used in other parts of the questionnaire, were supplied by the Institute for Sex Research at Indiana University.

Two Additional Small-Scale Surveys: 1986–87 and 1988

In more recent years I also directed two additional small-scale surveys in Guadalajara that gathered some information about male homosexual behaviors. The purpose of the surveys was to learn about the effects of the AIDS epidemic on the attitudes and homosexual behaviors of a judgment sample of 230 men living in Guadalajara in 1986–87 and 1988. The surveys were done in collaboration with the AIDS education staff of Guadalajara's gay liberation group (GOHL) and the staff of a citywide AIDS education program, Project Azomali. José Jimenez, who later died of AIDS, was in charge of the interview team in Guadalajara (made up of José Moreno, Cesar Cuevas, and Jesus Martinez) and conducted a majority of the interviews. During the time of the interviews, ongoing AIDS education programs were being conducted by both groups.

The first survey was conducted in two different time periods, late summer 1986 and spring 1987, with a very brief questionnaire administered face-to-face to 103 Mexican male participants in homosexual encounters. The second survey was conducted in the late summer and fall of 1988 with a revised and enlarged questionnaire administered face-to-face to another 127 male participants in homosexual encounters. The respondents were young Mexican men who frequented gay establishments or cruising areas in Guadalajara. They were mainly recruited in a gay youth center run by GOHL, two gay discos (Boops and SOS), and a downtown park (Parque de la Revolución). Although an attempt was made to develop equal samples of men by three sexual preference groups—*activo, pasivo,* and *internacional*—only a small number of the *activos* identified agreed to be interviewed.

Epidemiological Surveys: Homosexual Behaviors and HIV Status

Several epidemiological surveys of the homosexual behaviors and HIV status of Mexican men were conducted in the mid and late 1980s by Mexican social scientists and epidemiologists in both the public and private sectors. Although the primary purpose of these surveys was to learn about the relationship between types of homosexual practices and HIV infection, they provide some additional information on male homosexual behaviors not only in Guadalajara but also in other large Mexican cities. Though limited in scope, they are the first surveys dealing with Mexican homosexual behaviors that were staffed and directed by Mexican scientists.

One of the first of these epidemiological surveys was made in Guadalajara from the fall of 1984 to the fall of 1990 with the assistance of GOHL and directed by Eduardo Vázquez-Valls and his colleagues. Over the seven years of the survey, a judgment sample of 1,776 homosexually behaving men—gathered by the snowball technique—had a blood sample taken and responded in a face-to-face interview by staff members to a very brief questionnaire that elicited information about their vital statistics and sexual behaviors over the previous six months.

Another epidemiological survey of special interest was made in 1988 in six Mexican cities (Guadalajara, Mexico City, Mérida, Acapulco, Tijuana, and Monterrey) by staff members of the Mexican Ministry of Health and directed by José Izazola-Licea. A judgment sample of 658 men engaging in homosexual practices in the cities studied—recruited in gay bars, discos, and public parks, and through gay organizations—had a blood sample taken and responded in a face-to-face interview by staff members to a questionnaire that elicited information about their vital statistics, sexually transmitted diseases, and cruising and sexual behaviors over the previous four months.

Still another epidemiological survey of interest took place at the AIDS National Center in Mexico City where vital statistics, limited sex-life histories, and information about sexually transmitted diseases were elicited from 2,314 "homosexual and bisexual males" by survey staff members in face-to-face structured interviews. The men had come to be tested for HIV antibodies at the center during the period from January 1988 to June 1989.

Interview Survey Findings

The field research strategy of using both participant observation and a small-scale interview survey to map out Mexican male homosexual behaviors and their sociocultural setting in Guadalajara turned out to be an exceptionally useful one. I learned things about Mexican male homosexuality in the participant-observer phase of my field research that I would never have learned from the survey alone; and I learned things from the survey that would not have been apparent just from participant observation. These should be viewed, therefore, as useful and complementary methods. When studying the sexual behaviors of a population about which almost nothing is known, however, my years of study illustrate once again the usefulness of making participant observations prior to conducting an interview survey.

The following presentation of findings from the 1970–71 interview survey briefly summarize the important new information I learned from my respondents about Mexican male homosexuality. Relevant findings from the other interview surveys will also be presented and compared with the 1970–71 survey findings.

Homosexual Role Preference and Practices

The fifty-three sex-life histories I took as part of my 1970–71 survey support the notions developed from the participant-observation data that the sexual connection in most Mexican male homosexual encounters is anal; and that, on the basis of both sexual role preference *and* sexual practices over time, Mexican men who have sex with men can be sorted into three groups: anal insertive (*activo*), anal receptive (*pasivo*), and anal insertive and receptive (*internacional*). Although the sex-life histories of some respondents revealed changing sexual role preferences and practices over time—from anal insertive to anal receptive, for example, or vice versa—the sex-life histories of self-identified *activo* and *pasivo* respondents showed a remarkable stability in preference and sexual practices over time. And many respondents with historical changes in preference and sexual practices conceptualized themselves at one time or another as being *activo* or *pasivo* and then later expanded their sexual repertoires to include both sexual roles.

Findings from the two brief interview surveys in Guadalajara in 1986–87 and 1988 ($N = 230$) and the three epidemiological surveys in the mid and late 1980s ($N = 4,748$) provide additional confirmation of the high prevalence of anal sex in male homosexual encounters in Mexico, even in the time of AIDS. As was the case in my 1970–71 interview survey, only a small percentage of homosexually behaving Mexican men were identified in the surveys (less than 10 percent of the respondents) as practicing "no or almost no anal sex."

Findings from the three 1980s surveys conducted in Guadalajara (the two brief surveys and Vázquez-Valls's epidemiological survey) also confirm the existence of homosexually behaving Mexican men who have definite sexual role preferences. Respondents in the other two epidemiological surveys—the six cities survey and the Mexico City AIDS center survey—were not asked if they had a sexual role preference, so at best one can only infer something about the likelihood of their having sexual role preferences based on the limited historical information available on their sex practices. If we set aside the respondents reported as having no or almost no anal sex and just look at the sexual practices of those respondents who did have anal sex, then one can reasonably infer, I believe, that there is a strong likelihood that most of the respondents did have sexual role preferences and thus these two surveys do in fact provide additional confirmation of the notion that the subpopulation of Mexican men who have sex with men can be meaningfully divided into the culturally defined categories of *activo*, *pasivo*, and *internacional*. The six Mexican cities survey data show, for example, that of the respondents having anal sex ($N = 499$), the sexual practices of 40 percent ($N = 200$) were "mostly or only receptive"; 37 percent ($N = 283$) were "mostly or only insertive"; and 23 percent ($N = 116$) were "mixed," that is, they were "both anal insertive and receptive during half or more of the sexual encounters" (Izazola-Licea et al. 1991, 616–17). The Mexico City National AIDS Center survey data show that of the respondents having anal sex ($N = 2140$), the sexual practices of 20 percent ($N = 422$) were "mostly receptive or receptive only"; 36 percent ($N = 763$) were "insertive only or mainly insertive"; and 44 percent ($N = 955$) were "both insertive and receptive," that is, the "subject practiced both insertive and receptive behavior during half or more of sexual encounters."

It is important to note here that since *all* the surveys described above used judgmental nonprobability samples, their findings can be used only to establish the existence of different types of homosexual behaviors—like sexual role preference categories—and to make "guesstimates" about their possible distribution in a given subpopulation of Mexican men who have sex with men. They *cannot* be used to make statistical estimates of the percentage distribution of homosexually behaving Mexican men by the sexual role preference categories identified. The subpopulation of Mexican men who have sex with men would have to be framed, randomly sampled, and questioned in detail about their past homosexual behaviors in order to make statistically sound estimates of the distribution of behavioral phenomena. To my knowledge no one has made that kind of survey of sexual behavior in Mexico.

Setting aside the question of how the subpopulation of Mexican men who have sex with men may be distributed by anal sexual role played or preferred, the question still remains as to the best criterion to use to assign respondents to a particular sexual role group with whatever information is available on their homosexual behaviors. Should it be based on a majority of the sexual behaviors revealed in their sex-life histories, on the sexual behaviors recalled for a recent time period (three months? a year?), or just on the respondent's sexual role preference at the time of the interview?

One useful method I devised for the comparative analysis of my interview survey data was to group respondents according to the major kind of sex practiced during the *first sustained year* of postpubertal homosexual experiences. This grouping criterion has the important advantage of normalizing postpubertal homosexual experiences to the time frame of the first sustained year and thus allows inter- and intra-group comparisons of respondents based on an important part of their sexual life. To a large extent it removes the effect of differences in sexual experiences between respondents which may be due in part to age differences at the time of the interview. It also proved to be of value in predicting future homosexual activities of respondents, e.g., anal sex role preferred and played.

For any given respondent, the beginning of the first sustained year of postpubertal homosexual experiences may or may not have occurred at the same age as first homosexual contact. First homosexual contact is *not* used as the benchmark for the first sustained year since it may just be a one-time experience with no further, or only a few, sexual experiences for months or years. The basic criterion for determining the first sustained year is repeated homosexual experiences over a twelve-month time period after puberty. My 1970–71 survey respondents will be grouped by this criterion in many of the discussions that follow.

Differences Related to Sexual Role Played

Another important finding of the 1970–71 interview survey is that significant differences appear to exist between respondents according to sexual role played. Some of the important variables on which they differ are gender identity, prepubertal homosexual contacts with older males, family knowledge of homosexual behavior, postpubertal heterosexual contacts and feelings, and plans for marriage.

The grouping of respondents by sexual role played during the first sustained year of postpubertal homosexual experiences is as follows: twenty may be classified as predominantly playing the insertive sexual role; twenty-two as predominantly playing the receptive sexual role; and eleven as playing both the insertive and receptive sexual roles with about equal frequency. In terms of the kind of sex practiced, a little over 90 percent of the respondents (forty-eight of fifty-three) preferred anal over oral contacts. Seventeen respondents may be categorized as anal insertive (*activo*); twenty-two as anal receptive (*pasivo*); and nine as both anal insertive and receptive (*internacional*). Of the remaining five respondents, three may be categorized as oral insertive; one as both oral insertive and receptive; and one as mutual masturbator.

Sex-Typed Interests

One of the most significant differences between sexual role preference groups is related to sex-typed interests of the respondents. Those respondents who played the anal-receptive sexual role a majority of the time, or exclusively, during their first year of sustained homosexual experiences score on the feminine side of a number of factors which can be rated in terms of masculinity and femininity; whereas those who played the anal-insertive sexual role a majority of the time, or exclusively, score on the masculine side. Those respondents who played both sexual roles appear to score more in the masculine direction than the feminine but not as strongly as the insertive-only respondents.

Table 2 compares some sex-typed interests of respondents. It shows that, as compared to the *activo* group, more of the *pasivo* group respond in the feminine direction with regard to experienced "desire to be female," amount of doll play as a child, experimentation with wearing female clothes, and interest in sports. More *pasivo* than *activo* males also remember themselves as being slightly or very effeminate as a child and at puberty. Or to put it the other way, more *activo* than *pasivo* males remember themselves as being very masculine as a child (see table 3) and at puberty.

The semantic differential further supports the association of effeminacy with the *pasivo* group of respondents and masculinity with the

Table 2

Percentage Comparison of Respondents' Sex-Typed Attributes Compared by Sexual Role Played[a]

	Sexual Role Played		
Attribute	*Activo*	*Pasivo*	Total[b]
Desire to be female			
(at least once)	7	83	43
Played with dolls	40	83	55
SAMPLE NUMBER	(15)	(18)	(40)
Experimented wearing female clothes:			
Many times	0	18	8
Only during fiestas or as joke	35	50	45
SAMPLE NUMBER	(20)	(22)	(53)
Interest in sports:			
Some or much	65	50	61
Little or none	35	50	39
SAMPLE NUMBER	(20)	(22)	(53)

[a] Grouped by first sustained year of homosexual activity following first ejaculation.
[b] Total includes *internacional* respondents, i.e., those who played both insertive and receptive sexual roles.

Table 3

Percentage Comparison of Respondents' Self-Rating of Masculinity as a Child Compared by Sexual Role Played[a]

	Sexual Role Played		
Attribute	*Activo*	*Pasivo*	Total[b]
Very effeminate	5	43	22
Very masculine	53	14	32
SAMPLE NUMBER	(19)	(21)	(50)

[a] Grouped by first sustained year of homosexual activity following first ejaculation.
[b] Total includes *internacional* respondents, i.e., those who played both insertive and receptive sexual roles.

activo group. Figure 3 compares the mean profiles of the two groups of respondents' self-ratings on thirteen seven-step bipolar adjective scales. The self-ratings were based on remembered feelings up to the age of seventeen. A comparison of the two profiles suggests that, compared to the *activo* group, the *pasivo* group of respondents on the average remembered themselves as more feminine, passive, weak, depen-

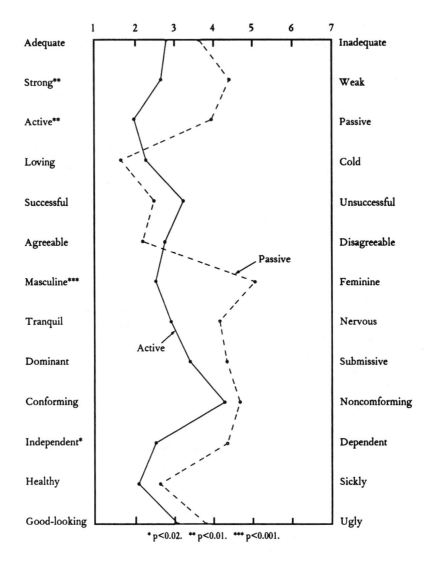

Figure 3.
Mean profiles of semantic differential of active and passive interviewees grouped by sex role played the first sustained year following first ejaculation.
*P<0.02.   **P<0.01.   ***P<0.001.

dent, and nervous. These were the only scales that show statistically significant differences.

Childhood Homosexual Contacts with Postpubertal Males

Another significant difference between the *activo* and *pasivo* groups is related to the percentage of respondents who had homosexual contacts with older postpubertal males before reaching puberty (as marked by their first ejaculation). A greater percentage of *pasivo* than *activo* respondents remember having had homosexual contacts with older postpubertal males (73 percent versus 10 percent). Table 4 shows the differences between groups by age of contact: five to eight and nine to twelve. It is of interest to note that, between the ages of five and eight, close to one-fourth of all the respondents had prepubertal homosexual contacts with postpubertal males.

The majority of the older male sexual contacts were friends and/or neighbors (46 percent), or relatives (36 percent). Only 18 percent were strangers. The homosexual encounters reported were more than a casual one-time sexual experience for most respondents. A majority (twenty-one of twenty-six) had, on different occasions, two or more sexual experiences with their older male partners, and six had sexual experiences with relatives or neighbors over extended periods of time, a few over one or more years. For example, a respondent in the *pasivo* group had weekly sexual encounters with a cousin for close to four years. He was eight and his cousin fifteen at the start of the relationship. Another *pasivo* respondent had weekly sexual encounters with his uncle for two years. He was ten when the relationship started, his uncle

Table 4

Respondents' Adult Homosexual Contacts as a Child by Sexual Role Played[a] (before, first ejaculation)

Contact Age	*Activo*	*Activo/Pasivo*	*Pasivo*	Total
5 to 8	5%	27%	41%	24%
9 to 12	5%	9%	32%	17%
SAMPLE NUMBER	20	11	22	53

[a] Grouped by first sustained year of homosexual activity following first ejaculation. More *pasivo* than *activo* respondents had adult homosexual contacts as a child between ages five to twelve: $\chi^2 = 14.37$ (1 df, P<.001).

eighteen. Still another *pasivo* respondent started a sexual relationship when he was six with an eighteen-year-old male neighbor. Their relationship lasted about two years.

As remembered by the respondents, the ages of the older males at the time of initial contact ranged from twelve to forty-three. The median age of the older males is eighteen. Whether the interviewees' age at the time of contact was in the five to eight range or the nine to twelve range, the median age of the older males was approximately the same. Table 5 shows the relationship and age of the older male contacts by respondents' age at time of contact.

A comparison of self-ratings of childhood masculinity between respondents with and without prepubertal adult homosexual contacts suggests that childhood effeminacy may be one of the factors associated with adult contact. Fifty-seven percent of the respondents with prepubertal adult contacts ($N = 21$), for example, remember themselves as being effeminate as children, whereas only 10 percent of those without prepubertal adult contacts ($N = 29$) remember themselves as being effeminate. Adults seem to identify "effeminacy" in males at a very early age. Green (1974), for example, reports Anglo-American parents being able to "clearly identify cross-gender behavior at the age of 3 years or younger." Moreover, as previously noted, in Mexico the adult population—sensitized by the folk concept of *machismo*—may be particularly alert to effeminate behavior in prepubertal males.

Setting aside the question of their effeminacy as children, of those respondents asked about the kind of sexual technique utilized in their prepubertal homosexual encounters (twenty-two of twenty-six), all but one reported that they played the passive receptive sexual role. One reported that his genitals had merely been fondled. Of the twenty-one who reported that they had played the passive sexual role, a majority claimed they had been anally penetrated by the penis of their older male partner. About one-third claimed their partner had performed sexual intercourse in some way between their thighs.

Although only an approximation of the age of puberty, first ejaculation is used to demarcate prepubertal from postpubertal experiences. None of my respondents said they had any difficulty remembering when they first "came." The ages remembered by respondents for first ejaculation varied between nine and eighteen. The median age of first ejaculation for all respondents was fourteen.

Table 5

Relationship and Age of Respondents' Older Male Homosexual Contacts

Relationship of Older Male[a]	Respondents' Age at Time of Contact										Total
	5 to 8					9 to 12					
Relative[a]	R12	R15	R17	R20	R25	R16	R18	R19			8
Neighbor/Friend	N18	F12	F19	F30	F43	N14	N18	N40	F15	F18	10
Stranger	S18	S25	S35			S30					4
SAMPLE NUMBER	13					9					22
Median Age of older males	19					18					18

[a] C_n = Contact "n" years old. C = (R) relative, (N) neighbor, (F) friend, or (S) stranger.

Family Knowledge About Homosexual Behavior

Another significant intergroup difference between *activos* and *pasivos* is related to family knowledge about their homosexual behaviors. At the time of the interview, respondents' ages ranged from fourteen to forty-seven (median age = twenty-two). Eighty percent (forty-five of fifty-three) were single and still living at home; six were single and living alone; and two were married and living with their wives. A large majority came from large families—three-fourths with six or more family members, over half with eight or more. The median number of siblings for all respondents was five.

Significantly more parents of *activo* than *pasivo* respondents neither knew nor suspected that their sons were homosexually involved: 65 percent versus 26 percent for the mothers, 86 percent versus 53 percent for the fathers. And significantly more siblings of *activo* than *pasivo* respondents did not know about the homosexuality of their brother: 75 percent versus 48 percent. Given the general correlation made by most Mexican people between effeminacy and homosexuality, homosexually involved masculine Mexican males obviously face a different set of family responses than do homosexually involved effeminate males. They are not as easily identified as "homosexual" as are feminine males; and, if they only play the anal-insertive sexual role and are not exclusively involved, they are not stigmatized to the same degree. However, they still do not want their parents or siblings to know about their homosexual behavior. It might be acceptable to talk about their homosexual experiences to friends at school and/or work, but almost never with members of the family. And they may maintain *novia* relationships with neighborhood girls to demonstrate their masculinity.

Masculine males who have extensive homosexual experiences over time are thus much more concerned about being exposed to their family as a "homosexual" than are their effeminate male counterparts. As a consequence, they must spend more time worrying about avoiding situations that might "burn" or "scorch" their reputation. The Mexican males who face the greatest amount of dissonance in their lives, however, are the masculine *internacionales*. They must worry about exposure *and* contend with the role conflict generated by being masculine and playing the female role. The interview survey data suggest that many masculine *internacionales* may start out first playing only the anal-insertive role. As they become more and more involved in homosexual encounters, they experiment with the anal-receptive role and begin incorporating it into their sexual repertoire. As previously noted, an interesting aspect of their behavior may be that they are generally not willing to play the receptive role with a male judged less masculine than themselves.

As a result of negative family attitudes, a majority of the respondents expressed concern over how much their parents and siblings knew about their homosexuality. Close to two-thirds said they definitely did not want their families to know. And even though one parent or sibling might know or suspect, they still felt the need to hide the behavior from the unknowing or unsuspecting family members. In response to the question of how frequently they were concerned about the possibility of being found out by unknowing or unsuspecting family members, a large majority (thirty-four of forty-three) replied that they were concerned at least occasionally; and 42 percent (eighteen of forty-three) said it was something they had experienced anxiety about frequently.

Heterosexual Encounters and Plans to Marry

The final two significant differences between the *activo* and *pasivo* groups to be discussed concern heterosexual encounters and plans to marry. As compared to Anglo men in the United States who have sex with men, a relatively larger percentage of Mexican men who have sex with men have also had sexual intercourse with women. This larger proportion is related in part to the fact that a much larger percentage of males in the *activo* than in the *pasivo* group have had sexual intercourse with women (88 percent versus 32 percent), and in part to the fact that even with the large difference, close to *one-third* of the *pasivo* respondents have had at least one heterosexual contact. In terms of number of heterosexual encounters, 90 percent of those in the *activo* group have had more than one heterosexual contact compared to only 18 percent of those in the *pasivo* group.

Interviewee responses to a set of questions about sexual arousal or repulsion from heterosexual stimuli provide some evidence as to why there are group differences in percentage of males having heterosexual contacts. Table 6 compares responses to heterosexual stimuli with respondents grouped by sexual role played during the first sustained year of homosexual activity. In general, a much larger percentage of respondents in the *activo* group claim that the heterosexual situations

Table 6

Interviewee Response to Heterosexual Stimuli Compared by Sexual Role Played[a]

Stimulus[b]	Activo		Pasivo	
	A	R	A	R
Seeing attractive female in social situation	82%	0	23%	14%
Seeing naked breasts of female in real life	76%	6%	27%	23%
Seeing photographs of nude female	65%	23%	9%	41%
Seeing female genitals in drawings or photos	41%	41%	14%	36%
Thought of having genitals fondled by sexually aroused female	82%	6%	45%	23%
Sample Number	17		22	

[a] Grouped by first sustained year of homosexual activity following first ejaculation.
[b] The respondents were asked whether they would be aroused (A) or repelled (R) by the stimulus. The difference percentagewise between E + R and 100 represents those respondents who were neither aroused nor repelled.

described arouse rather than repel them. For example, 82 percent of these said the thought of being touched on the genitals by a sexually aroused woman excited them whereas only 45 percent of the respondents in the *pasivo* group said they would be excited. Yet even with the large difference, close to *half* of the *pasivo* respondents said they would be excited. Added to other factors, such as family and peer pressure for a male to demonstrate his masculinity by having sex with a woman, this helps explain why so many men even in the *pasivo* group have had heterosexual intercourse.

Respondents' marriage plans also provide some evidence that helps explain group differences in the level of heterosexual encounters of Mexican men who have sex with men. A much larger percentage of the *activo* than *pasivo* respondents (76 percent versus 27 percent) said they planned to marry. All respondents were asked why they planned to marry, why they planned not to marry, or why they did not know one way or the other. Of those responding affirmatively, the most frequently cited reason was fear of loneliness (35 percent of *activo* respondents). Several said they wanted children and a few said they would marry for the sake of appearance, but most were not able to give a specific reason. None of those in doubt was able to give a reason for his position. Of those responding negatively, the most frequently cited reason was that they did not like women sexually or it was not possible sexually (two-thirds of *pasivo* respondents). The rest were unable to cite a specific reason.

Regardless of marriage plans, a large majority of all the respondents had at some level courted women. Between the ages of fourteen and eighteen, 95 percent of the *activo* respondents and 82 percent of the *pasivo* respondents had social relations with at least one girl either as an *amiga* or *novia*. Since the age of eighteen, 85 percent of the *activo* respondents and 47 percent of the *pasivo* respondents have had at least one *amiga* or *novia;* and 65 percent and 29 percent respectively have had more than one.

Relationship Between Sexual and Gender Roles

This appendix shows that significant differences appear to exist between participants in homosexual encounters in regard to several important characteristics when they are grouped according to sexual role played during the first sustained year of homosexual activity. Some of the characteristics in which significant differences appear further suggest that a high correlation exists between sexual role played and gender role. Over time, however, the relationship between sexual role and gender role may or may not be a stable one. A comparison of figures 4 and 5 shows, for example, that over time the sexual preferences and practices of some participants in homosexual encounters remain the same, whereas for others they change.

From the available data a judgment cannot be made about the stability of the relationship between gender and sexual roles over time. In general, however, the participants with the most rigidly developed sex-typed interests in either direction, masculine or feminine, appear least likely to change their sexual preferences and practices (i.e., their sexual role) over time. That is, those participants with strongly developed feminine sex-typed interests continue to maintain those interests and to exclusively, or primarily, play the anal-receptive sexual role, and vice versa. Further, the data on family relationships support this notion in that the more observably effeminate a male, for example, the more likely he is to become accepted by his family over time, and pressures to change his effeminate choices are diminished. For the very masculine male (i.e., the male with strongly developed masculine sex-typed inter-

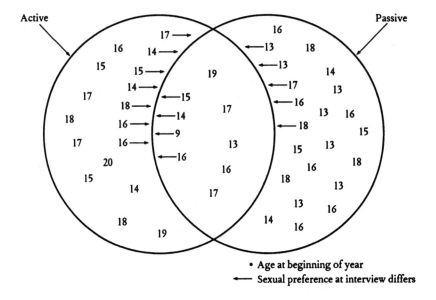

• Age at beginning of year
◄── Sexual preference at interview differs

Figure 4.
Interviewees grouped by major sexual activity during the first sustained year of homosexual encounters.

ests and masculine bearing), the family pressures more likely reinforce his masculine choices. His heterosexual interests may thus be reinforced to the point where marriage plans, for example, are carried out.

More sex-life histories need to be taken on those males who over time play both the anal-insertive and anal-receptive sexual roles. Several different behavior patterns are nevertheless suggested by the available interview survey data. In one pattern, males from an early age appear to have no developed preference, in spite of the cultural pressure to play only the *activo* sexual role or undergo the stigmatization associated with playing the *pasivo* role. In another pattern, males have an early preference and thus for a given time period play only one role. As they expand their sexual experiences over time, however, they also start playing the opposite role. They may thus eventually discover equal enjoyment in playing both sexual roles. In a third pattern, males have an early preference for, and over a given time period play, only one role—usually the anal-insertive role. When they expand their sexual repertoire and start playing the opposite role, however, they often do so (as previously mentioned) in a stylized way: they rank their prospective partners as either more masculine or more feminine than themselves and play the *activo* or *pasivo* role accordingly. They usually do not play both sexual roles with the same partner. Several Mexican respondents who had a considerable number of homosexual encounters with North American Anglo men noted that they do not face the problem of dichotomized sexual roles as do Mexican men. The respondents wished that they had had that advantage.

The changes in sexual role preference and homosexual behaviors that took place between the interview survey respondents' first meaningful sustained year of postpubertal homosexual experiences and the time of interview are shown in the aggregate by table 7, and figures 4 and 5. Of the seventeen respondents who were anal *activo* in a majority of their first-year experiences, 59 percent by preference and practice were still anal *activo* when interviewed on average eight years afterward; 41 percent had changed and incorporated both sexual roles between their first year of homosexual experiences and the time of interview. Of the twenty-two respondents who were anal *pasivo* their first year, 77 percent by preference and practice were still anal *pasivo* when interviewed on average five years afterward; 23 percent had changed

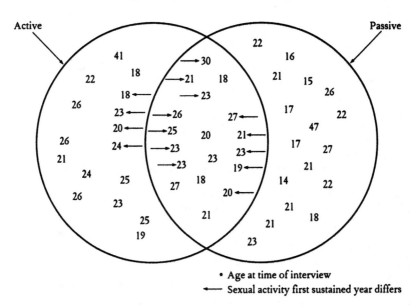

Figure 5.
Interviewees grouped by sexual preference at time of interview.

Table 7

A Percentage Comparison of Respondents' Sexual Preference and Majority of Homosexual Experiences at Time of Interview[a]

At Time of Interview	Majority of Homosexual Experiences First Sustained Year			Total[b]
	Anal			
	Activo	*Activo/Pasivo*	*Pasivo*	
Sexual preference				
Anal				
Activo	59	44	0	26
Activo/Pasivo	41	33	23	28
Pasivo	0	0	77	32
Oral	0	0	0	8
Masturbation (mutual)	0	0	0	2
No preference	0	23	0	4
TOTAL	100%	100%	100%	100%
Majority of homosexual experiences				
Anal				
Activo	59	22	0	22
Activo/Pasivo	41	78	23	36
Pasivo	0	0	77	32
Oral	0	0	0	8
Masturbation (mutual)	0	0	0	2
TOTAL	100%	100%	100%	100%
Median age of respondents at time of interview	24	20	21	22
Median years between first sustained year and time of interview	8	5	5	5
SAMPLE NUMBER	17	9	22	53

[a] Grouped by major homosexual activity first sustained year following first ejaculation. For example, the first column shows that of the respondents who were anal *activo* in a majority of their first year experiences, 59% by preference and practice were still anal *activo* at time of interview; 41% had changed and incorporated both sexual roles between first year and time of interview.

[b] The total includes four respondents whose major homosexual activities during the first sustained year following first ejaculation were oral-genital and one respondent whose major sexual activity was mutual masturbation. Their sexual preference and majority of homosexual experiences at the time of interview remained the same as first-year experiences.

and incorporated both sexual roles during the intervening time. Of the nine respondents who played both sexual roles their first year, at the time of interview four preferred to be anal *activo* and three *internacional;* two said they had no preference. In terms of homosexual experiences, however, only two of the nine were *activo* most of the time.

Changes that take place over time in sexual role preferences and homosexual behaviors of members of the subpopulation of Mexican men who have sex with men illustrate once again the need for collecting large numbers of sex-life histories in order to map out the various patterns of sexual behavior and to help understand the differences that exist between what people say they prefer doing as compared to what they actually do. Because of the changeability of the Mexican men making up the *internacional* group, they are particularly in need of this kind of in-depth study.

The fifty-three ethnosexual life histories of Mexican men I recorded in Guadalajara in 1970 are the first of their kind in Mexico. Previously mentioned findings from AIDS-related interview surveys in the mid to late 1980s in Mexico, conducted some sixteen to eighteen years after my 1970 interview survey, provide more recent information about Mexican male homosexual behaviors. But since none of these surveys elicited in-depth sex-life histories of respondents—specific sexual practices or techniques are recorded only for four to six months before the survey—they add little to our knowledge about the lifelong patterns of sexual behavior of Mexican men who have sex with men. This is particularly unfortunate in view of the fact that one of the important changes that may have taken place in Mexican male homosexual behaviors in the recent past has been an increase in the number of *internacionales*—and because the spread of HIV may be facilitated by homosexually behaving men playing both the anal-insertive and anal-receptive sexual roles.

References

Alonso, A. and M. Koreck. 1989. Silences: "Hispanics," AIDS, and sexual practices. *Differences: A Journal of Feminist Cultural Studies* 1:101–24.

Arboleda, M. 1987. Social attitudes and sexual variance in Lima. In Murray 1987, 101–17.

Carrier, J. 1971. Participants in urban Mexican male homosexual encounters. *Archives of Sexual Behavior* 1:279–91.

Carrier, J. 1972. Urban Mexican male homosexual encounters: An analysis of participants and coping strategies. Ph.D. diss., University of California, Irvine.

Carrier, J. 1976a. Cultural factors affecting urban Mexican male homosexual behavior. *Archives of Sexual Behavior* 5:103–24.

Carrier, J. 1976b. Family attitudes and Mexican male homosexuality. *Urban Life* 5, no. 3:359–75.

Carrier, J. 1985. Mexican male bisexuality. In F. Klein and T. Wolf, eds., Bisexualities: Theory and research, 75–86. New York: Haworth Press.

Carrier, J. 1989a. Gay liberation and coming out in Mexico. In G. Herdt, ed., Gay and lesbian youth, 225–52. New York: Haworth Press.

Carrier, J. 1989b. Sexual behavior and spread of AIDS in Mexico. *Medical Anthropology* 10:129–42.

Carrier, J. and J. R. Magaña. 1991. Use of ethnosexual data on men of Mexican origin for HIV/AIDS prevention programs. *Journal of Sex Research* 28, no. 2:189–202.

Chiñas, B. 1985. Isthmus Zapotec berdache. ARGOH (Anthropological Research Group on Homosexuality) Newsletter. San Francisco.

Del Rio, E. 1988. *El amor en los tiempos del SIDA*. Mexico City: Editorial Grijalbo.

Diaz-Guerrero, R. 1955. Neurosis and the Mexican family structure. *American Journal of Psychiatry* 112:411–17.

Diaz-Guerrero, R. 1967. Socio-cultural premises, attitudes, and cross-cultural research. *International Journal of Psychiatry* 2:79–87.

Escobar Latapí, A. 1993. The connection at its source: Changing socioeconomic conditions and migration patterns. In A. Lowenthal and K. Burgess, eds., *The California Mexico Connection*, 66–81. Stanford, Calif.: Stanford University Press.

Fry, P. 1987. Male homosexuality and Afro-Brazilian possession cults. In Murray 1987, 55–91.

García, M. et al. 1991. Bisexuality in Mexico: Current perspectives. In R. Tielman et al., eds., *Bisexuality and HIV/AIDS*, 41–58. Buffalo, N.Y.: Prometheus.

Gomezjara, F., E. Barrera, and N. Perez. 1978. *Sociologia de la prostitución*. Mexico City: Ediciónes Nueva Sociologia.

González Block, M. and A. Liguori. 1992. EL SIDA en los estratos socioeconómicos de Mexico. Pespectivas en salud pública 16. Cuernavaca: Instituto Nacional de Salud Pública.

Green, R. 1974. *Sexual identity conflict in children and adults*. New York: Basic Books.

Hernandez, M. et al. 1992. Sexual behavior and status for Human Immunodeficiency Virus Type 1 among homosexual and bisexual males in Mexico City. *American Journal of Epidemiology* 135, no. 8:883–94.

Hooker, E. 1965. An empirical study of some relations between sexual patterns and gender identity in male homosexuals. In *Sex research: New developments*. New York: Holt.

Ingham, J. 1968. Culture and personality in a Mexican village. Ph.D. diss., University of California, Berkeley.

Izazola-Licea J. et al. 1991. HIV-1 seropositivity and behavioral and sociological risks among homosexual and bisexual men in six Mexican cities. *Journal of AIDS* 4:614–22.

Jiménez, A. 1971. *Picardía Mexicana*. Mexico D.F.: Editores Mexicanos Unidos.

Kiev, A. 1968. *Curanderismo: Mexican-American folk psychiatry*. New York: Free Press.

Kinsey, A., W. Pomeroy, and C. Martin. 1948. Sexual behavior in the human male. Philadelphia: W. B. Saunders.

Kinzer, N. 1973. Priests, machos, and babies: Or, Latin American women and the Manichaean heresy. *Journal of Marriage and the Family* 35:300–311.

Klapp, O. 1964. Mexican social types. *American Journal of Sociology*, 69:409–15.

Kutsche, P. and B. Page. 1992. Male sexual identity in Costa Rica. *Anthropological Review* 3:7–14.

Lancaster, R. N. 1988. Subject honor and object shame: The construction of male homosexuality and stigma in Nicaragua. *Ethnology* 27:111–25.

Leyva, J. 1970. *El perfil de Mexico in 1980*. Vol. 2, *El problema habitaciónal*. Mexico City: Siglo XXI Editores.

Lumsden, I. 1991. *Homosexuality, society, and the state in Mexico*. Toronto: Canadian Gay Archives.

McGinn, N. 1966. Marriage and family in middle-class Mexico. *Journal of Marriage and the Family* 28:305–13.

Magaña, J. R. and J. Carrier. 1991. Mexican and Mexican-American male sexual behavior and spread of AIDS in California. *Journal of Sex Research* 28, no. 3:425–41.

Maldonado, J. 1969. *Después de todo*. México D.F.: Editorial Diógenes, S.A.

Metzger, D. and M. Black. 1965. Ethnographic description and the study of law. *American Anthropologist* 6:141–65.

Mother: Confesiones de mi madre acerca de mi homosexualidad. 1984. *Crisálida: De y para la comunidad gay*. Guadalajara, México: Grupo Orgullo Homosexual Liberación A–D.

Murray, S. 1984. *Social theory, homosexual Realities*. Gai Saber Monograph, no. 3. New York: Gay Academic Union.

Murray, S. 1987. The family as an obstacle to the growth of a gay subculture in Mesoamerica. In S. Murray, ed., *Male homosexuality in Central and South America*, 118–28. Gai Saber Monograph, no. 5. New York: Gay Academic Union.

Murray, S. and M. Arboleda. 1987. Stigma transformation and relexification: "Gay" in Latin America. In Murray 1987, 130–38.

Nexos (Mexico City). 1989. *El Sexo en Mexico*. Published in *Nexos* 12, no. 139 (Special Issue, July): 29–80.

Parker, R. 1989. Youth, identity, and homosexuality: The changing shape of sexual life in contemporary Brazil. *Journal of Homosexuality* 17, nos. 3–4:269–89.

Parker, R. 1991. *Bodies, pleasures, and passions: Sexual culture in contemporary Brazil*. Boston: Beacon Press.

Paz, O. 1961. *The labyrinth of solitude: Life and thought in Mexico*. New York: Grove Press.

Peñalosa, F. 1968. Mexican family roles. *Journal of Marriage and the Family* 30:680–89.

Quijada, O. 1977. *Comportamiento sexual en Mexico*. Vol. 1, *El hombre*. Mexico City: Editorial Tinta Libre.

Redfield, R. 1953. *The primitive world and its transformation*. Chicago: University of Chicago Press.

Riding, A. 1984. *Distant neighbors: A portrait of the Mexicans*. New York: Knopf.

Roebuck, J. and P. McNamara. 1973. *Ficheras* and free-lancers: Prostitution in a Mexican border city. *Archives of Sexual Behavior* 2, no. 3:231–44.

Ross, S. 1966. *Is the Mexican Revolution dead?* New York: Knopf.

Saghir, M. and E. Robins. 1973. Male and female homosexuality: A comprehensive investigation. Baltimore: Williams and Wilkins.

Stevens, E. 1971. Marianismo: The other face of machismo in Latin America. In ?. pp. 89–101.

Taylor, C. 1974. Preliminary report on homosexual subculture in Mexico. Presented to the American Anthropological Association Symposium on Homosexuality in Cross-cultural Perspectives, Mexico City, November 23, 1974: mimeographed.

Taylor, C. 1978a. El Ambiente: Male homosexual social life in Mexico City. Ph.D. diss., University of California, Berkeley.

Taylor, C. 1978b. How Mexicans define male homosexuality: Labeling and the *buga* view. *Kroeber Anthropological Society Papers*, nos. 53 and 54 (University of California, Berkeley):106–28.

Taylor, C. 1986. Mexican male homosexual interaction in public contexts. In E. Blackwood, ed., *The many faces of homosexuality*, 117–36. New York: Harrington Park Press.

Trichopoulos, D., L. Sparos, and E. Petridou. 1988. Homosexual role separation and spread of AIDS. *Lancet* (October 22, 1988):965–66.

Van Druten, H., F. Van Griensven, and J. Hendriks. 1992. Homosexual role separation: Implications for analyzing and modeling the spread of HIV. *Journal of Sex Research* 29, no. 4:477–99.

Vázquez-Valls, E. 1989. Prevalence of HIV antibodies in homosexual Mexican males in Guadalajara during period 1984–1988. Paper presented at the International AIDS Conference, Montreal, Canada.

Velázquez, M. 1967. *Spanish and English dictionary*. New York: Follett.

Whitam, F. 1987. Os entendidos: Gay life in Sao Paulo. In Murray 1987, 24–54.

Wiley, J. and S. Herschkorn. 1989. Homosexual role separation and AIDS epidemics: Insights from elementary models. *Journal of Sex Research* 26:434–49.

Williams, W. 1986. *The spirit and the flesh: Sexual diversity in American Indian culture*. Boston: Beacon Press.

Wilson, C. 1995. *Hidden in the Blood: A Personal Exploration of AIDS in the Yucatán*. New York: Columbia University Press.

Zapata, L. 1979. *Las aventuras, desventuras y suenos de Adonis Garcia, el Vampiro de la Colonia Roma*. Mexico City: Editorial Grijalbo.

Designer: Linda Secondari

Text: 11.5/13.5 Fournier

Compositor: Impressions, a div. of Edwards Brothers, Inc.

Printer: Edwards Brothers, Inc.

Binder: Edwards Brothers, Inc.